Buñuel and Mexico

Buñuel and Mexico

The Crisis of National Cinema

ERNESTO R. ACEVEDO-MUÑOZ

University of California Press

University of California Press
Oakland, California

© 2003 by the Regents of the University of California

All rights reserved.

First Paperback Printing 2025

Library of Congress Cataloging-in-Publication Data

Acevedo-Muñoz, Ernesto R., 1968–.
  Buñuel and Mexico : the crisis of national cinema / by Ernesto R. Acevedo-Muñoz.
      p.   cm.
  Includes bibliographical references and index.
  9780520239524 (cloth); 9780520419292 (pbk.);
  9780520930483 (ebook)
  1. Buñuel, Luis, 1900–   .—Criticism and interpretation.   2. Motion pictures—Mexico.   I. Title.
PN1998.3.B86A64   2003
791.43'0233'092—dc21   2003044766
GPSR Authorized Representative: Easy Access System Europe,
Mustamäe tee 50, 10621 Tallinn, Estonia,
gpsr.requests@easproject.com

A Mamá, Papá, y Carlos R.
Por quererme y apoyarme sin pedir nada a cambio, y
por siempre ir conmigo al cine

And in loving memory of Stan Brakhage
(1933–2003)

Contents

List of Figures	ix
Acknowledgments	xi
Introduction	1
1. Mexican Cinema in the Time of Luis Buñuel	15
2. Buñuel and Mexico	32
3. *Los Olvidados* and the Crisis of Mexican Cinema	57
4. Genre, Women, Narrative	80
5. On the Road: *Subida al Cielo* and *La Ilusión Viaja en Tranvía*	111
6. Masculinity and Class Conflict: Buñuel's Macho-Dramas	124
Conclusion. From Buñuel to "Nuevo Cine"	143
Filmography of Luis Buñuel	153
Notes	159
Bibliography	177
Index	187

Figures

1. Luis Buñuel playing around with Fernando Soler and Fernando Soto "Mantequilla" on the set of *The Daughter of Deceit* (1951). 9
2. Libertad Lamarque and Jorge Negrete almost kissing in *Gran Casino* (1947). 47
3. Rosario Granados and Fernando Soler perfectly happy in *The Great Madcap* (1949). 53
4. Roberto Cobo, Alfonso Mejía, and Javier Amezcua posing for *Los olvidados* (1950) in "the very real slums of Mexico City." 66
5. Pedro's mother and Jaibo consummate the Oedipal narrative in *Los olvidados*. 75
6. Pedro is inevitably lost in the labyrinth of violence and solitude in *Los olvidados*. 78
7. Don Guadalupe and Susana dramatize the nature of their initial relationship in Buñuel's *Susana* (1950). 87
8. Nacho Contla and Fernando Soto "Mantequilla" pose with Buñuel's counterfeit *cabareteras* in *The Daughter of Deceit* (1951). 97
9. Rosario Granados in Buñuel's "classic" maternal melodrama, *A Woman Without Love* (1951). 103
10. Every Sunday brings a killing and all men have guns in Buñuel's *Death and the River* (1954). 109
11. In *Mexican Bus Ride* (1951) the locals put up a "traditional" fiesta to amuse foreign tourists. 118

12. The narrative detours in *Illusion Travels by Streetcar* (1954) stress the many financial difficulties that came with development and modernization under President Alemán.   121

13. Class conflict and masculinity are fatally linked in *El Bruto* (1950).   127

14. Patriarchy, masculinity, and insanity are the same thing in Buñuel's *Él* (1952).   135

15. Ernesto Alonso as the troubled title character in *The Criminal Life of Archibaldo de la Cruz* (1955).   141

16. Buñuel directing *Nazarín* (ca. 1958), one of his independent films produced by Manuel Barbachano Ponce.   145

17. Silvia Pinal in *The Exterminating Angel* (1962).   146

18. Gabriel Figueroa and Buñuel on the set of *Nazarín*.   151

Acknowledgments

Many institutions and individuals have helped me in the long process that has led to this book. At the University of Iowa, where this work began as a dissertation, Lauren Rabinovitz was a generous advisor, mentor, and supporter. Kathleen Newman provided much guidance, and Rick Altman, Dudley Andrew, Corey Creekmur, and Joy Hayes were wise critics of the first version. The Graduate College and the University of Iowa Foundation, the University of Colorado's College of Arts and Sciences, and its Graduate Committee on the Arts and Humanities all gave me fellowships, grants, or time off that took me to Mexico City, Guadalajara, New York, and London for research. In Mexico City, I thank the personnel of the Library of the Cineteca Nacional, the Lerdo de Tejada library, and the Library at the National Autonomous University of Mexico. Lourdes Zamudio at the Mexican Film Institute (IMCINE) gave me copies of documents, books, and other sources. The people at the Cinema Research and Teaching Center (Centro de Investigación y Enseñanza Cinematográfica) of the University of Guadalajara deserve special thanks. Emilio García Riera was kind enough to honor my requests for an interview. Eduardo de la Vega Alfaro put all the resources of the CIEC at my disposal, and their research staff—Ulises Íñiguez Mendoza, Carlos Torrico, and Ana María Armengol—opened their files and their minds to my curiosity. Mary Corliss at the New York Museum of Modern Art Film Stills Archive was of great help, and Samantha Grabowski gave me valuable research assistance.

My students in Buñuel courses at the University of Colorado and the University of Iowa provided many thought-provoking comments when I tested these ideas with them. Melinda Barlow, Stan Brakhage, José Manuel Del Pino, Suranjan Ganguly, Bruce Kawin, Marian Keane, Kathleen Man, Jim Palmer, Eric Smoodin, and Phil Solomon have been generous in many ways. Some brief but meaningful conversations with Carlos Monsiváis in Iowa City, Matilde Landeta in Mexico City, Marvin D'Lugo, Ángela Molina, Víctor Fuentes, and Juan Luis Buñuel in London helped me, however vicariously, to think about Luis Buñuel as "a friend."

Carl J. Mora and Claire F. Fox read earlier versions of the manuscript and gave me intelligent and generous criticism and many wise suggestions. They contributed significantly to making this a better book. All remaining errors and omissions are my sole responsibility.

I am grateful to Mary Francis, Kate Warne, and Colette DeDonato at the University of California Press, who were very kind and patient guides through the editing process.

My deepest thanks go to Anne and Aaron Han-Joon Magnan-Park and Carol Schrage for their support, friendship, and advice. And to Ella Chichester—friend, colleague, and partner—for the ideas, the laughs, the cups of coffee, and so much more.

Introduction

> Many of [Buñuel's] films made in Mexico are inconsequential. Only five of the nineteen films of this period can be considered memorable.
>
> —Virginia Higginbotham, *Luis Buñuel*

In this book I analyze in context the relationship between Luis Buñuel's career as a filmmaker in Mexico, Mexican politics, and the Mexican film industry. Buñuel's Mexican films need to be understood, both in relationship to questions of national cinema and the nationalist orientation of classical Mexican cinema, and within the structure of the Mexican film industry in which Buñuel worked from 1946 to 1965. My purpose is to place Buñuel's Mexican films, from *Gran Casino* (1946) to *Ensayo de un crimen* (1955), within the historical, political, and industrial contexts in which they were made. My purpose is to "nationalize" Buñuel's "lesser" Mexican films and to reposition in their national context the Mexican movies that are usually associated with his "better" French and Spanish films. Some of Buñuel's Mexican films are popular in psychoanalytic and auteurist criticism, particularly *Los olvidados*, *Él*, and *Ensayo de un crimen*, but they are rarely seen as "Mexican" movies. Without abducting them from their rightful place within international film criticism, I place these films in a prominent space vis-à-vis Mexican cinema, showing how Buñuel specifically questioned and addressed the ideology and imagery of classical Mexican cinema and found ways of referring to Mexican national issues.

This study departs from the usual perspectives that ground Buñuel's work solely in surrealism. Buñuel's surrealist formation certainly justifies his creative and ideological independence from any concept of "national cinema," especially the melodramatic/folkloric style of Mexican cinema. Yet, by rethinking auteurist and psychoanalytic approaches to Buñuel's work as critical standards of evaluation for such a transnational, highly individualistic director, I will show how functions of genre and "national cinema," state politics, and national identity contribute to a deeper, richer understanding of his work. Furthermore, Buñuel's incorporation into the genre system of Mexican cinema was particularly successful, insofar as the director was able to consolidate surrealist aesthetics and ethnographic interests within popular formats that resulted in what we may call a "popular surrealism." Buñuel's Mexican films thus raise questions about the definition of national cinema as it was exemplified by the nationalist project of the Mexican Revolution through its most celebrated (and diffused) products, such as the films of Emilio Fernández and other directors.

BUÑUEL AND FILM STUDIES

Most Buñuel scholarship centers primarily on two peaks in the director's career: his "surrealist trilogy" *(Un chien andalou,* 1928; *L'Age d'Or,* 1930; and *Las Hurdes,* 1932) made in France and Spain, and the French and Spanish films made from 1961 *(Viridiana)* to 1977 *(Cet obscur objet du désir).* Traditionally, Buñuel scholarship tends to pursue two main lines of discourse and critical methodology: psychoanalysis and, most often, auteur criticism. In her book *Figures of Desire: A Theory and Analysis of Surrealist Film,* for example, Linda Williams concentrates on *Un chien andalou, L'Age d'Or, Le fantôme de la liberté,* and *Cet obscur objet du désir.* The book offers a much-needed (if narrowly focused) theory of surrealist film that is mostly based on the films' dream-structures and their relation to the unconscious according to Freudian and Lacanian psychoanalysis. According to Williams, the Mexican films provide only "an occasional *bizarre juxtaposition* or *incongruous desire* that intrudes upon the smooth surface of social relations," characteristics that Williams finds only in "surrealism proper."[1] Williams states that precisely because the Mexican movies were made under the constraints of a well-organized commercial genre system (from *Gran Casino* in 1946 to *Nazarín* in 1958), they bear little interest for an analysis of Buñuel's work and her theory of surrealist film. *Figures of Desire,* as much as it sheds welcome light on the director's most difficult works, is a clear instance of the scholarly neglect of most of Buñuel's Mexican films because they do not conform to the accustomed critical and theoretical approaches.

The exclusion of Buñuel's Mexican period from scholarship is rather the norm, not the exception. Paul Sandro, in his book *Diversions of Pleasure: Luis Buñuel and the Crises of Desire,* concentrates on the films made "early and late" in Buñuel's career and their perversion of classical narrative structure. Sandro's analysis of Buñuel's work addresses how Buñuel's films violate the conventions of spectatorship and "wish fulfillment" in classical narrative. Both in their diegeses (the protagonists' angst in not possessing their "objects of desire") and in their narrative structures, the films Sandro cares for work to frustrate spectators' desires. This model, however, once again serves to exclude most of the commercial Mexican films, which were narratively coherent and conventional compared to Buñuel's other work. In Sandro's study there is no place for works with such linear, cause-effect narrative structure, such as *Una mujer sin amor*, *El gran calavera*, *La ilusión viaja en tranvía*, or *Susana*. These movies, however, served well their narrative, generic, and structural purposes in the context of the state of Mexican cinema when they were produced.

In *The Discreet Art of Luis Buñuel*, Gwynne Edwards seeks uniformity in Buñuel's work, with a clearly auteurist method, by associating his movies with struggling and opposing forces in the director's personality: Catholicism and surrealism. Edwards flirts with some notions of nationality that are important in shaping the director's "unity of vision." But she subordinates Spanishness to Catholicism, putting the weight on the director's struggle between his *upbringing* (Spanish, Catholic, bourgeois) and his *formation* (French surrealism). When it comes to the Mexican movies, though, Edwards (like other auteurists) is also in search of Buñuelian "moments" that largely disregard the production context of the Mexican movies to which the book pays attention, namely *El ángel exterminador*, *Subida al cielo*, and *La ilusión viaja en tranvía*.

Similarly, in her critical biography, *Luis Buñuel*, from which I picked this chapter's opening epigraph, Virginia Higginbotham dedicates only one chapter to the bulk of the Mexican movies because "many of [Buñuel's] films made in Mexico are inconsequential. Only five of the nineteen films of this period can be considered memorable."[2] Higginbotham's seems to be the uniform position of film scholarship when dealing with Buñuel's Mexican movies. The only importance Higginbotham grants to the Mexican films is that the Mexican film industry taught Buñuel to work in "commercial," accessible genres and narratives that allowed him to reach greater audiences when he re-emerged in the 1960s. While Higginbotham's observations are genuine and true to Buñuel's own observations,[3] I believe that learning a more accessible film style was hardly a difficult task for Buñuel. While he admitted to having learned much from his earlier Mexican movies *Gran Casino* (1947) and *El gran calavera* (1949), Buñuel was already going through a process of revision of his own style a decade before he moved to Mexico.

In any case, if Buñuel in fact admitted learning classical narrative structure and stylistic refinement with his Mexican movies, that is already a way to expand the influence of his Mexican experience to his subsequent films, from *Viridiana* (1961) to *Cet obscur objet du désir* (1977). In other words, auteur criticism can take Buñuel out of Mexico, but it cannot take Mexico out of Buñuel. Buñuel's biggest commercial success of the early 1950s was *The Adventures of Robinson Crusoe*, a Mexican/U.S. co-production that was already a departure from his Mexican production base. This suggests that after a very early period of adaptation the director was in full command of his resources and of a commercial style of filmmaking by the time he made most of his Mexican films.

The tendency to overlook many of Buñuel's Mexican films made before *El ángel exterminador* (1962), because they are inconsistent with psychoanalytical analyses of surrealist filmmaking, also occurs in classic auteurist criticism. Originating with works published in *Cahiers du Cinéma* in the 1950s, auteurist critics deemed most of Buñuel's Mexican work too "commercial" or creatively crippled precisely because it emerged from the tightly structured, often generic, national film industry. With the occasional exceptions of *Los olvidados, Él, Ensayo de un crimen,* and *El ángel exterminador,* auteurist critics set the precedent for disregarding the industry-oriented, commercial Mexican movies as a whole. Attention to these conventional, commercial (that is, Mexican) films was limited to the search for isolated "moments" of surrealism. Their production history, context, and content depart from Buñuel's appreciated style, authorial independence, and clear ideological positions in the European films.

Part of this critical prejudice comes from the fact that some of Buñuel's best and least-known Mexican works, movies like *Subida al cielo* and *La ilusión viaja en tranvía*, are too dependent on their historical context to fit any classic definition of "Buñueliana." In addition, an argument could be made for Buñuel's Mexican films based on clear matters of national prejudice against Latin American cinema in the 1950s. The elitist, "center-periphery" cinematic metaphor could explain somehow why Buñuel, the exiled Spanish surrealist, became the focus of what little critical attention Mexican cinema (and Latin American cinema, in general) got in the European film journals before the "new cinema" movements started emerging in the late 1950s in Brazil. With the exception of a few crossover films coming primarily from Japan (Akira Kurosawa's *Rashomon*, 1950; Yazujiro Ozu's *Tokyo Story*, 1953) and India later in the 1950s (exclusively the Apu trilogy of Satyajit Ray), only Hollywood and European directors received consideration in the critical journals. Even when Latin American cinema started getting attention in the late 1950s, it was often in relation to European styles of filmmaking and to the filmmakers' direct links with European training. Such was the case of the first generation of Latin American auteurs, mostly schooled at the Centro Sperimentale de Cinematografia in Rome and the Moscow Film School.[4] Thus, Latin American cinema, with the notable exception of films by Mexican director Emilio Fernández, remained mainly at the margins of serious critical consideration until the *cinema nôvo* movement emerged in Brazil. Before that, only Fernández in 1947, and Buñuel after 1951, made it into the pages of *Cahiers du Cinéma*.

André Bazin (the co-founder of *Cahiers du Cinéma*) was extremely supportive of Buñuel's Mexican movies, and he even predicted the shift in critical attention from the "classical" style of Emilio Fernández and Gabriel Figueroa to that of Luis Buñuel in a 1951 article in *L'Observateur*.[5] Even Bazin, however, soon lost interest in Buñuel's movies of the 1950s—with the exception of *Los olvidados* and *Subida al cielo*—and gave just lukewarm reviews to *Él* and to *Ensayo de un crimen*. These films would eventually emerge as among the director's best works.[6]

Buñuel criticism and scholarship—including Fernando Cesarman's *L'Oeil de Buñuel*, Jenaro Talens' *The Branded Eye*, Maurice Drouzy's *Luis Buñuel: Architecte du rêve*, and even Ado Kyrou's classic, *Luis Bunuel*—emphasize "the man" (his "vision," formation, anxieties, desires), the films as individual texts (their thematic and stylistic continuity, their "Buñuelian" motifs), and the convergence of these two subjects ("the man" and "his films"). This is what defines classic auteur criticism. What seems to be most often lacking, especially in relation to the "inconsequential" Mexican films, is the importance of context, whether it be historical, national, or industrial. My purpose here is to analyze and understand Buñuel's films from 1946 to 1955 as "Mexican" movies, insofar as they relate to issues and concerns, and often even to the styles and genres, of Mexican "national" cinema.

THE CRISIS OF MEXICAN CINEMA

The best known of Buñuel's Mexican films *(Los olvidados, Subida al cielo)* help us define a transitional phase of crisis in the "image" of the "national" and of the Revolution in Mexican cinema. These are films that identify the aesthetic and stylistic conversion from "classical" (epic in scope, ideologically conservative, formally generic) to "new" cinema (auteurist, politically progressive, formally experimental) in Mexico, making Buñuel the principal transitional figure between two successive generations of Mexican filmmakers.

As with any national cinema, issues of genre are instrumental for understanding the operations of the Mexican film industry. Mexican and American film historians agree on a number of genres that are specific to the country's cinema: the *comedia ranchera*, the revolutionary/historical epic, the family melodrama, the *cabaretera* musical, and the "social comedy." These genres are classified in terms of their social functions and atmosphere even more than their structural peculiarities. For example, the *ranchera* is customarily a romantic story set in a rural, bucolic setting. It invents a world full of innocent peasants; gentle, landowning patriarchs; hyper-masculine, honorable *charros*; and virginal, beautiful women—thus idealizing country life before the era of modernization. It can be a comedy or a drama, and more often than not it is both, adding comic characters and situations to the romantic plot. While its generic "brand" may vary (since it can be called a "romantic comedy" or a "musical drama"), what remains static is its idealization of a preindustrial era, its freezing of Mexico "on the margins of modernity."[7]

In contrast, the revolutionary epic usually exploits dramatically a segment of the Mexican Revolution (1910–20). It focuses on that period to articulate a synecdoche of the nation that dictates specific conceptions of the male hero and his indispensable role in the constitution of the modern nation. The revolutionary epic has a consistent style; it proposes a pictorial version of the themes of the nation and the male hero. In its epic scale, desert landscapes, and spectacular battle sequences it condenses stylistic traits of Mexican muralism and socialist realism.

The family melodrama disguises as titillation the traditional moral values of Catholicism and patriarchy. Its function is to restate the safety of church, family, and the state (often symbolic of one another) while attracting its faithful audiences with the magnets of promised lewdness, incest, or adultery. Paradoxically, its technique is to suggest that the safekeeping of patriarchal morals at home helps to secure the longevity of modern society.

In response to the family melodrama, the *cabaretera* films, set in the marginal spaces of bars, cabarets, bordellos, and dance halls, propose the difficulty of sustaining traditional morals in the era of urban growth and modernization. Consequently, the *cabaretera* films, which flourished during President Miguel Alemán's administration (1946–52), expose the retrograde positions of the family melodrama and the *ranchera* as untenable by calling attention to the necessary revision of Mexican society imposed by the post–World War II economy.

Finally, the function of classic social comedy in Mexican films was to give the working classes the illusion of being represented in the nation's cinematic imaginary. The great comedians Cantinflas and Tin-Tán became famous by typifying working-class characters whose own misadventures were the butt of every joke: it was fine to be poor if it was with a sense of humor and self-righteousness.⁸ Comics like Cantinflas and Tin-Tán were enormously successful at home and abroad playing the two basic types of comedic characters of Mexican cinema: the "pelado," or streetwise, small-time hustler, and the "pachuco," the border town, pseudo-assimilated zoot-suiter.

Buñuel's Mexican movies are clearly distinct from classical cinema in Mexico. Yet they are comparable to those genres that are specific to their cultural context. In fact, Buñuel's films gain new meaning within the historical context of the traumatic, accelerated push toward an industrial economy that characterized the administration of President Alemán in Mexico. Buñuel's great Mexican films can all be recognized as part of the contemporary currents of Mexican national cinema. This holds true, arguably, of his best Mexican films, such as *Los olvidados, Él*, and *Subida al cielo*. The minor films—*Una mujer sin amor, El río y la muerte, La ilusión viaja en tranvía, Ensayo de un crimen*—are revisionist versions of the "family melodrama," the *cabaretera*, and the classic comedy.

Some serious scholarly approaches to Buñuel's Mexican films as genre pictures have recently emerged. Gastón Lillo's *Género y transgresión: El cine mexicano de Luis Buñuel* analyzes five of Buñuel's Mexican films to argue rather convincingly that they transgress the genres to which they seemingly belong (somewhat along the lines of Paul Sandro's argument in *Diversions of Pleasure*). What really distinguishes Lillo's book is the emphasis on the Mexican movies *Los olvidados, El gran calavera, Ensayo de un crimen, El bruto* and *Nazarín*. However, Lillo's analysis overlooks important contextual information regarding the historically specific traits of Mexican cinema—the relationship of Buñuel's movies to, say, the *cabaretera* subgenre of melodrama, as well as to some literary sources (for example, Rodolfo Usigli's novel *Ensayo de un crimen*) that inform these movies in a very specific light. As relevant as Lillo's book is, it is principally concerned with Buñuel's Mexican movies in relation to classical genre theory in cinema and literature (his sources range from Christian Metz to Jean-Louis Baudry, from Peter Brooks to Julia Kristeva, from Mikhail Bakhtin to Michel Foucault). Lillo pays less attention to the specifically Mexican variants of classic genres, which is what I emphasize in this book. Furthermore, Lillo finds that *El ángel exterminador* and *Simón del desierto* are incompatible with the rest of Buñuel's Mexican films, which is in some ways true, but, I would argue, they also represent the logical conclusion, the closure, of that period of Buñuel's career.⁹ It is precisely these "rare" Mexican films that ultimately link Buñuel to the "new" Mexican cinema.

Other relatively recent books have rescued some of the forgotten

Mexican films and helped raise them into the Buñuelian canon. Peter W. Evans, in *The Films of Luis Buñuel: Subjectivity and Desire,* analyzes five of Buñuel's Mexican films *(Una mujer sin amor, Los olvidados, Susana, Ensayo de un crimen,* and *Él)* from the perspective of psychoanalytic and sexual theory, logically connecting them to the categories of Freudian "family romance," the Oedipal trajectory, the "uncanny," and articulations of desire.[10] Víctor Fuentes, in his book *Buñuel en México: Iluminaciones sobre una pantalla pobre,* pays special attention to Buñuel's Mexican films as well. Fuentes takes us through Buñuel's generic, cultural, and intertextual context, tracking, collecting and analyzing the director's moral views, rich literary allusions, stylistic motifs, and personal experiences scattered throughout his Mexican films. What emerges from Fuentes's book is Buñuel's struggle and resolve to survive as an artist against many odds and the allegorical meanings of that struggle for the Spanish exile community. Fuentes underscores at once Buñuel's Spanishness and the universality of his work. Finally, the Brazilian collection of essays, *Um jato na contramão: Buñuel no México,* offers separate close readings of individual films, once again without making many direct connections to Mexico or its cinema. It is, rather, another list of "Buñuelian" motifs, and some new hypotheses of the overall surrealist meanings of *Simon of the Desert, The Exterminating Angel,* and other films.

But Buñuel's Mexican films are also an important part of Mexican cinema in the critical transitional period from the end of the classical era in the 1950s to the beginnings of the "new cinema" in the 1960s. Instead of approaching a select group of "Buñuelian" movies made in Mexico as if they existed in a historical vacuum, I see Luis Buñuel's experience in Mexico as a reflection on the crisis of national cinema. It is also a turning point in the negotiation of the cultural debates about Mexican politics and Mexican cinema between 1950 and 1965. Buñuel's significance is, in part, to have contributed to a perspective on Mexico which, filtered through his distant position as an exile and a surrealist, allowed for a careful observation of "the nation," of the cinematic narratives of nationalism, and of the flaws of popular arts and national cinema. With this interest in Mexico during the crisis of the 1950s, Buñuel became part of a cultural debate (taking place in journals, newspapers, books) which called for an economic, historical, and cultural revision of the achievements of the Mexican Revolution throughout the late 1940s and 1950s. The symptoms of "crisis" that Buñuel identified were present in works of contemporary criticism, in developments in other artistic genres, and in the genre and style revisionism of Mexican cinema. These markers of "the crisis of the national" in Mexican cinema thus incor-

FIGURE 1. Luis Buñuel *(center)* playing around with Fernando Soler *(left)* and Fernando Soto "Mantequilla" on the set of *The Daughter of Deceit* (1951). Museum of Modern Art / Film Stills Archive.

porate the peculiarities of Buñuel's work into what seems like a pattern proper to its parallel context. The pattern is manifest in contemporary films of "transitional" genres (such as Alberto Gout's *cabareteras*) and can help us understand Buñuel as part of an undeclared "movement" of revisionism in Mexican cinema between 1945 and 1955.

BUÑUEL AND MEXICAN CINEMA

In Chapter 1, I will explain what the term "national cinema" represents in Mexican film, the general state of the nation's film industry in the decade prior to Buñuel's exile, and the importance of cinema in Mexico's overall cultural and political context in the 1930s and 1940s. In Chapter 2, I analyze the historical and cultural context that precedes and surrounds Buñuel's 1946 move to Mexico to accept a job with a friendly producer in a genre picture, a move that resulted in Buñuel taking up Mexican nationality in 1949. The chapter concludes with observations on Buñuel's first two Mexican movies, which are among his least-known films, *Gran Casino* (1946–47) and *El gran calavera* (1949).

Chapter 3 analyzes the Mexican film by Buñuel that is most often acclaimed by scholars and critics: *Los olvidados*—although such acclaim almost always disregards the context of the Mexican film industry and Mexican society at the time. My analysis of *Los olvidados* demonstrates Buñuel's original clash with Mexican classical cinema (in style and content) and how the movie is illustrative, even symptomatic, of the crisis of national cinema after the decline of the Golden Age. *Los olvidados* was Buñuel's first Mexican film that participated in the critical revision of the revolutionary social projects championed under President Lázaro Cárdenas (1934–40). It conforms to other contemporary cultural and political events in Mexico (the rise of *cabaretera* films and the work of Daniel Cosío-Villegas and Octavio Paz, for example) that were indeed questioning and challenging "the myth of the Revolution."

Chapters 4, 5, and 6 concentrate on the bulk of Buñuel's Mexican films, the "inconsequential" generic comedies and melodramas that put in evidence Buñuel's close relationship to popular Mexican cinema. Some of the movies analyzed in these chapters (with the notable exception of *Él*) are the ones most often neglected by Buñuel scholars because they do not fit the usual critical and interpretive models. In Chapter 4 I analyze Buñuel's female-centered melodramas. I initially focus on *Susana* and *La hija del engaño* with respect to the Mexican *cabaretera* melodrama of the late 1940s and 1950s. Then, I turn to the "maternal" melodramas *Una mujer sin amor* and *El río y la muerte* and their relation to Mexico's national metanarrative of La Malinche, a figure prominent in popular literature and films. In Chapter 5 I look at Buñuel's more eloquent and more specifically Mexican movies, the national allegories-as-road-movies *Subida al cielo* and *La ilusión viaja en tranvía*. Finally, in Chapter 6 I address the "macho-dramas" *El bruto*, *Él*, and *Ensayo de un crimen*, in which Buñuel examines the question of *machismo* and male identity that is so important in Mexican society, a question that would also be taken up by the new Mexican cinema directors a decade later. One of the prominent thematic features that all these movies share is their commentary (sometimes subtle, sometimes direct) on Mexican society at the threshold of the traumatic modernizing, developmentalist, and industrialist efforts of the administration of President Miguel Alemán. Consequently, these films, along with *Los olvidados*, are the movies that most clearly demonstrate the depth of Luis Buñuel's relationship to Mexican culture and the Mexican nation.

In his popular movies of the 1950s, Luis Buñuel elaborated his critical position vis-à-vis the currents of Mexican cinema and articulated a systematic revisionist treatment of contemporary social and political issues. As he did in *Los olvidados*, his most celebrated Mexican movie, Buñuel criticized in the popular "forgotten" films Mexican cinema's generic conventions while showing a serious awareness of contemporary politics, of social concerns, and always in some way of Mexican cinema's management of crisis. There are very specific references to cultural, social, historical, and political context in *Los olvidados, Susana, La hija del engaño, Una mujer sin amor, El río y la muerte, El bruto, Él, Ensayo de un crimen, Subida al cielo,* and *La ilusión viaja en tranvía*. From that perspective, the films show that Buñuel's immersion in Mexican cinema was not only as a clever dissembler of standard genre movies (which is the leading critical opinion) but also as an informed, careful analyst of Mexican society. Furthermore, even when Buñuel was more interested in character study, whether seriously, as in *El bruto* and *Él*, or comically, as in *Ensayo de un crimen*, he showed a clear concern for placing his commentary in contextual and narrative formats that were familiar to his potential Mexican audiences.

For instance, patriarchal characters in Buñuel's Mexican films are morally and politically ambiguous (as evidenced by the evil Don Carmelo in *Los olvidados;* the demagogue politician Don Eladio in *Subida al cielo;* Francisco, the pathetic paranoid in *Él;* and the effeminate dilettante Archibaldo de la Cruz in *Ensayo de un crimen*). They all show some form of sexual "dysfunction" in macho Mexico, ranging from pedophilia, to rejection by women, to homosexuality: portrayals that cast a shadow over the pristine depictions of gentle patriarchs and gallant *charros* of Mexican cinema's Golden Age. Moreover, by violating the strict, righteous image of men in Mexican cinema with these characters, Buñuel raised questions about the moral and political codes that imprint patriarchy and machismo with symbolic nationalist meanings. As Charles Ramírez Berg has written, this critical practice was adopted in the 1970s by directors such as Arturo Ripstein and Jaime Humberto Hermosillo.[11]

The problem raised by Buñuel's small Mexican movies—the studio potboilers *(Gran Casino)*, the conventional pictures *(Una mujer sin amor)*, the flamboyant melodramas *(Susana)*, and the socially aware satires *(Subida al cielo, La ilusión viaja en tranvía)*—is that, seen in the context of the industry in which they were made, these films respond to generic conventions and the specificity of their context. These movies can give us a more complete view of the career of Luis Buñuel, but they can also upset our image of Buñuel as the European surrealist phenomenon who was always ill-at-ease within a national film industry.[12]

What these movies clearly indicate is Buñuel's immersion into the currents of Mexican cinema. Even with his critical, satirical eye, most of

Buñuel's films of the 1950s are careful renditions of Mexican film genres that are also especially sensitive to political and economic issues. They address the crisis of the Revolution *(Los olvidados)*, machismo *(El bruto, Él, Ensayo de un crimen)*, the ineptitude of social and political initiatives *(Subida al cielo, La ilusión viaja en tranvía)*, violence, and even the narrative dependency on "La Malinche" *(El río y la muerte, Una mujer sin amor)* to mediate national identity.

Buñuel refined his mastery of popular cinema, both narratively and technically, in Mexico. He rehearsed characters like Belle de Jour (of the homonymous 1966 film), Don Jaime of *Viridiana* (1961), and Don Lope of *Tristana* (1969) with rudimentary Mexican versions like Archibaldo de la Cruz *(Ensayo de un crimen,* 1955) and Francisco Galván de Montemayor *(Él,* 1952). Buñuel appropriated and adapted traits of the Mexican *cabaretera* to his later films about relationships between men and women, such as *Tristana* (1969) and *Cet obscur objet du désir* (1977). He tested in Mexico the issue of the irrational purity of violence in *El río y la muerte* (1954), a topic he would later retake in *Le fantôme de la liberté* (1974). Thus, while mastering his skills as a narrative filmmaker, Buñuel found ways of analyzing topics and characters in Mexican cinema to which he would return in the third, most popular period of his career, from 1961 to 1977 (specifically, in the films from *Viridiana* [1961] to *Cet obscur object du désir* [1977]).

Nevertheless, the popular movies of the 1950s were important not only in giving Buñuel a prolific training ground, but also in making his contribution to Mexican cinema more tangible. Buñuel was openly irreverent toward the ideology and prevalent images of Mexican cinema. Yet, in these movies, Buñuel often referred to specifically identifiable contexts that were sometimes too detailed or obscure for foreign audiences, but undoubtedly Mexican. For example, the city of Guanajuato plays a symbolic role in *Él*. The casting of actor Manuel Dondé, who was said to resemble President Alemán, is meaningful in *Subida al cielo*. In *El bruto* and *Ensayo de un crimen,* the star discourse of Pedro Armendáriz and Ernesto Alonso suggests hidden meanings. Even the posture of a female character in *La hija del engaño* and the rhetorical style of a monologue in *Subida al cielo* are referential nods to Mexican films, politics, and culture.

Thus, in these movies Buñuel was indeed speaking to his Mexican audience, practicing his criticism in ways that were significant to his immediate audience and to the industry where the films were produced; in short, he was making Mexican movies. These nuances of context and content differentiate *Susana, Una mujer sin amor, Subida al cielo,* and *Ensayo de un crimen,* for instance, from movies like *The Adventures of Robinson Crusoe,*

Nazarín, Viridiana, and *El ángel exterminador.* In these latter films, produced independently from the Mexican studios, Buñuel was finally looking for his way out of Mexican cinema.

Therefore, I only briefly refer to the independent and foreign co-productions. *The Adventures of Robinson Crusoe, Abismos de pasión* (Buñuel's adaptation of Emily Brontë's *Wuthering Heights), Nazarín, Cela s'appele l'Aurore, La mort en ce jardin,* and *La fièvre monte à El Pao* were made independently of the Mexican film industry or intended for festivals and international distribution. Although some of these films were made in Mexico and coincide chronologically with the Mexican movies, they were produced in Mexico for reasons of finance or convenience, because Buñuel lived in Mexico, but they are films that are particularly non-Mexican. Still, the early films, *Abismos de pasión* (1953) and *Nazarín* (1958), help to bridge the "generic" films of the early 1950s with the more mature, more independent movies of the early and mid-1960s. *El ángel exterminador* (1962) and *Simón del desierto* (1965), for example, positively leave behind the specifically Mexican period of 1946 to 1955.

The release of *El ángel exterminador* and *Simón del desierto* coincided with the emergence of "new cinema" in Mexico in the 1960s. These two films are privileged in a critical literature that otherwise neglects Buñuel's work in Mexico. That is because they are considered to be unlike anything in Mexican cinema, stylistically consistent with the director's surrealist period from 1929 to 1932, and Buñuel himself was adamant about making them outside of the Mexican film industry. However, whether Buñuel desired it or not, they suggested, if not initiated, the wave of independent experimental films of the Mexican "new cinema," which is historically placed precisely in the period 1964–65. Furthermore, the rise of auteur criticism in the 1960s and of the auteurist journal *Nuevo Cine* (1961–62), which picked Buñuel as a symbolic, inspirational figure, confirm the bridging function of Buñuel's films between two distinct eras of Mexican cinema. Buñuel was not an anomaly, but an instrumental piece in the complex puzzle of the nation's film history.

This book perhaps follows a similar line of thought as the relatively recent "industrial auteur" criticism. I think of Judith Mayne's book, *Directed By Dorothy Arzner,* where a systematic approach to that director's work and life paints a telling portrait of a great filmmaker's style, the meaning of her films, and her struggle to assert herself, with all the limitations imposed on her by the Classical Hollywood context. In this book, I aspire to discover the ways in which Buñuel managed to function inside the Mexican film industry while remaining always a challenge, a rebel, and generally misunderstood by his contemporaries (and eventually by his critics).[13] My intention with this work is both to see how much Buñuel's work differed from some contemporary directors in Mexican film, and how it depended upon, spoke to, addressed, and even helped to shape the filmmaking context itself. Hence, my choice of title. There are some writings out there that bear the title "Buñuel *in* Mexico" (or some variation of it), such as Víctor Fuentes's or Michael Wood's works, cited below. But the meaning of the preposition "in" does not convey how I judge Buñuel's Mexican career. What "in" suggests is a position or location in relation to something "else" or "other." By contrast, to me, the conjunction "and" signifies a connection with something. For Buñuel, it was not always an easy connection or a smooth one, but it was a connection, an association, a link, all the same.

1 Mexican Cinema in the Time of Luis Buñuel

> In contemplating the murals of Rivera, Orozco and Siqueiros, President Cárdenas imagined a cinematographic correspondence with such a celebrated plastic manifestation.
> —Francisco Sánchez, *Crónica antisolemne del cine mexicano*

In order to reconsider Buñuel's Mexican movies, we need first theorize what a national cinema is and how this concept of national cinema applies to and helps us to understand the film industry into which Luis Buñuel incorporated in 1946. We must look at the status of the Mexican film industry in the 1940s, the relationship of Mexican cinema to the country's cultural institutions, and the relevance of "national cinema" in the cultural, educational, and political project of the Mexican Revolution. It is important to understand some of the social and political functions of cinema in Mexico in order to see the complexity of the structure which Buñuel entered and to better appreciate the impact of his participation and contribution to Mexican cinema.

Mexican film genres were conceived in the 1930s as popular tools of propaganda, and films often dealt with topics and characters that were part of the historical and moral imaginary of the Revolution. By the turn of the decade of the 1940s, the genres of Mexican cinema included: (1) the *comedia ranchera* (for example, *Out at the Big Ranch* by Fernando de Fuentes [1936]); (2) the historical/patriotic epic, or revolutionary melodrama (for example, *Enamorada* by Emilio Fernández [1948])[1;] (3) the family melodrama (for example, *When the Children Leave* by Juan Bustillo Oro [1941])[2;] and (4) comedies with some social message such as those of Mario Moreno (Cantinflas) and Germán Valdés (Tin-Tán).

Of these genres, the *comedia ranchera*, the family melodrama, and the Cantinflas comedies were not only enormously popular in Mexico, but they established Mexican cinema as the most popular in many other Spanish-speaking countries. Nevertheless, it was the historical epic, with revolutionary and "indigenist" themes, that became inscribed with the official label of "national" cinema and that was privileged to be shown at the European film festivals of the late 1940s. The cinema laws decreed by Congress in the 1940s specified that films had to respect the Mexican nation, Mexican authorities, and Mexican law. These laws also favored the production of films that would "achieve ... a labor of adequate propaganda locally and abroad in favor of the national film industry."[3] This language established one of the constants of Mexican cinema when it came to defining "the national": at the center lay the "respectful" revolutionary dramas; at the margins (as far as the international image of Mexico was concerned) lay the comedies and several variations of musical drama.[4]

Moreover, the genres of the "old" Mexican cinema had also solidified around a strict star system. Specific actors became identified with the character types they played: the patriarch (the brothers Domingo and Fernando Soler, Joaquín Pardavé), the mother (Sara García), the singing *charro* (Jorge Negrete, Pedro Infante, Tito Guízar), Indians and soldiers (Pedro Armendáriz, Emilio Fernández), the "femme fatal" (María Félix, Andrea Palma), the sexy *cabaretera* (Ninón Sevilla, María Antonieta Pons), and the saintly virgin (Dolores del Río, Columba Domínguez). Thus has the tradition of classical cinema in Mexico been characterized,[5] and these genres serve as a model with which to compare and contrast Luis Buñuel's direct impact and contribution to Mexican film history. Ultimately, when Luis Buñuel arrived in Mexico, there did not exist anything like the independent, "artisan" mode of production he had known in Europe in the 1930s.

The genres and narratives of the Mexican film industry related to the state and state ideology, actually making them something of an official "national cinema." Practically every feature film in the classical period (roughly 1935–55) was produced within the national film industry, and many represented the political project of national cinema in Mexico. Although the Revolution began in 1910, the articulation of a homogenizing nationalist ideology could not occur until the Institutional Revolutionary Party finally consolidated power in the 1930s. A decade later, Mexican cinema had adopted its revolutionary image, exemplified by the award-winning epic films directed by Emilio Fernández and photographed by Gabriel Figueroa.

NATIONAL CINEMA: A BLUEPRINT

In her book *French National Cinema*, Susan Hayward asks two pertinent questions about cinema and nationalism: "What are the texts and what meanings do they mobilize?" and "What typologies must be traced into a cartography of the national?"[6] Hayward argues that the canonization of certain film-texts and products (their archival status, the forums in which they are made public and/or housed), as well as how they are managed, diffused, and preserved, helps to associate and relate these films to national politics and culture. In other words, Hayward's model helps us to understand how a cinema becomes "national," in the official sense of the word, and what it is that cinema contributes to the codes, myths, and ideologies that define a nation. In the search for a working concept of national cinema, according to Hayward, specific questions emerge: "How is the national enunciated? . . . *How* to enunciate the national? . . . What is there, what does it mean, and how do we write its meaning?"[7] Furthermore, Hayward's blueprint for a national cinema helps us to understand the hierarchization of different styles and genres in national cinema:

> Here the concern is not simply with art and popular cinemas' cultural production, but with mainstream and peripheral cinemas, with *the* cinema . . . that which is at the center of the nation. This shifts according to which particular nation is being referred to because the concept of a nation's cinema will change according to a nation's ideology.[8]

Hayward identifies the coexistence of "central" and "peripheral" film styles and genres that serve different functions within a national cinema. She proposes studying a national cinema through: "(a) narratives; (b) genres; (c) codes and conventions; (d) gesturality and morphology; (e) the star as sign; (f) cinema of the center and of the periphery; and (g) cinema as the mobiliser of the nation's myths and of the myth of the nation."[9] Each of these categories can be used as a model to reach a working definition of national cinema in Mexico.

Hayward goes on to explain the relationship between state ideology and film styles:

> Filmic narration, calls upon the available discourses and myths of its own culture. It is evident that these are not pure and simple reflections of history, but a transformation of history. Thus, they work to construct a specific way of perceiving the nation. Cinema . . . is no exception to this nation construction . . . and the question becomes, what myths does a national cinema put in place and what are the consequences?[10]

In the process of perceiving and constructing the nation, of centralizing the Mexican state, and of "institutionalizing" the revolutionary government (Mexico is, after all the country of the "Institutional Revolution"), national cinema appropriated a mythology of the nation through motifs and symbols. These symbols, in film and other media, became both official and popular. In the case of Mexican cinema, nation-construction translated into a visual imagery that was quickly reproduced in the movies in the mid-1930s. It was not until the mid-1950s that this image of the Mexican nation and the cultural and political processes that forged it began to collapse.

CULTURE AND THE MEXICAN REVOLUTION

Benedict Anderson, from whom Hayward draws part of her model, describes some of the symptoms of the particular brand of nationalism proper to the Mexican Revolution and present in Mexican cinema. In his book, *Imagined Communities: Reflections on the Origin and Spread of Nationalism*, Anderson explains the importance of codification and "aging" for creating a sense of nationhood, that is, of finding an "imagined" past to legitimize a nation's origins. In the case of Mexico, this past was the heritage of the Aztecs, the Mayas, and the Mexicas, which became the departure point for the fictional historical continuum out of which the Revolution evolved.[11] According to this story, in Mexico, as in other Spanish territories in the Americas, the Indian heritage was absorbed into the dominant creole (the Mexican-born, white bourgeoisie) social structure, becoming the glue, so to speak, that bonded together the different components of the national identity. In addition, the practice of hierarchizing, preserving, and diffusing this adopted national/cultural heritage became integrated into government cultural institutions. As Anderson says, "These ... institutions were the census, the map, and the museum: together, they profoundly shaped the way in which the colonial state imagined its dominion—the nature of the human beings it ruled, the geography of its domain, and the legitimacy of its ancestry."[12] The management of cultural products is thus one of the areas to which Anderson pays attention in order to illustrate his theory and account of the "imaginary" nature of nationalism and national identities.

In the case of Mexico, Anderson's argument is especially important because one of the most successful areas of revolutionary-historical management occurred through the design and diffusion of cultural production.[13] Renowned anthropologist Néstor García Canclini has studied Mexican museums, painting, and the plastic arts, and he concludes that in Mexico the adoption of cultural production as a tool of nationalism has emphasized the visual arts: "Although Mexico has a powerful literature, its cultural profile was not established primarily by writers. From codices to muralism, from the death's-heads of José Guadalupe Posada to paintings and short stories, from the handicraft markets to the mass audiences of the museums, the conservation and celebration of the patrimony, its knowledge and its use, is basically a visual operation."[14] Although García Canclini fails to mention it,

Mexican classical cinema, with its enormous popularity at home and abroad, its nationalist leanings, and its cultural-propagandist mission, was one of the great achievements of Mexico's project of "visual culture."[15]

Beyond exposing the relationships among art, hegemony, mythology, and the state as they are reproduced at the Mexican National Museum of Anthropology, García Canclini has analyzed the ways "culture" has been codified, structured, and hierarchized in the Mexican state's "revolutionary" program:

> Among Latin American countries, Mexico, because of the nationalist orientation of its postrevolutionary policy, should be the one that has been more concerned with expanding visual culture, preserving its patrimony, and integrating it into a system of museums, archeological and historical centers. In the first half of the twentieth century, the documentation and diffusion of the patrimony was done through temporary and traveling exhibits, cultural missions and muralism.[16]

The systematic expansion of visual culture and its integration into a system of public cultural diffusion was exemplified by the rise of state museums and similar forums. To these spaces and forms of cultural flux, we must add the cinematheque, film archives, film festivals, and theaters. García Canclini is concerned with theorizing the tension between modernism, modernization, and tradition in Latin American countries (an issue also raised in Buñuel's "urban" comedies and melodramas), and he draws examples from postrevolutionary Mexican politics and its manipulation of culture, a practice in which cinema participated actively.

In Mexico, narratives of resistance to tyranny and foreign invasion have been useful for centuries in the creation of the patriotic imaginary. During the Latin American independence movements of the early nineteenth century, creole-dominant ideology was justified in part by associating the independence movements with Indian resistance to the Spanish conquest in the sixteenth century. Naturally, the heroes of the 1810 provincial/nationalist revolt that led to Mexican independence became part of the fictional-historical continuum, and they were invoked during the Revolution one hundred years later.[17] In other words, the precolonial empire, the independence movement, and the Revolution became part of a single, imaginary linear history. Interestingly, this imaginary continuity of the nation's heroes is one of the consistent traits of the management of culture in revolutionary Mexico. Thus, the Aztec emperor Cuauhtémoc, who led the 1520 insurrection against Hernán Cortés—Miguel Hidalgo and José María Morelos, the leaders of the independence movement of the 1810s—and the twentieth-century revolutionary leaders Francisco Madero, Francisco "Pancho" Villa, and Emiliano Zapata are all protagonists of the same story.[18]

In the 1930s and through the 1940s, the articulation of the "cultural nation" was transmitted locally through the educational system and through public radio. And Mexican films were simultaneously significant international ambassadors for Mexico's revolutionary image as well as agents of internal cohesiveness, at least until the advent of the economic and social crisis of the late 1940s. Because of the state's involvement as an arbiter of cultural production, some films in the 1940s were sent to represent Mexico in a number of international film festivals. This allowed these films to be further legitimized as representatives of Mexico's culture and identity, and the international praise and recognition they received was second only to that of the Mexican muralists José Clemente Orozco, Diego Rivera, and David Alfaro Siqueiros. The historical scenario championed by the government through public education, muralism, radio, and the cinema was thus strengthened at home and exported abroad.

In her book *The Myth of the Revolution*, Ilene V. O'Malley analyzes the codification of men, historical episodes, popular culture, and images that, filtered through the mentality of Mexican machismo, have come to represent Mexico locally and abroad. The focus on men and national history matured during the process of "mythification" of the Mexican Revolution, O'Malley argues—a process further strengthened by public education in the 1930s. The Revolution, then, was responsible for sparking a "tremendous subjective change of national consciousness":

> The revolution brought a surge of creativity to the arts unparalleled since the pre-Columbian era, provoked a mania for the "truly Mexican," and inspired countless ballads and stories which have become the modern Mexican folklore. This folklore has in turn been taken up as themes in movies, comic books, novels, and even in the decor of discotheques and restaurants. . . . It is necessary to understand [Mexico's fascination with the 1910 Revolution] . . . in order to understand Mexican society today. The revolutionary motif that pervades it is no mere curiosity or fluke of style. The Revolution has a fundamental ideological role.[19]

O'Malley analyzes the public image of the four patriarchs of the Mexican revolution: Francisco Madero, Emiliano Zapata, Francisco "Pancho" Villa, and Venustiano Carranza. Madero led the initial revolts of the November 1910–June 1911 period against the old dictatorship of Porfirio Díaz. Emiliano Zapata led the following surge of peasant revolts against Madero from November 1911 to February 1913, and along with Pancho Villa, headed up the *constitucionalista* armies that took Mexico City in December

1914. Finally, Venustiano Carranza is credited with enforcing the first land-reform decrees, in 1915, thereby achieving one of the major goals of the Revolution. O'Malley shows how, by marrying the concept of "the State" with that of "the Revolution," these men became symbols of what was to become the "national culture":

> The propaganda surrounding these four heroes had a number of common traits: the claim that the government was revolutionary; the promotion of nationalism; the obfuscation of history; the denigration of politics; Christian imagery and the promotion of Catholic values; and patriarchal values and the "masculinization" of the heroes' images. These characteristics form the internal ideology and psychology of the myth of the Mexican Revolution.[20]

A checklist of what defined the revolutionary spirit of Mexico shows that the Revolution ratified a patriarchal system that perpetuated many ideological positions of the ancien régime,[21] even as the ideology was merged into that paradoxical concept known as the "Institutional Revolution."[22]

The ideological processes of the Mexican Revolution and its effective incorporation and homogenization of a national imaginary took definite form after the foundation of the Secretaría de Educación Pública (SEP), or Public Education Secretariat, in 1921. The SEP provided an almost systematic model for establishing Mexican revolutionary nationalism, for giving it an "official" imprimatur, for forging a coherent rhetoric and symbolic system. It occupied a central place in the discourse of Mexican cinema before the time of Luis Buñuel. As Jesús Martín-Barbero discusses, the Mexican government saw in the public education system "the opportunity to civilize the masses under the direction of the state . . . [and to articulate the nation as] not only what the state has identified and brought into existence but the way in which the masses have experienced . . . the social legitimacy of their aspirations."[23] Public radio, for example, was an instrumental medium in "touching the sentiments of everyone" through broadcasts that emphasized national and regional music in search of "the roots of an 'authentic' ethnic identity."[24] The cinema, however, provided a popular visual expression of Mexicanness, and as Martín-Barbero concludes, it gave "national identity an image and a voice."[25] Logically, cinema did not invent this image; it was passed on to the cinema from the revolutionary mythology that had been in the making since 1910 and from the public education system's rationalization and diffusion of "the myth of the Revolution."

One of the great achievements of the government's cultural project in the 1930s was combining a sense of creole patriarchy with Indian arts and crafts and Catholic morals. As several historians have observed, the ideological project of the Mexican Revolution was always a negotiation that included diverse forms of media and the arts. In her book, *Cultural Politics in Revolution*, Mary Kay Vaughan characterizes the "cultural nationalist movement" of public education under Minister José Vasconcelos as the construction of "the cultural nation."[26] Furthermore, the homogenizing cultural initiative of public education expanded to promote national music, literature, arts, and education. The government even attempted to amend popular culture practices, like sports and religious rituals, so that they would fit the plans of the Revolution, becoming lay and "institutionalized" in accordance with the revolutionary state.[27]

Classical Mexican cinema became part of that project in the 1930s, partially supported by government incentives (primarily in the form of taxes on film imports) and subventions. There was, as well, the recognition of a "central" cinema (the historical/patriotic epics) and a "peripheral" cinema (the comedies of Cantinflas and, later, Tin-Tán, the musical dramas, and the *cine de arrabal*). The epic/historic dramas, the ones that best represented a certain code of visual/aesthetic and narrative/thematic motifs and were chosen to represent Mexico in the international film festivals, were like other Mexican revolutionary art (muralism, for example) that could be distinguished from "popular" manifestations. In other words, like muralism, the revolutionary epics were considered examples of the "cultural nation" worthy of international consumption. Specifically, film legislation in the 1940s stated that the National Film Institute was to "cooperate with the Public Education Secretariat to increase the use of the cinema as a means of scholarly instruction and extra-curricular cultural diffusion."[28]

Some of the visual themes of Mexican cinema had been legitimized by the muralist tradition that helped "invent" and diffuse the visual image of revolutionary Mexico. Among the exemplary films from this period are Carlos Navarro's *Janitzio* and Fred Zinnemann's *Redes*, both Indian-theme dramas released in 1934. Director Emilio Fernández is said to have once called himself "the fourth muralist," and it is acknowledged that his work with cinematographer Gabriel Figueroa owes a tremendous stylistic debt to the pictorial style of José Clemente Orozco.[29] From the writings of José Vasconcelos (specifically, his book *The Cosmic Race*, which made a theoretical argument that Mexicans were a mestizo race with European culture and values, a concept at odds with most revolutionary ideology), to the "indigenismo" of the muralists, the revolutionary image of Mexico was codified in museums, in literature, and in the plastic arts. That image, as Vaughan has written, "rested heavily on the achievements of the Indian past and contemporary Indian aesthetics, which were nationalized as symbols, objects, and artifacts."[30]

Furthermore, part of the Revolution's program to inculcate a mythological narrative was officially incorporated into the public education system in the (failed) "socialist education" programs of the 1930s. As Vaughan points out, the Mexican Revolution's "imagined community," which rendered only faulty results, was the product of the SEP, instituted in 1921, whose first minister was the writer and philosopher José Vasconcelos. Vaughan goes on to explain the "bottom-up" approach of the Secretariat and its specific attempts at creating a state of cultural and political homogeneity, an "imagined community," to which Mexicans of all walks of life could abide. Succinctly put, Vaughan writes that "notions of national identity and membership were indeed nurtured at the local level by the revolutionary process through the school."[31]

Understanding the agenda of the public education system in rural Mexico in the 1930s is instrumental for understanding the trajectory of Mexican national cinema, another product of the systematic incorporation of the Revolution into Mexican society, arts, and popular culture.

> The real cultural revolution of the 1930s lay not in the state's project, but in the dialogue between state and society that took place around that project. A common language for consent and protest was forged. It was enabled by a simultaneously emerging institutional structure (represented by the official party, popular organizations, state agencies, and the school system); and it was facilitated by a proliferating infrastructural network of communication in the State and private economies (including roads, cheap modes of transport, the print and electronic media, and schools).[32]

As parts of that project was the rural teachers' common curriculum and *El maestro rural*, SEP's journal for teachers involved in the nationalization project. This brings to mind Jesús Martín-Barbero's assessment of the public education system as a means to "civilize the masses," as well as his analysis of the popularity of Mexican cinema, a bridging point between the project of "the cultural nation" and the popular classes. In his analysis of Mexican classical cinema, Martín-Barbero echoes cultural critic Carlos Monsiváis, who stresses the key role of cinema in "mediating" the official images of culture and the public's subscription to them.

> Going to the movies was not a purely psychological event, but the point of encounter between the collective lived experience generated by the Revolution and the mediation which, even though it deformed this experience, gave it social legitimacy. . . . Cinema was the living, social

mediation that constituted the new cultural experience, and cinema became the first language of the popular urban culture. Beyond the reactionary subject matter and the rigidity of its form, film connected with the yearnings of the masses to make themselves socially visible.... People went to the movies more to see themselves in a sequence of images that gave them gestures, faces, manners of speaking and walking, landscapes and colors than to identify with the plots.[33]

For Martín-Barbero and Monsiváis, the power of Mexican cinema lay in its success in giving the nation a mirror in which people could see themselves.

In an attempt to consolidate these forces of education and nationalism in the cinema, Emilio Fernández's 1947 film *Río Escondido (Hidden River)* took up the topic of the rural schools program of the 1930s. In the film, María Félix plays a rural teacher who instructs her students on revolutionary history, the lives of the heroes of the revolution, and the myth of the historical continuum from the Aztecs to the present. She also teaches her eager pupils the ways to achieve the Revolution's goals through hard work and discipline, as well as the ideology of ethnic incorporation known as "indigenismo" in intellectual circles and government policy. The movie is itself a reflection on both the state's cultural project and the role of national cinema in that project's incorporation and diffusion.

In one of the most dramatic scenes in the movie, the teacher-protagonist received her instructions from President Miguel Alemán. As she walks into the National Palace and upstairs to the president's office, the camera flows leisurely over one of Diego Rivera's most famous murals, *Mexico Yesterday, Today, and Tomorrow,* finished in 1945. The panning shot gives the audience a condensed history lesson, in which the Aztecs, the *pater patriae* of the Independence, and the revolutionary titans (Villa, Zapata, Madero) all seem to be fighting the same war. In that single shot, Emilio Fernández and cinematographer Gabriel Figueroa seem to be articulating three theses: that there is a historical-cultural bias to the Revolution; that public education is important in helping that project adhere together; and, finally, that the national cultural establishment, of which Diego Rivera was a foolproof symbol, played a substantial role in ensuring the success of that project.[34] The mural is not only a grand condensation of Mexican history and revolutionary mythmaking, but it has a clearly iconic status in the movie. Emilio Fernández's *Río Escondido* was not only a movie that dealt directly with the revolutionary projects of acculturation from the educational perspective, or as Vaughan calls it, "the modernization of patriarchy."[35] *Río Escondido* was also a kind of self-reflexive glimpse at the mythical significance of the revolutionary cultural project which expanded to multiple areas of Mexico's life.

With his most famous film, *María Candelaria* (1943), as with *Río Escondido*, Emilio Fernández wanted to make it clear that the cinema was an active part of the country's enormous cultural undertaking. Through his work, he believed, the cinema could aspire to be "a poem" that would embody "the history of a people."[36] (In fact, in Mexican cinema history the most consistent adjective that describes Fernández's cinema of the 1940s is "lyrical.") Unfortunately, the construction of the "cultural nation" was not as simple as Rivera's poetic murals or Fernández's lyrical movies make it appear: the state initiative to adopt and diffuse specific cultural notions was not smooth, and it met with different forms of opposition and resistance in some communities.

Alan Knight analyzes the state's attempts at molding popular culture to fit the plans of the Revolution. He explains that this plan, along with that of the SEP, also incorporated a "social clean-up" project, with known ideological convergence with social Darwinism, and that the plan alienated so many Indian and popular communities that it led to resistance and boycotts rather than active participation.[37] Among other things, Indian communities were expected to recognize the Aztec and Mayan cultures as the accepted, privileged Indian heritage, which often undermined their own ethnic and tribal origins. The fact that these efforts were absolute failures in Yaqui communities in the state of Sonora, for example, shows how arbitrary and misguided the popular/cultural/social assimilation project was from the beginning.[38] Even when public education attempted to "redeem the Indians"[39] through education and assimilation (as *Río Escondido* shows), the reality of many Indian and rural communities was incompatible with government plans.[40] Furthermore, Emilio Fernández's movies were among the few that dealt with Indian topics and characters, but generally the focus of classical cinema was on creole-centered narratives about the Revolution and the manly heroes of Mexican patriarchy.[41]

In recent years, historians and anthropologists have scrutinized the scope, strategy, and faults of Mexico's attempt to construct the "cultural nation."[42] They have built on the initial critical revisionist critique of the Revolution, politics, the PRI, and the economy that cultural critics like Daniel Cosío-Villegas, Octavio Paz, Rodolfo Usigli, and others were rehearsing in the 1940s and 1950s.[43] That first wave of revisionism was part of a larger intellectual pursuit of the meaning and identity of Mexicanness *(lo mexicano)* in the face of the crisis of the Revolution. Yet, as Homi Bhabha states in *Nation and Narration*, the "image of the nation—or narration— might seem impossibly romantic and excessively metaphorical, but it is from those traditions of political thought and literary language that the nation emerges as a powerful historical idea in the west."[44] And Doris Sommer, in her essay on the "national romances" of Latin America, observes the Latin American weakness for "pretty lies" in fiction when it comes to dealing with history, nationalism, and patriarchy. "The Latin Americans," writes Sommer, "tended to patch up [the cracks in the bourgeois ideal of family] with the euphoria of recent successes or with the sheer will to project ideal histories."[45] This undertaking was more originally redefined in Mexican cinema by the "revolutionary epics" and family melodramas of Emilio Fernández, Fernando de Fuentes, Juan Bustillo Oro, and other classic directors. The Mexican Revolution provided the building blocks for a new "foundational fiction" in Mexico, even one hundred years after independence.

CINEMA AND THE CULTURAL NATION

The issues of nationalism, state cultural policy, and the public role of the cinema are important for understanding Mexican cinema's openly nationalist position concurrent with the flow of official culture and the institutionalization of the Revolution in the 1930s. The emergence of classical cinema in Mexico was facilitated by the consolidation of political power into the Institutional Revolution Party (the Partido Revolucionario Institucional, or PRI.) The 1930s constituted the first decade of political stability since the end of Porfirio Diaz's dictatorship in 1911.[46] This stability in the 1930s coincides with methodical efforts to invent the "cultural nation," with the establishment of a cinematic aesthetic, and with a specific set of "revolutionary" topics, genres, and heroic figures that became the classical-national cinema.[47]

Political stability and the financial viability of the genres of classical cinema in Mexico evolved into the state production incentives that were subsequently granted in the early 1940s and 1950s. This was further facilitated by the importation of U.S. raw film stock during and around the time of World War II. Classical Mexican cinema, in its nationalist-epic mode, was thus an active participant in the revolutionary program as early as 1934, clearly abiding by the aesthetics of the "cultural nation" as rehearsed and put into practice by the intelligentsia and the cultural establishment.

Some of the stylistic motifs of classical cinema are historically traced back to films like Sergei Eisenstein's ¡Que Viva México!, parts of which Fernández probably saw in Hollywood before returning to Mexico in 1934.[48] Eisenstein's footage was clearly of great influence on indigenist Mexican films. Fernández, who also worked as an extra in American films in the late 1920s and early 1930s, once said that when he saw the Eisenstein footage (probably from Sol Lester's version, *Storm Over Mexico*) he thought to himself, "This is the cinema Mexico should make," and that the film caused such an impact in him that he decided to study and dedicate himself to making films.[49] But Eisenstein was said to have been influenced himself by the "monumental" painting style of Diego Rivera, so his relationship to Mexican cinema was as symbiotic as it was influential.[50] Carlos Navarro's *Janitzio* (1934)—the original "indigenist" film , as well as the work of the muralist painters Rivera, Siqueiros, and Orozco, and even Fred Zinnemann's *Redes* (1934) are all identified as stylistic and thematic influences in the cinema of the following decade.

The combination of a characteristic visual style and a specific set of themes led to the original classics of sound Mexican cinema: Fernando de Fuentes's *Vámonos con Pancho Villa (Let's Go with Pancho Villa*, 1935*)* and *Allá en el Rancho Grande (Out at the Big Ranch*, 1936*)*. The lyrical style of filmmaking of Emilio Fernández and the cinematography of Gabriel Figueroa that followed gave Mexican cinema international recognition a decade later.

Official national film culture became part of the revision of the image of Mexico that followed the Revolution and was popularly exemplified by the mural paintings of Rivera, Siqueiros, and Orozco. Other than the fame of the muralists, one can argue that the films that the government exported to international film festivals, especially Emilio Fernández's *Flor silvestre* and *María Candelaria*, both produced in 1943, were some of the most eloquent emissaries of Mexican culture to the rest of the world. In 1946 and 1947 these two films received wide distribution and critical acclaim in the postwar European film festivals, particularly at Cannes. They went on to win diverse technical awards (with the sponsorship of the state, since only officially selected movies could represent their country in the international festivals).[51] Furthermore, these movies were made possible by the availability of loans from the National Cinematographic Bank (Banco Nacional Cinematográfico), established in 1942. The triumphs of the epic, melodramatic, and often preachy movies directed by Fernández and photographed by Figueroa represent the peak of the Classical or Golden Age of Mexican cinema. At the same time, they mark the beginning of the end of an industry that then slowly declined in quality, quantity, and critical esteem through the 1950s.[52]

In his book, *Crónica antisolemne del cine mexicano*, Francisco Sánchez agrees not only with the correspondence of the Golden Age with this period, but also with the international recognition of the Fernández–Figueroa team as the incontestable yardstick of the style and quality of Mexican cinema. As film scholar Susan Hayward has schematized in her book on *French National Cinema*, Fernández–Figueroa exhibited certain recognizable "narratives, genres, codes and conventions, gesturality and morphology, and stars as signs." Sánchez puts it in these terms for Mexican cinema:

> In the so-called Golden Age some intelligent directors made their debut and, after the armistice, some international awards started falling [this way], but not for all the cinema that was being made here . . . but almost exclusively for the pictures directed by Emilio "Indio" Fernández and photographed by Gabriel Figueroa.[53]

Furthermore, Jorge Ayala Blanco, one of Mexico's most respected film historians, finds that after appearing as an actor in the classic "indigenist" drama, *Janitzio*, in 1934, Emilio Fernández made many contributions to Mexican cinema. First, he helped to "liberate" the Indians from their supporting roles in dramas of strong creole content, and second, to "internationalize" the image of the cinematographic Mexico, even if, in retrospect, his films seem rather shallow in content:

> With *María Candelaria* the panorama [of Mexican cinema] was modified. The thick moustache . . . of Pedro Armendáriz and the delicate braids . . . of Dolores del Río imposed themselves internationally. This universally celebrated classical work of Mexican cinema . . . has decreased very little in its lyricism. . . . Nevertheless, the exploration of the film was more directed toward photogenic [quality] than to the historical-social moment.[54]

The undisputed classics of the history of Mexican cinema, in particular *María Candelaria* and *Flor silvestre*, established and consummated the international image of Mexican cinema and Mexican culture, in part based on the governmental initiatives to absorb popular culture into the "plan" of the revolutionary government. Furthermore, the film *María Candelaria* itself comments on the "officialization" of the image of the Indian into the Revolution's cultural imaginary. In the movie, the title character, played by Dolores Del Río, is an Indian woman who is hired to pose nude for an artist (perhaps a thinly disguised reference to some famous work by Diego Rivera) because she represents, according to the painter, "the essence" of Mexican beauty.

The fictional scenario of *María Candelaria* is rather self-reflexive: a reference to the Mexican cultural establishment's appropriation of the image of the Indian as a surrogate for Mexican nationality, or at least as the visual representation of *mexicanidad*, of "the essence" of Mexico. Furthermore, the Mexican nation's other major components are represented by the presence of the white creole artist (Alberto Galán) who idealizes the Indians' "image," and the evil mestizo shopkeeper (Miguel Inclán) who exploits the Indians and is put in charge by the government.

In the 1930s there had been an important ongoing philosophical and intellectual debate in literary magazines and books about *mexicanidad* and *lo mexicano*. Some of the most prominent thinkers of the time (Leopoldo Zea, Samuel Ramos, Jesús Silva Herzog, Alfonso Reyes, and later Daniel Cosío-Villegas and Octavio Paz) had publicly debated, if only for an elite readership, the question of "Mexicanness" and had tried to define theoretically what it was to be "Mexican."[55] As was to be the case with *Río Escondido* a few years later, *María Candelaria* was also, in its own naive way, bringing Mexican cinema right into the crux of that debate and the rich cultural life of Mexico City in the 1940s.[56]

Thus, *María Candelaria* was not only a movie about an Indian woman who lends her image to an artist (she dies for it, too), but it was also a comment on official cultural policy that participated in a documented cultural debate. Appropriately, it also became the film most internationally acclaimed and recognized in the entire history of Mexican classical cinema. *María Candelaria*, along with *Flor silvestre*, interestingly marks the peak in the national and international film scene and thus the beginning of the end of Mexican classical cinema. Significantly, it was at this juncture, when national cinema had reached its peak, that Luis Buñuel's films intersected the path of Mexican cinema and forever changed the trajectory of Mexican film history.

BUÑUEL IN MEXICO

Luis Buñuel's work often contrasted with the virile mythological heroes of the Revolution.[57] For example, the effeminate leading-man character Archibaldo de la Cruz in *Ensayo de un crimen* and the young Alberto in *Susana* do not fit the depiction of the Mexican "macho." In *Los olvidados*, Buñuel directly addresses the matter of social Darwinism, when the protagonist is sent to a reformatory-trade school where he is the subject of a "social-scientific" project that is itself doomed to failure. These and many other instances exemplify Buñuel's spirit of parody of the imaginary of Mexican cinema. But they also ground Buñuel's work unequivocally within the currents of revisionism of the themes and genres of Mexican cinema, exemplary of the decline of the Golden Age.

The crest of creativity in revolutionary art of the 1920s and 1930s was followed by a phase of crisis, also reflected in national cinema. It was during the time when Luis Buñuel's best Mexican films were produced that Mexican cinema also saw the proliferation of more "feminine" genres and more active female protagonists. The images of the patriarch and the macho—images that were instrumental to the conception of the Mexican revolutionary myth—were somewhat corroded.

Luis Buñuel's Mexican films are of utmost importance for understanding the two defining periods of Mexican cinema that they help link, the Classical and New Mexican cinema. When *Los olvidados* became an international success after its 1951 release at the Cannes Film Festival, Buñuel achieved recognition as a prominent figure *within* Mexican cinema, but not necessarily a figure *of* Mexican cinema. After *Los olvidados* and until the early 1960s, only a few of Buñuel's movies achieved outstanding positions in Mexican cinema, both in the critical journals and on the festival circuits. Indeed, Buñuel's definitive departure from Mexican cinema after *Simón del desierto* coincides with the beginning of the "new" era of Mexican cinema in the mid-1960s.[58] Buñuel's influence was acknowledged in the works of the "New Cinema" directors of the 1960s. The future names of Mexican cinema, directors like Alberto Isaac (*In This Town There Are No Thieves*, 1964; *Tívoli*, 1974), Arturo Ripstein (*El castillo de la pureza*, 1972; *El lugar sin límites*, 1977), and Jaime Humberto Hermosillo (*María de mi corazón*, 1982) knew and respected Buñuel.

Because of Luis Buñuel's inquiry into the mythical images of Mexico in classical cinema, much of his work is deeply related to Mexican cinema's historical development from the classical era to the "New Cinema" of the 1960s. It is necessary that we try to understand Buñuel's pivotal relationship to disparate periods of Mexican cinema (in its thematic, historical, and aesthetic contexts) in order to better understand Buñuel's incontestable importance for the history of Mexican cinema as a whole.

National cinema in Mexico was significant in the making of the "cultural nation." The unifying "idea" of the nation was a legitimate attempt at political solidarity and social coherence and was manifested in literature, painting, education, and the cinema. The "myth" of the Mexican Revolution, presently the target of postrevisionist analyses, is one of the things that had been under scrutiny in Mexican cinema since the time of Buñuel. Some of Buñuel's contemporaries, like *cabaretera* film director Alberto Gout for example, are now acknowledged to have offered critical and revisionist portraits of Mexican society in their films during the pivotal decade of the 1950s. The subsequent generation of filmmakers in Mexico, the "New Cinema" directors of the 1960s and 1970s, specifically, confirm the significance of Buñuel's period as a turning point in the nation's cinema.

One of the surrealists' favorite topics was the unpredictable designs of chance and how they arbitrarily could change a person's life forever. Chance brought Buñuel to Mexico, and eventually his life, and arguably the face of Mexican cinema, were altered thereafter. In the following chapter, I will analyze the personal and professional trajectory of Luis Buñuel's career, from his filmmaking training in France, the United States, and Spain, to the historical circumstances that landed him and his family in Mexico, a country where he said he could never be found.[59]

2   Buñuel and Mexico

> Should I suddenly drop out of sight one day, I might be anywhere except there.
>
> —Luis Buñuel, *My Last Sigh*

> In what way is Luis Buñuel, Aragonese man of good stock, immersed in the French cultural tradition, going to find Mexico and its drama?
>
> —Miguel Ángel Mendoza, 1947

After his landmark debut film *Un chien andalou* in 1929 and the controversial *L'Age d'Or* in 1930, Luis Buñuel had a somewhat irregular career, until he reemerged from relative obscurity in 1950 with his third Mexican feature, *Los olvidados*. That film enjoyed international acclaim and, as André Bazin stated in 1951, it rescued Buñuel from being "swallowed up by the commercial cinema of the New World."[1] Between his early surrealist phase (1929–32) and his "late" phase of European movies (1966–77), Luis Buñuel produced the largest body of his work, seventeen of his thirty-two films, in Mexico. Critics agree that for someone who had achieved such *succès de scandale* with his first two movies, the transition to work in the commercial Mexican film industry must have been a difficult one.[2] Working in Mexico, however, may have been easier for Buñuel than working in Hollywood, which was the only other option for a filmmaker from a devastated, slowly recovering postwar Europe. Nevertheless, Luis Buñuel's training and his activities in the period from 1932 to 1946, some of his interests, and the historical circumstances that took him to Mexico may be more logical than they seem at first glance.

Buñuel's incorporation into Mexican cinema was originally "generic," not very political, and his early movies, *Gran Casino* (1947) and *El gran calavera* (1949), were distinctly harmless in their apparent submission to the conventions of the musical melodrama and the "social" comedy. These genres themselves, however, were under revision at the time of Buñuel's incorporation into the Mexican film industry, and Buñuel's films reflect this revisionist inclination. Furthermore, Buñuel's move to Mexico was a logical continuation of his filmmaking training. He was familiar with some genres of Mexican cinema, and his process of "conversion" to popular cinema had already begun in the middle 1930s, when Buñuel was in charge of the production of several comedies and melodramas at Filmófono studios in Madrid. Thus, this chapter is concerned with the processes and the circumstances that preceded, prepared, and led Luis Buñuel to Mexico and to his relatively smooth transition into the Mexican mode of production.

The fact that Buñuel had no problem incorporating into Mexico's classic "genre" film industry may have been because he came from a traditional European bourgeois background, which included an education with plenty of access to Spanish, French, and English literature. As Gwynne Edwards argues in *The Discreet Art of Luis Buñuel*, Buñuel was a Spanish Catholic who had directed classic Spanish theater even before becoming a surrealist. Those aspects of his education are likely to have made his eventual transition to Mexican cinema easier than a judgment based on a viewing of *L'Age d'Or* would lead us to believe. In other words, it was *Un chien andalou* and *L'Age d'Or* that were really (and literally) extraordinary. *Una mujer sin amor*, for example, Buñuel's 1951 Mexican melodrama based on Guy de Maupassant's 1887 novel *Pierre et Jean*, more logically continued Buñuel's cultural trajectory and his transition toward popular forms, begun in Hollywood and Madrid in the early 1930s. Even some of Buñuel's best-known late-surrealist films *(Le Journal d'une femme de chambre*, 1963; *Belle de jour*, 1966; *Tristana*, 1969; *Cet obscur objet du désir*, 1977) are genuine offspring of the classical melodramatic tradition in the literature of the nineteenth and early twentieth centuries (just like *Pierre et Jean*). Their sources are classical, even if the movies themselves are not particularly traditional melodramas in their final film adaptations.[3] What makes Buñuel's use of melodramatic format extraordinary is not the literary sources on which his movies are based, but the subversion of classic structure that Buñuel exercised.

THE WORLD ACCORDING TO BUÑUEL

> Surrealism was a kind of call heard by certain people everywhere who, unknown to one another, were already practicing instinctive forms of irrational expression.
> —Luis Buñuel, *My Last Sigh*

Luis Buñuel was born in 1900 to an upper-middle-class family in the town of Calanda, in the northeastern Spanish province of Aragón. His father had made his fortune in Cuba, as a shop owner, before returning in 1898 to Spain, shortly after the Island's war of independence. Luis attended a Jesuit school in the provincial capital, Zaragoza, where his family had moved soon after Luis was born. Under the Jesuits' strict regimen of education and religious doctrine, there was no opportunity to question the arbitrary judgments of Catholicism, until, due to his constant conduct problems, Luis was transferred to the local public high school at age fifteen. There, Buñuel remembers, he first encountered the classics of lay science and literature that forever shaped the course of his intellectual (and spiritual) life: "I discovered Spencer, Rousseau, Marx! Reading Darwin's *The Origin of Species* was so dazzling that I lost what little faith I had left."[4] After graduating from the Instituto, Buñuel went to Madrid and enrolled in the prestigious college Residencia de Estudiantes from 1917 to 1925, where, after experimenting with sciences and agronomy, he finished a philosophy degree.

The formative years at the Residencia de Estudiantes were the most important in the young Luis's intellectual life before joining the surrealists in the late 1920s. At the college, he met and befriended people who were to have a profound impact on his life, as well as some of the most influential Spanish artists and intellectuals of the century. Besides his friendship and associations with Federico García-Lorca (whose personal library Buñuel shared), Salvador Dalí, and Rafael Alberti, Buñuel met in those Madrid years the revered "Generation of '98," writers and philosophers like Miguel de Unamuno, José Ortega y Gasset, and Benito Pérez-Galdós. He studied with Spain's leading entomologist, Ignacio Bolívar, and became active in the café discussions of Madrid's self-proclaimed intellectual avant-garde, "the Ultraists." According to Buñuel, the group provided an excuse for aspiring anarchist writers and artists who were "admirers of Dada, Cocteau, and Marinetti" but who lacked a coherent political position to meet.[5]

Trying to organize their thoughts, the Ultraists—many of whom would later be named the "generation of '27" in Spanish letters—started publishing a journal called the *Gaceta Literaria*. In the *Gaceta*, Buñuel published some film criticism and a collection of poems and prose under the prophetic title *Un perro andaluz (An Andalusian Dog)*.[6] As a film critic for *Gaceta Literaria* in Madrid, Buñuel stated his admiration for American silent screen comics Buster Keaton, Harold Lloyd, Charles Chaplin, and others whom he considered to be "the only surrealist equivalent in the cinema."[7] Among Buñuel's peers at *Gaceta Literaria* were professor Ernesto Giménez Caballero, poet and playwright Federico García-Lorca, poet Rafael Alberti (who later converted to surrealism proper with Buñuel), and, in exile, Chilean poet Pablo Neruda.[8] The *Gaceta Literaria* is credited with the establishment of Madrid's first cine-club, chaired by Luis Buñuel, and, which, in turn, is credited with the first Spanish public screening of *Un chien andalou*.[9]

Dissatisfied, however, with what seemed to him a limited, provincial cultural atmosphere, Buñuel longed above all to leave Spain.[10] Thus, after his father's death in 1925, Buñuel made his first trip to Paris, a city that would change his life and with which he would forever be associated.

Between 1925 and 1929 in Paris (although he would return to Spain periodically in that period), Buñuel found himself surrounded by writers, painters, and artists; he stayed close to old friends like Rafael Alberti and made new ones, most notably Pablo Picasso. He wrote criticism for the *Cahiers d'Art* in Paris and continued to contribute, from abroad, to *Gaceta Literaria*. He directed amateur and professional (classic Spanish) theater, and he saw more movies than he had ever dreamed of in Spain. He became an admirer of Sergei Eisenstein, G. W. Pabst, and F. W. Murnau, and was especially affected by the work of Fritz Lang: "When I saw *Destiny [Der müde Tod,* 1921], I suddenly knew that I too wanted to make movies.... Something about this film spoke to something deep in me; it clarified my life and my vision of the world."[11]

Determined to get into films, Buñuel enrolled in Jean Epstein's acting school, where the director promised his students small roles in his movies. When plans for the production of Epstein's *Mauprat* were announced in 1927, Buñuel was hired as a production assistant, which allowed him to do "a little bit of everything." Buñuel was most impressed, however, with the job of the cinematographer, Albert Duverger, whose work he observed, "fascinated."[12] After *Mauprat,* Epstein kept Buñuel on for his next film, *The Fall of the House of Usher* (1928), where Buñuel was named second assistant to the director. Nevertheless, Buñuel's association with Epstein ended abruptly. At some point, Epstein asked Buñuel to assist Abel Gance (whose wife, Marguerite, starred in the film) in auditioning some actors, and Buñuel refused categorically because he disliked both Gance and his films. Even after firing him for that reason, Epstein thought he recognized "surrealist tendencies" in Buñuel's anarchic rebelliousness, his disregard for respected figures (like Gance and himself), and he warned him to stay away from the surrealists.[13] Yet, a number of circumstances prompted Buñuel in 1928 both to pursue his own interests as a film director and to become involved with an artistic and political movement like surrealism.

The surrealists, greatly influenced by Karl Marx's *Capital* and Sigmund Freud (particularly his major 1900 treatise *The Interpretation of Dreams)* were an offshoot of the other European "isms" (expressionism, futurism, Dadaism) of the late 1910s and 1920s. They were largely interested in articulating an idea and practice of "freedom" that would open the doors to the unconscious mind. In a way, the surrealists wanted to skip over the "superego" and thus do without societal constrains, morals, and social manners, which they thought of as arbitrarily imposed, hypocritical, and repressive. Thus, to exercise their liberation of the unconscious mind, surrealist expression took form as a kind of homage to irrational thought in painting, music, photography, literature, and in the celebrated surrealist "pranks" (dressing up as Lindbergh's murdered child for a costume party, for example)—offensive practical jokes designed to scandalize everybody in bourgeois and Catholic society. In part, that was the more political side of surrealism: they believed that the social revolution that Marx foresaw would have to happen both as an economic/political liberation from the oppression of capitalism and as a psychological liberation of the mind from rules, reason, repression.

Buñuel had met many of the "right" people in the surrealist movement since moving to Paris, but his inclinations were perhaps more toward an undisciplined anarchism (which Epstein took for "surrealist tendencies") than toward the orthodoxy of surrealism.[14] Unemployed after being fired by Epstein and with the help of cinematographer Albert Duverger, Buñuel found work as an assistant in the Josephine Baker vehicle *The Siren of the Tropics* (directed by Henri Etievant), then being filmed in Paris. According to Buñuel, two events converged to tip the balance toward the search for artistic independence and a more articulate form of political activism. He was appalled by the star's dramatic tantrums on the set of *The Siren of the Tropics*, which gave Buñuel a warning of some of the drawbacks of working under a star-studio system. Meanwhile, the execution of Italian immigrant anarchists Nicola Sacco and Bartolomeo Vanzetti on 23 August 1927 in the United States and the subsequent international outrage awoke the young Buñuel's anarchist inclinations. Against the background of the American Red Scare of the 1920s, the case of Sacco and Vanzetti became something of a cause célèbre. Its implications seemed enormous, in terms of xenophobia, a "witch hunt" against anarchist immigrants, and of the mighty, arbitrary power of the law to convict and execute two men whose case seemed to have had lots of legal holes. For the young Buñuel in Paris the execution of Sacco and Vanzetti (anarchists, atheists, foreigners) dramatized what was wrong with the direction of dominant society and must have made the surrealist promise of political and mental freedom truly appealing.[15]

By then greatly interested in films and politics, Buñuel was impressed by the frankness of articles, photographs, and interviews in the journal *La Révolution Surréaliste*. The style and content of *La Révolution Surréaliste*, where surrealists theorized and practiced "irrational expression," brought Buñuel ever closer to members of the movement. Thus, when Buñuel made *Un chien andalou (The Andalusian Dog)* in 1928 with the help of Salvador Dalí and the actor Pierre Batcheff (whom he had met on the set of *The Siren of the Tropics)*, he was introduced to surrealism proper. Man Ray and Louis Aragon brought Buñuel to the attention of the "card-carrying" surrealists Max Ernst, André Breton, Paul Eluard, and others.[16] Buñuel found in the surrealists an outlet for his anger, a form for his rejection of bourgeois values, and by extension of Catholicism, that represented what he most wanted to escape: the "medieval" moral and social ways of Spain. Unlike the vague ramblings of the Spanish Ultraists in the early 1920s, surrealism, wrote Buñuel, "was a coherent moral system that, as far as I could tell, had no flaws. It was an aggressive morality based on the complete rejection of all existing values."[17] Buñuel's scandalous attacks on bourgeois values and Catholic morals in *Un chien andalou* found a home within surrealism. As Charles Tesson writes, "Buñuel did not make a film to become a surrealist, but he was a surrealist in making the film."[18]

Un chien andalou, which Buñuel made independently with his mother's money, became a surprising success in its Paris run of eight months. Buñuel was recruited by legendary aristocratic arts patrons Charles and Marie-Laure de Noailles to make another film. Buñuel was given complete independence within the limited budget, and the result of that venture, *L'Age d'Or* (1930), remains a classic of surrealist cinema. The film provoked such a strong reaction from right-wing, anti-Semitic, and conservative sectors in Paris that the theater where the movie was showing, Studio 28, was closed after six days. It provoked riots, protests, and violence, and the film was banned by French authorities and withdrawn from public circulation for many years.[19]

L'Age d'Or (The Golden Age) was released at a time when surrealism itself as a movement, as well as Buñuel's relationship to the surrealists, was changing. Among the surrealists, divisions emerged over whether the movement should define itself through aesthetic means or political action, through an organized political agenda or artistic, literary expressions. Furthermore, Buñuel was becoming increasingly unhappy with what he perceived as the snobbish manners and the hypocrisy of the surrealists.[20] Surprisingly, it was the notoriety of *L'Age d'Or*, the ultimate surrealist film, with its equation of sex, irrational violence, and death, and its brutally pure attacks on religion and society,[21] that brought Buñuel to the attention of Hollywood. This was the cause of further distance from the surrealists and eventually changed the course of his personal and artistic life.

HOLLYWOOD: FIRST CONTACTS

After the completion of *L'Age d'Or* in 1930, and to Buñuel's surprise, an MGM executive who had seen the movie offered him an apprenticeship deal with that studio. This was not uncommon during the unpredictable transition from silent to sound cinema between 1927 and 1930. Still not knowing what to do with the challenges that dialogue and vernacular music imposed on the Hollywood dominion of world markets, the American studios attracted and hired European directors and actors who could be employed in dubbing and re-shooting foreign-language versions of American films. Reportedly, in the interest of not violating his personal "convictions," Buñuel chose not to direct movies in Hollywood, first in 1930, and later between 1938 and 1946. However, and regardless of the claims of many an auteurist study, it seems clear that Buñuel was interested in the technical proficiency of Hollywood movies (to which Dalí compared *L'Age d'Or*) and in the possibility of working under better economic conditions than he had found as an independent director.[22] This may explain his (reluctant) acceptance of the 1930 MGM six-month contract.

Buñuel's early experiences at MGM as an observer in 1930 (where he met Eisenstein, Grigori Alexandrov, and Edward Tissé, then en route to Mexico for the original failed attempt at *¡Que Viva México!*) were tremendously disappointing. Buñuel was supposed to learn the making of Hollywood movies, but he was ousted from his first visit to a set, having been branded an anonymous loiterer in the eyes of star Greta Garbo. He later witnessed in awe (presumably on the set of *Shanghai Express*) how even the prestigious director Joseph Von Sternberg apparently had little or no creative control on the set. Buñuel saw how, under the Hollywood studio system of vertical integration, producers and executives ruled.

> What was more upsetting . . . was to see [Von Sternberg's] set designer positioning the cameras while [he] seemed content just to shout "Action!" In fact, most of the directors I watched seemed little more than lackeys who did the bidding of the studios that had hired them; they had no say in how the film was to be made, or even how it was to be edited.[23]

Buñuel's earlier experiences in film production, when he worked with Epstein, were in a much more artisanal mode of production, decidedly different from his experiences in Hollywood. In any case, Hollywood's mode of production negatively impressed Buñuel far more than Hollywood's dependence on the conventions of genres like melodrama, which Buñuel knew all too well.[24] Thus, it was the issue of creative independence and not necessarily his previous career as a director of surrealist movies that alienated Luis Buñuel from the Hollywood film industry during his first visit there in 1930. Convinced that he would neither find work nor be happy in Hollywood, Buñuel returned unemployed and in financial ruin to Spain in 1930, months before the institution of the Spanish Republic.

FILMÓFONO, HOLLYWOOD, THE SPANISH WAR

After returning briefly to Spain in 1930 and independently producing *Las Hurdes (Land Without Bread)* in 1932, Buñuel worked in Paris in the dubbing operations of Paramount Pictures. Later, in 1934, he married Jeanne Rucar and went to Madrid to work in the Warner Bros. dubbing studios there. By then, Buñuel was disappointed with the surrealists. He had left the movement in 1933, saying later that surrealism "was successful in its details and a failure in its essentials."[25] Buñuel feared that some members of the group who had chosen to seek publicity and celebrity (Eluard, Breton, Dalí) were in fact betraying surrealist principles. They had succumbed to "the total separation of life from art"; rather, they were doing "art for art's sake," ignoring the political principles that had originally governed their philosophy.[26]

Buñuel was recruited in 1935 by the company Filmófono as executive producer for several musical comedies and melodramas. Some of these were tremendously popular and apparently technically well accomplished.[27] Filmófono had been founded in 1929 and was the pioneer company of Spanish sound film technology. Filmófono's own sound system was invented and developed by entrepreneur Ricardo María Urgoiti, who had been involved with radio stations in Spain since 1925 and who had met Buñuel at the famed Residencia de Estudiantes in the early 1920s. Although its own sound system failed to get off the ground, Filmófono achieved great success in distribution and exhibition with, among other things, Disney's "Silly Symphonies" in the early 1930s. After establishing a solid distribution and exhibition chain in Madrid, Urgoiti felt that Filmófono was ready to try its hand at production. In 1935, when Buñuel was in Madrid supervising and directing Spanish dubbing for Warner Bros., Urgoiti hired him to produce Filmófono's home-grown products, giving Buñuel his first hands-on experience in a decision-making position in commercial film production. According to film historian Manuel Rotellar's interviews with members of the cast and crew of the Filmófono studios, Buñuel's only condition was that his involvement with these pictures and his name be kept in complete anonymity, apparently in fear of damaging his reputation as a surrealist. Another, even more practical reason for wanting to remain unknown was Buñuel's status as persona non grata with the Spanish censors after *Las Hurdes*.[28] Rotellar insists, however, "the truth is that it was Luis Buñuel who directed the Filmófono productions."[29]

Director José Luis Sáenz de Heredia, who went on to pursue a notable career in Spanish cinema as the foremost director under Franco, was credited as director of Filmófono's *La hija de Juan Simón* (1935). But he stated that it was Luis Buñuel who "explained to [him] every morning what he wanted.... We looked at the takes together and it was Buñuel who chose the shots, and in editing, I wasn't even allowed" to be present.[30] Rotellar also insists that Buñuel personally admitted that he did give specific instructions to the "nominal" directors under his command and that he often showed them, in situ, "how to direct rapidly" if they were behind schedule.[31] In any case, there seems to be no documented evidence to show whether Buñuel actually directed the Filmófono movies, since he never took credit for them, or whether he acted only as an executive producer with supreme powers over a fixed cast and crew. What we do know is that Buñuel was "in charge of production" at Filmófono and that the director avoided speaking about those movies and often stated later that he had nothing to say about that period. But by the time he took his second trip to Hollywood in the late 1930s, the two years he spent working with Jean Epstein and the two years he spent as head of production at Filmófono gave Buñuel much experience in studio, genre, and commercial production.

Buñuel's Filmófono experience between 1935 and 1936 (before his return to Hollywood) suggests that he became familiar with rapid studio shooting and post-production, which were the general working conditions he would find in the Mexican film industry a decade later. At Filmófono he also came in contact as a producer with the genres he would first encounter in Mexico in 1946—the musical melodrama and the comedy. For example, Buñuel's early Mexican melodrama, *La hija del engaño* (1951) was a remake of Buñuel's Filmófono production of *Don Quintín, el amargao* (1935).[32] In fact, the producers changed the title of Buñuel's Mexican *Don Quintín, el amargao*, and Buñuel protested that at least under the original title "all the Spanish would have come to see it"[33] because this was a tremendously popular Spanish farce by Carlos Arniches both on stage and in print. Buñuel's statement reveals his gradual recognition of the importance of achieving some degree of popular audience appeal.

Scholars have differed in their opinions on the impact of Buñuel's Filmófono years for his subsequent career. The testimonials and documents gathered by the Spanish critics Manuel Rotellar and Luis Gómez Mesa suggest that Luis Buñuel was ready for a gradual shift to popular genres, in part due to his displeasure with the surrealists, in part due to his real need to make a living. Marsha Kinder, citing different sources but with exactly the same information, is more inclined to believe that Buñuel's training in popular genres was always in a revisionist, transgressive mode. The thought of a complacent Buñuel is untenable.[34] Yet, Kinder sees an extraordinary set of heroines who are characterized as "agent[s] of subversion of the patriarchal symbolic order."[35] In any case, whether women in Buñuel's films are "agents of subversion" or whether they are victims of the flaws of patriarchy, the evidence suggests that while at Filmófono Buñuel made popular genre pictures and agreed to return to Hollywood and pursue his career as a director there (however unsuccessfully). The logic of Buñuel's trajectory between *Las Hurdes* and *Gran Casino* does not rule out the possibility of his willingness to compromise,[36] at least until Buñuel's position was more secure, which only happened after the commercial success of *El gran calavera*, his second Mexican movie, in 1949.

In any case, Buñuel's decision to work at Filmófono already involved a compromise, one that stressed a key point of this transitional stage of Buñuel's career: he was moving away from the orthodox, uncompromising positions of surrealism[37] and toward further popular acceptance and a more accessible cinematic language. In *My Last Sigh*, Buñuel reflects nostalgically, "It wasn't only the political dissension among the surrealists that cooled my ardor for the movement, but also their increasing snobbery, their strange attraction to the aristocracy."[38] After all, Buñuel had already accepted a Hollywood contract to train at MGM and to learn the Hollywood mode of production, and he had established contacts at that studio and at Warner Bros., as well as with Hollywood personalities like Charles Chaplin and producer Frank Davis.[39]

During Buñuel's years at Filmófono in Madrid, Spain was in political turmoil. The Republic established in 1931 was weakened by the rise of Fascism and civil war broke out in 1936. Buñuel remained in Madrid and loyal to the Republic, since the Fascists, under the leadership of General Francisco Franco, were aggressively repressive of artistic activity and Buñuel was something of a local celebrity among intellectuals and artists.

In September 1936 Buñuel was recruited by the Spanish ambassador to Paris, Luis Araquistain, to help with the distribution of Republican propaganda. While in Paris, Buñuel is credited with supervising the compilation film ¡*España, leal en armas!* (1937), a rare piece of Republican propaganda made with the help of Pierre Unik (who also collaborated in *Las Hurdes* and *Wuthering Heights*) and which is often compared to *Las Hurdes* in its ironic and tragic tone.[40] Buñuel's actual involvement with the film is uncertain. However, as with the Filmófono comedies, he refused to speak about it or take credit, but it is Buñuel's last known work before he left for the United States again in 1938.

In her memoirs, Buñuel's widow, Jeanne Rucar, remembers the period when her husband was in his diplomatic post in France in 1938, as the defeat of the Spanish Republic against the Fascists seemed imminent.

> We could not return to Spain, nor did Luis want that. Since his trip to the United States [in 1930] he had always wanted to return: he thought it was a marvelous country. Los Angeles was the place for filmmakers [. . .] there was technology, money, opportunities. Somebody suggested to Luis: "Go to the United States, there are magnificent opportunities." He was attracted to the idea.[41]

Thus, for Buñuel, the thought of incorporating into a commercial film industry, such as Hollywood, for instance, in order to have access to technology and opportunities, and perhaps to escape the uncertain future of Spain, was not entirely inconceivable.

In 1938 the Spanish government sent Luis Buñuel to Hollywood as a "technical adviser" for American movies about the Spanish Civil War that were mainly favorable to the Republican cause. The pretext may have been a diplomatic mission, but he came to Hollywood at his own request. Buñuel states that the American movies about the civil war, like *Cargo of Innocence* (unfinished at MGM in 1938) and *Blockade* (from United Artists and directed by William Dieterle, also 1938) were "full of good intentions; [but] with errors, and did not take part in certain political questions."[42] Thus, Hollywood was not as sympathetic to the Republican cause as Buñuel had thought; even known "leftist" figures like Charles Chaplin refused to openly support any side. In addition, Catholic groups opposed any form of U.S. involvement in the Spanish war, the defeat of the Republic seemed imminent, and the production of these films was soon shut down.[43] Neither Buñuel's diplomatic mission nor his professional ambitions seemed destined to bear fruit. Besides, in 1939, when Franco's Nationalist armies won the Spanish Civil War, the stage was set and the scenario rehearsed for World War II, and like many other Spanish Republican sympathizers, Buñuel was forced to remain in exile. The transition to directing his own films proved even more difficult.

Buñuel's Filmófono experience and technical jobs at Warner Bros. prove that he was willing to experiment, to give up some formal aspects of his style of filmmaking in favor of both job security and a more "accessible" language (necessary if he wanted to reach popular audiences). In addition, he was willing to observe the making of Hollywood movies (first at MGM, then at Warner Bros.) and to dedicate himself to learning film editing, screenwriting, dubbing, executive-producing, budgeting, scheduling, technical responsibilities, and possibly even directing at Filmófono and Warner

Bros. in order to gain greater technical proficiency. As Virginia Higginbotham and Spanish critic José Agustín Mahieu have observed, Buñuel's credits as a director alone (two surrealist avant-garde films, of which only one was feature length, and a short, unorthodox documentary) were hardly enough to interest Hollywood (or the Mexican film establishment) in hiring him to direct a feature.[44] Furthermore, the monotony of Hollywood genres and the Hollywood lifestyle bored Buñuel.[45]

Buñuel subsequently moved to other sorts of film-related jobs in the United States, unable to return to warring Europe. Through some old connections he found work at New York's Museum of Modern Art, where he stayed from 1939 to 1943. In forced exile from Franco's Spain, his job was, very appropriately, editing anti-Nazi and pro-American propaganda for Nelson Rockefeller's Office of Inter-American Affairs.[46] He resigned under the threat of being fired due to pressure from conservative elements, who worried about his scandalous European films. There were also rumors that Dalí's comments about Buñuel's association with Communist surrealists in his 1942 autobiography, *The Secret Life of Salvador Dalí*, were also a factor in his dismissal from MoMA. After that, he worked briefly as dubbing director back at Warner Bros. before becoming definitively unemployed in 1946.

Because he was out of work, Buñuel briefly considered returning to Europe. He had an offer from producer Denise Tual (the former wife of Pierre Batcheff, the leading actor in *Un chien andalou*) to adapt his friend Federico García-Lorca's play, *The House of Bernarda Alba*. En route to Paris, where the film was to be made, Tual and Buñuel stopped in Mexico City. But they had not secured the rights to García-Lorca's play, and Tual's project was eventually canceled. Almost by chance, Buñuel found himself unemployed in Mexico City and with no real options. Perhaps the opportunity to find work in Mexico seemed genuine to Buñuel: after all, Mexico's was a solidly established film industry that had been friendly to Spanish talent and occasionally sympathetic to exiled Republicans during and after the Civil War. Furthermore, many Spanish exiles worked in Mexico's film industry and knew Buñuel's work from the 1929–32 period.

THE LOGIC OF MEXICO

During the Spanish Civil War of 1936–39 and after the defeat of the Republic, thousands of Spanish Republicans, among them numerous artists and intellectuals, sought exile in Latin America. No other country welcomed so many Spanish exiles as Mexico. Furthermore, Mexico had been friendly not only to all sorts of Spanish exiles during the Civil War, and to Europeans generally during the second World War, but also to the remainder of the surrealist movement. Víctor Fuentes explains that Mexico was attractive to Buñuel in the world historical and cultural context between 1939 and 1945 (regardless of the actual chance happenings that landed him there):

> Mexico, especially the capital, occupied the place of the world's artistic and cultural center, while the war turned the European Metropolis into holes ... the visits of the surrealists, Artaud in 1936 and Breton in 1938, and the manifesto "For an Independent Revolutionary Art," written by Trotsky [sic], Breton and Diego de Rivera [sic]; the incorporation of refugee Spanish intellectuals into the literary and cultural Mexican life in 1939, and the surrealist exposition of 1940.[47]

Many Spanish exiles came from the film industry that had briefly flourished in Spain during the Republic and which included Filmófono and other small production companies.[48]

Mexico and Argentina were the Spanish-speaking countries with the largest, best established film industries, and Mexico had benefited enormously from its political position during World War II, since it declared war on the Axis nations in 1942. Second only to Hollywood on the American continent during the war years, the Mexican film industry went through a period of solid growth that led to its domination of the Latin American film markets. There were financial and development incentives, such as the open importation of raw film stock from the United States (a privilege denied Argentina because of its neutral position in the war). Mexico also benefited from the return of Hollywood-trained film talent and technicians, among them actress Dolores del Río, actor/director Emilio "El Indio" Fernández, and cinematographer Gabriel Figueroa, who had studied with Greg Toland.[49] Even putting aside these facts about the Mexican film industry, for a Spanish exile who had solid, indisputable ties to literature and the arts, Mexico was, politically and culturally speaking, the place to be in the 1940s.

When Luis Buñuel arrived in Mexico in 1946 and took producer Óscar Dancigers's job offer to direct *Gran Casino*, Mexican artistic production not only was at a peak, but there was extraordinary activity in the national film industry. Mexico had just emerged from a period in which the Revolution was popular, when nationalist feelings were high during the Lázaro Cárdenas administration (1934–1940), peaking in 1938 with the nationalization of the oil industry. The cinema establishment saw itself as another expression of Mexico's preeminent position in the world's cultural environment.

Luis Buñuel was always critical of cinema conventions, as his film criticism of the 1920s confirms,[50] and he initially chose not to make any more films after his surrealist documentary *Las Hurdes* (1932), because he did not want to "fall" into commercial cinema.[51] His early movies in Mexico were, however, as Buñuel put it later, strictly commercial and responded to financial necessity. In spite of having originally worked in Mexico for need, Buñuel insisted that in these early Mexican movies he never shot "a single scene that was contrary to [his] convictions or personal morality."[52] However, for Buñuel to betray his convictions at this transitional phase in his career would have been to give up his creative independence, regardless of the actual form or content of his work. Buñuel was much more willing to work with formulaic genres than to give a producer control over what any picture was going to look like or how it was to be edited. As Buñuel's words suggest, what remained inviolable through his Mexican years was the director's "personal morality." This is significant because, for Buñuel, surrealism was a moral system that stood for "the complete rejection of all existing values"[53] and Buñuel's Mexican movies were generically correct but always morally ambiguous. The important thing here is that Buñuel subscribed to generic conventions as a means to gain access to Mexico's film industry while keeping a critical distance, so as not to "violate his convictions." That critical distance was what allowed Buñuel to become part of the revisionist current of Mexican cinema that preceded the fall of the Golden Age and the old genre system.

In Mexico, producers did not have to respond directly to studios' demands since movies were often funded through direct loans from the Banco Nacional Cinematográfico, which financed independent producers and production companies. That would have been a similar situation to the one Buñuel had found at Filmófono a decade earlier: an independent production company that responded directly to audience appeal and box-office returns, to financial security and credit, to the logic of a "genre" system but not to organized studio politics, as Hollywood did.

Nevertheless, because of the previous decade's general economic boom in Mexican cinema, government involvement made producers increasingly dependent on subventions and backing from the Banco Nacional Cinematográfico. One of the most interesting features of Mexico's film industry in this period was that it was not the studios who had the power (they were for hire, along with their unionized labor), but the government-operated Banco Cinematográfico. Producers' dependency on Banco Nacional Cinematográfico loans forced them to be faithful to the genres of proven commercial viability since these were the only pictures that the bank would finance.[54] This was due, in part, to the fact that the Bank's goal was to make itself financially autonomous, which required that producers pay back their loans with interest. Thus, the genres of Mexican cinema (and the public's response to those genres since the 1930s) dictated the types of movies that were to be made, which is why producers, dependent on government loans, remained faithful to proven formulas. Therefore, without actually having the tightly structured mode of production of the Hollywood studios of the classical era, Mexican cinema rather found itself in a financial structure of government dependency that evolved into what can be properly called a "genre" system. The steady output of genre pictures led the public to expect the conventions of the familiar genres: patriotic epics, family melodramas, and comedies. Genre dependence and familiarity led to a lack of variety, stagnation, and eventually to a decline in domestic public movie attendance and in foreign critical esteem.

Not surprisingly, then, the "turning point" of classical cinema occurred under President Miguel Alemán. The economic policies of *alemanismo* clashed with the positions of classical cinema, and this collision led to some revisionism in content, form, and genre. The industrial, modernizing drive of the state challenged the ideological positions of classical cinema, generally summarized as (1) the idealization of the provinces and the countryside, (2) admiring condemnations of the city, (3) exaltation of the patriarchal regime, and (4) excessive defense of conservative values.[55] The "transitional" moment framed by *alemanismo* coincided with the production and release of Buñuel's first Mexican movie, *Gran Casino (In Old Tampico)*, which was filmed in late 1946 and opened in Mexico City on 12 June 1947.

With producer Dancigers's help (through his independent production company, Películas Anáhuac), Buñuel soon proved himself a competent director at studio filmmaking and at popular genres. However, it came as a surprise to its producers that *Gran Casino* was a commercial and critical failure, which has since been the subject of much critical discussion about Buñuel's aptitude for and attitude toward "conventional" film narratives, genres, and forms. Yet, according to Mexican film historians, *Gran Casino*'s commercial failure was due as much to the poor quality of the script as to Buñuel's inability and lack of interest in commercial filmmaking.[56] However, it may as well have been due in part to the tiredness of the musical subgenre of melodrama, in crisis in the late 1940s. Not only was Buñuel new to Mexican cinema (if certainly not to the musical melodrama), but Mexican cinema was changing. Despite the stability of "family" melodramas and *comedias rancheras*, the conservative classical musical was evolving into the more risqué *cabaretera* film that was so culturally specific to the *sexenio* of President Alemán between 1946 and 1952.[57]

Under Alemán, a gradual shift of governmental policy was taking place,

FIGURE 2. Libertad Lamarque and Jorge Negrete almost kissing in *Gran Casino* (1947). Museum of Modern Art/Film Stills Archive.

one that turned away from the pseudo-socialist, nationalist economic policies of the late 1930s (among which, the expropriation of the railroads and the oil industry from American, British, and other private interests were the most dramatic turns). *Alemanismo*'s shift from the previous decade's policy of nationalization of resources suggested the Revolution's failure to serve its proclaimed purposes of equality and progress for the agrarian communities and organized labor. In that context, the *cabaretera* film served as a response to these critical times, in which images of women and the urban cityscape were reconceptualized in contrast to those found in bucolic family melodramas and *comedias rancheras*.[58] After the late 1940s, the *cabaretera* presented a great counterpoint to the classic *comedia ranchera* (of which Fernando de Fuentes's *Allá en el Rancho Grande* is the best known example). The *cabaretera* films dealt with Mexico's fast-growing urban population through the 1940s and into the 1950s and with the growing disillusionment of the working classes over the slow rate of their own economic growth.[59]

While *Gran Casino* was more "musical" than "melodrama," and its aging stars were approaching the end of their careers as leading figures, a new breed of musical melodrama was rapidly and successfully emerging. The use of more sex, lurid plots, faster "tropical" musical scores, and younger, fresher stars like Ninón Sevilla and María Antonieta Pons in skimpy outfits and provocative dancing numbers made the *cabaretera* subgenre of musical melodrama a favorite of the public by the turn of the decade. Some old genres (the *comedias rancheras*, family melodramas, and especially the revolutionary melodramas) were still popular, but they seemed strikingly anachronistic with their inept Porfirian moralisms and their populist aesthetics.

Consequently, despite the star-power of Argentine tango diva Libertad Lamarque, Mexican singing *charro* Jorge Negrete (both of them fading musical stars at the time *Gran Casino* was made), and cinema patriarch Fernando Soler, *Gran Casino* both predicted and symptomatically represented the fall of classical cinema in Mexico. Arguably, *Gran Casino*, and later *El gran calavera*, already incorporated Buñuel into the historical and social discourse of cinema in Mexico. These were quickly made "B" movies, and Buñuel was only expected to "block" actors and camera set-ups (particularly for *El gran calavera*) because the films were not expected to break from the generic conventions in which they were conceived. They were what the Mexicans call *churros:* cheap, badly and quickly made, conventional genre movies that practically directed themselves. Those generic conventions, particularly in the case of *Gran Casino*, were becoming increasingly untenable in the late classical era.

Even before *Gran Casino* opened, it seemed to have been doomed. When the movie was still in production in early 1947, critic Miguel Ángel Mendoza of *Cartel*, who visited the set, predicted its failure and with it the end of Buñuel's career. In an article published on 14 January 1947 and entitled "Buñuel Fracasa en México" (Buñuel Fails in Mexico), Mendoza wrote:

> Failure. A wreckage from the aesthetic point of view. And, later: insatisfaction and regret. Buñuel cannot find Mexico. At least not in this picture. . . . In spite of everything, Buñuel is more a victim than he is guilty. . . . The fundamental exculpatory fact is that Buñuel was hired by . . . Jorge Negrete . . . [and] in the final decisions one does what the boss says. . . . [But Buñuel] should have never made concessions to bad taste, nor mortgage his real prestige to mediocrity.[60]

Mendoza thus inaugurated the negative criticism toward Buñuel's Mexican movies—of the very films that were more in tune, stylistically and generically, with popular Mexican cinema. That history of negative criticism has since become the norm when it comes to critical appreciation of Buñuel's

"Mexican" movies. The result is that ever since *Gran Casino*, these films are characterized not only as oddities in Buñuel's filmography but also as ill-fitting within Mexican film history.

"DOWN WITH THE 180-DEGREE RULE!"

With the little control that Buñuel exercised, he nevertheless found ways to self-reflexively mock the conventions of romantic musical melodrama in *Gran Casino*. Adapted by Mauricio Magdaleno, Emilio Fernández's distinguished collaborator,[61] from a novel by Michel Weber, *Gran Casino* tells the unbelievable story of an escaped convict (Gerardo, played by Jorge Negrete) who ends up working in the oil fields of Tampico in the first decades of the century (before oil nationalization). There, he meets Mercedes, a tango singer (played by Libertad Lamarque) whose "oil baron" brother has disappeared. Mercedes suspects Gerardo of foul play against her brother (presumably because he is an ex-convict who works in the oil fields). Gerardo soon learns that there is a plot, led by the evil Mr. Van Eckerman (Charles Rooner), to take over the oil fields, and this explains Mercedes's brother's disappearance. After uncovering the plot, Gerardo kills one of Van Eckerman's tough-guys, and he is promptly arrested. Mercedes intervenes on his behalf, clears things up with Van Eckerman, and exchanges Gerardo's freedom for the rights to the oil fields. In the end, Gerardo and Mercedes sabotage the oil fields before escaping from Tampico.

There is certainly nothing extraordinary about the plot, its execution, or the dramatic arc of *Gran Casino*. After all, screenwriter Magdaleno was the person who gave proper narrative structure to Fernández's careless early screenplays.[62] Thus, as far as the conventions of Mexican melodrama are concerned, *Gran Casino* is a satisfactorily executed movie. Buñuel was more wary about the treatment of his singing stars and unhappy about the six songs in the soundtrack. He declared the movie "a tournament to see who sang more tangos, Lamarque or Negrete."[63] Emilio García Riera explains that Buñuel deliberately toyed with the rules of the genre by playing up the musical moments (making them even more evident and implausible), and especially by avoiding the cliché kiss of the lovers at the dramatic climax of the movie.[64] Another one of the most celebrated moments of self-reflexive genre criticism in the film is the presence of the musical group Trío Calaveras that plays for Jorge Negrete. They arbitrarily (and sardonically) walk onto the set and are graciously greeted by Negrete every time one of his songs is introduced. The on-screen presence of the Calaveras makes the musical accompaniment evident, yet still not diegetic, since it is clear that the musicians walk in on cue for each musical scene and their narratively unjustified presence is readily acknowledged by the leading man.

Buñuel even told his interviewers, José de la Colina and Tomás Pérez Turrent, that he deliberately violated the formal convention of the 180-degree rule: "Let them go to hell! After making thirty films I still have doubts about the relation of the gaze to the shot-reverse shot."[65] Besides, Buñuel's resistance to closing the love story with the inevitable kiss of the protagonists led him into further parody. In the climactic scene, the camera turns away from the couple as they are about to kiss, re-framing on a muddy puddle on the ground, which Negrete (off-screen) stirs with a stick, turning the scene literally into something "slushy," in bad taste. In *Gran Casino*, Buñuel violates generic standards and turns them into parody within a genre that was at the time already becoming a parody of itself.

The first signs of Buñuel's concern with Mexican cinema are thus quite visible in *Gran Casino*, making the movie consistent with Buñuel's surrealist films, particularly with *Las Hurdes*. Classic "genres" and formats can be useful for the purposes of surrealist critique, making Buñuel's early movies a form of popular surrealism. *Las Hurdes*, Buñuel's famous "surrealist ethnographic" documentary made in Spain in 1932, was a reflection on Spain, civilization, and prejudice, a look at "the violence that is at the heart of life."[66] It was also a very conscientious parody of social and ethnographic documentaries in the tradition of John Grierson and Robert J. Flaherty. Buñuel's *Gran Casino* effectively served as a parody of popular cinema conventions by exploiting their presence and accentuating the audience's own insecurities and morbid character, which is how surrealist ethnography worked in *Las Hurdes*. In *Las Hurdes* the gritty images of the lives of the people in the region, filmed in solid documentary fashion, are shockingly juxtaposed to the dry, inhuman commentary written by Buñuel and Pierre Unik. The narration, concordant with surrealism, violates the bourgeois morality that commands pity toward the *hurdanos*, the subjects of the film. By slightly overemphasizing and parodying the management of the musical numbers, the violence (by portraying comically the death of the villain), and the romantic conventions (with the notoriously slushy kiss)[67], Buñuel turns *Gran Casino* into a parody of itself and of its dying genre. In a similar way, *Las Hurdes'* disturbingly distant voice-over narration and its judgmental claims about its "subjects" brings to the fore the audience's own prejudices. Both movies are culturally specific to their contexts: *Gran Casino* is effective as parody only insofar as it is also faithful to the very genre conventions that it is dissecting; *Las Hurdes* is especially effective because it is superficially in its form and mode of production a "legitimate" documentary. In a year when the *cabaretera* film had matured into a version of the Mexican musical melodrama more in tune with Mexico's momentum for modernization, *Gran Casino*'s self-reflexive form of parody and prerevolutionary setting may have been too remote for the Mexican urban audience.

Gran Casino's leading stars came from singing careers, family melodramas, and *comedia ranchera*. Negrete was one of the leading *charros* of Mexican cinema. *Gran Casino*'s rural setting and improbable morality seemed not only anachronistic, but uninspired and gratuitously disengaged from the social and political concerns of more popular films like the *cabareteras* and the urban melodramas known as *cine de arrabal* (which, in turn, came to contrast with the old "family melodrama"). *Gran Casino* was indeed out of sync with the contemporary musical variations of Mexican cinema, which besides the *cabaretera* included the brand of cabaret-set musical comedy of the *pachuco* character of comedian Germán Valdés, known as Tin-Tán. The failure to comply with its immediate cultural context was hardly due to Luis Buñuel's ineptitude as a genre director, as classic Buñuel criticism would lead us to believe, but rather with the ill-conception of the film that preceded Buñuel's involvement with the project. Buñuel, indeed, could not "find Mexico," as Mendoza properly stated in his *Cartel* article, but it was because "Mexico" could not be found in *Gran Casino:* because "Mexico" was moving in the direction of different settings, plots, characters, and situations; because Mexico could not find itself in Mexican cinema. Parody was, however, difficult to convey in Mexico, as Buñuel's later experience with *Susana* proved.[68] Thus, when it came to criticism of the politics and aesthetics of classical cinema, "revisionism" meant the transformation of genres into new variations and not just the uses of parody that Buñuel admittedly rehearsed in *Gran Casino*.[69]

Gran Casino flopped in 1947. *El gran calavera (The Great Madcap)* was a modest success in 1949, possibly because it easily flowed into the conventions of the "family" melodrama, albeit in a comedic variation, a format that took much longer to fade out in the complex scheme of Mexico's film genres and subgenres. *El gran calavera* was based on a *sainete* (one-act farce of transparent morals) by Adolfo Torrado and adapted by Buñuel collaborators Luis Alcoriza *(Los olvidados, Él, El Bruto, La mort en ce jardin)* and Janet Alcoriza *(La hija del engaño)*. A shallow, simple "moral" comedy, *El gran calavera* was not unlike the movies that Buñuel had supervised at Filmófono a decade earlier.[70] In the movie, the rich widower drunkard Ramiro, played by one of the stereotypical patriarchs of Mexican cinema, Fernando Soler (who also appears in Buñuel's *Susana* and *La hija del engaño*), is fooled by his parasitic family into believing that his unruly ways have prompted the family's financial ruin. While Ramiro is unconscious, recovering from an apparent heart attack, the family relocates to a poor neighborhood. Upon his recovery, family members make him believe that they are now poor and have had to take jobs (carpentry, shoe-shining, cooking, laundry) in order to support themselves. Ramiro soon discovers the farce and, with the help of his manager, succeeds in making the family believe that, in fact, they are ruined and that their false new life as working-class folk is real. The deception-within-the-deception teaches everyone a lesson: Ramiro learns the virtues of sobriety and temperance, and his family learns the moral superiority of earning a living. In the process, Ramiro's daughter Virginia (Rosario Granados, also in Buñuel's *Una mujer sin amor*) breaks her engagement to the spoiled playboy Alfredo (played by Luis Alcoriza) and falls in love with a young, "poor but honest" electrician, Pablo. After order is restored, Virginia leaves Alfredo at the altar and runs away with Pablo, to her father's satisfaction.

The movie was filmed in sixteen days at a cost of 400,000 pesos (a little over $46,000 U.S. at the 1948 exchange rate), and it was a commercial success. In directing a "formula" melodramatic comedy, Buñuel was unable to experiment much formally. Instead, and perhaps to avoid the long dry spell that followed the poor critical and box-office performance of *Gran Casino*, Buñuel was more faithful to a formulaic narrative. Since the movie's "moral farce" format allowed for comic moments, Buñuel seemed to be content with harmless interventions that did not disrupt the story's generic efficiency, as was not the case with the "slushy" melodrama of *Gran Casino*. At the same time, Buñuel learned to film quickly and effectively, with few takes and little waste of expensive studio time and post-production facilities. He was to follow this style of production through most of his career, to the relief of his producers.

Buñuel's humor is recognizable in *El gran calavera*. The opening shot of Ramiro's feet entangled with those of his jail mates has been established as a "Buñuelian" motif. Likewise, Buñuel's avoidance of an emotional moment by mockingly setting the unavoidable love-declaration scene inside an advertising truck which blares the dialogue through loud-speakers helped to gently tone down what would have otherwise been the romantic climax of the movie. Unlike the kiss-*cum*-muddy-puddle shot in *Gran Casino*, which seems openly satirical, the love scene in *El gran calavera* comes across as both funny and believable, helping ease the tensions of a potentially melodramatic exchange. In that way, Buñuel did not "violate" his own convictions against emotional manipulation, while allowing the story to come to

FIGURE 3. Rosario Granados and Fernando Soler perfectly happy in *The Great Madcap* (1949). Museum of Modern Art/Film Stills Archive.

a satisfactory narrative conclusion. Neither the plot nor the theatrical format of *El gran calavera* is serious enough to demand much effort for it to be exploited for farcical effect.

Recent criticism of *El gran calavera*, specifically in Gastón Lillo's *Género y transgresión*, puts too much emphasis on the film's satiric tone, treating it strictly as a melodrama in which Buñuel took creative liberties for the sake of irony. Lillo argues that *El gran calavera* "disarticulates melodrama without destroying its format," and that in a *guiñolesca* fashion (from the Spanish verb *guiñar*, "to wink"), it "disarticulates the effect of reality ... showing the threads of the fiction."[71] This perception, however, seems contradictory. It foregrounds the movie's relation to Spanish *guiñol* (puppet) theater, suggesting that this "decodification of irony" is Buñuel's commentary on melodrama. Yet it ignores the fact that the *guiñol*, like the Spanish *sainete* (the original form of *El gran calavera*) is defined by the unidimensional puppetlike constitution of its characters and the simplicity of its dramatic structure and morals.[72] As a *sainete*, the original play on which the movie is based already implies the plot's deceptions (the farce-within-the-farce) as *guiñolesca*. Thus, instead of reading *El gran calavera* as a parody of melodrama in which Buñuel winks a sardonic eye at his complicit audience,[73] as Lillo suggests, it seems that Buñuel simply executed *El gran calavera* as dictated by the tradition of the Spanish theater from which it came. *El gran calavera* is by no means devoid of ironic spirit. Nevertheless, the irony does not disrupt the flow of the narrative, nor does it violate the diegetic realm, as do Negrete's musicians in *Gran Casino* for example; after all, the movie is about putting up a fictional world.

Consequently, the conception of *Gran Casino*, and not what Buñuel did with it, was the reason for its famous failure. Yet, Buñuel's appropriate execution of generic and narrative standards in *El gran calavera* (in tune with those of the Arniche comedy-dramas filmed at Filmófono in the mid-1930s) ensured that movie's success and thus opened the door for him to eventually obtain more creative independence. *El gran calavera* is a satisfactory movie: good-looking, well-paced, coherently structured, narratively satisfying, funny, commercially successful. It's certainly not the film of an amateur of popular cinema. And, finally, we must consider that commercial success was the key issue of Mexican cinema in the time of President Alemán, when the Banco Nacional Cinematográfico was only willing to support movies that seemed to be secure investments, namely, movies in the "old," proven genres of the Golden Age. Had *El gran calavera* failed commercially, that would have doomed Buñuel's chances to work again in Mexico, and perhaps anywhere else. *El gran calavera*'s success did, in fact, open the doors of Mexican cinema for Luis Buñuel.

Luis Buñuel's professional, personal, and political career between 1932, the year of *Las Hurdes*, and 1946, the year of *Gran Casino*, was consistent with the chance decision of working in Mexico and with his incorporation, even if reluctantly, into the contemporary currents of Mexican cinema. These early films of Buñuel's Mexican career should be considered "marginal," not only in relation to Buñuel's past glory as the controversial mind behind *Un chien andalou* and *L'Age d'Or*, but also in relation to the canon of Mexican cinema. The canon by then could only aspire to replicate the success of *María Candelaria* and *Flor silvestre*. But as classical cinema was in its latter stages in the late 1940s, the tendency toward "revisionism" increased.

While seemingly operating within the expectations of the genre system in Mexican cinema, Buñuel was very good at the subtle "transgression" of classical genres. However, the revisionist initiative that critics identify in *Gran Casino* and *El gran calavera* was part of a limited yet definitive inclination of Mexican cinema toward new aesthetics, characters, settings, and narrative formats. Along with the *cabaretera* films of Alberto Gout and the *arrabalera* films of Alejandro Galindo, among others, Buñuel's early

Mexican films were symptomatic of the crisis of both Mexican cinema and Mexican society at the brink of modernization. After stumbling into Mexican film with the failed open parody of *Gran Casino*, Buñuel succeeded in his integration with *El gran calavera*.

The assumption that Luis Buñuel saw in the Mexican film industry a continuation of his "popular" training at Filmófono and a secure way to distinguish his work from what surrealism "proper" had become (Dalí's narcissistic celebrity, for example) is not so far-fetched. In fact, it makes Buñuel's observational and learning trips to Hollywood also consistent with his alienation from the surrealist movement, if not necessarily from surrealist aesthetics (as *Gran Casino*'s attempts at self-parody suggest). Subsequent Mexican films, like *Subida al cielo*, *La ilusión viaja en tranvía*, and *Susana* help to emphasize what is more revealing of Luis Buñuel's Mexican career: the conjunction of surrealist aesthetics with popular narrative formats and with the particular political and social context of Mexico in the 1950s. *El gran calavera*'s commercial success opened the doors for Buñuel's acceptance by the Mexican film establishment and adoption by the Mexican nation (he became a Mexican citizen in 1949, legally, the only way he could get steady work). With *Los olvidados* the following year, Buñuel effectively secured his position as Mexico's foremost director, while consolidating his ties with Mexican cinema, Mexican society, and the intellectual community.

CODA: REPRESSED MEMORIES

Buñuel's own assessment of his life and films in *My Last Sigh* sheds significant light on any critical work on his Mexican years. In the memoir, written with long-time collaborator Jean-Claude Carrière in 1982, Buñuel treats the thirty-seven years he spent in Mexico (much like his marriage to Jeanne Rucar) as a detour. The lack of attention given to the seventeen Mexican films seems disproportional compared to the focus on briefer periods, personal pleasures, and prejudices that Buñuel thought were the highlights of his life: his student years, Paris, surrealism, a good martini.

Like most critics of his work, Luis Buñuel did not want to be (mis)taken as part of Mexican cinema. He disowned, ignored, or claimed to have forgotten most of these movies. He had little to say about the actors with whom he worked, about popular reactions to his films, about what, if anything, they meant in his career. In short, as Buñuel read the balance of his life in his autobiography, Mexico emerged as an obstacle. Most of his

Mexican films are treated as an inevitable detour in an otherwise stylistically and thematically interconnected body of work.

Buñuel's declared marginality from the mainstream of Mexican cinema, his position as an outsider, gave him a privileged perspective. Interestingly, in the chapter on Mexico in *My Last Sigh* Buñuel speaks more about Mexico than about his Mexican films. However, what is missing about the Mexican films in *My Last Sigh*, namely the connection between those films and the rest of his oeuvre, I believe, is readily apparent in the body of the work itself, as I will demonstrate in the chapters that follow.

Buñuel's memoir serves to state, from the safe perspective of a fifty-year career and an assured place in world cinema history, his own critical opinion about his work. The book tells us for which work Buñuel wishes to be remembered. Appropriately, as the work of a surrealist, *My Last Sigh* seemingly flows as stream of consciousness, with the deceptive unpredictability of automatic writing. But like a dream, it speaks figuratively; it represses and projects that which the conscious mind of the filmmaker fears, such as the significance of his Mexican period. As a work of self-critique, *My Last Sigh* confirms the generalized neglect of Buñuel's Mexican work. As part of his artistic production, it aims at being consistent with the detached wit of the surrealist artist, downplaying the aspects of his life where he may have seemed more vulnerable—his family and his involvement with Mexico.

3 *Los Olvidados* and the Crisis of Mexican Cinema

> I am the Mexican Cinema.
> —Emilio Fernández

> I feel profound horror for Mexican hats.
> —Luis Buñuel

Luis Buñuel's first Mexican films, *Gran Casino* (1946–47) and *El gran calavera* (1949) were self-reflexive yet mild forms of genre parody, and they were harmless, almost experimental. In the former case, Buñuel worked generic conventions for producer Óscar Dancigers (not to mention star Jorge Negrete, also one of the producers of the movie) and, in the latter case, he worked under powerful star-producer Fernando Soler. It took the commercial success of *El gran calavera* to guarantee Buñuel enough independence to pursue the serious social, political, and aesthetic issues of *Los olvidados (The Young and the Damned)*, his third Mexican movie.

Widely regarded by European film critics as Buñuel's "return" to notoriety after a period of prolonged inactivity and apprenticeship (between 1932 and 1946, when he moved to Mexico), the release of *Los olvidados* was an important historical marker of the "crisis of nationalism" in Mexican cinema. Sometimes seen as a foreigner's distanced view, *Los olvidados* also relates directly to cultural, political, and economic concerns among contemporary Mexican intellectuals and artists. Furthermore, *Los olvidados* gains importance to Mexican issues in light of its close formal and historical relationship to Octavio Paz's 1950 cultural essay, *The Labyrinth of Solitude*, itself a turning point in Mexican literary and culture studies. Grounding *Los olvidados* in its Mexican context helps us to better understand Luis Buñuel's impact on the tradition of Mexican cinema and the contribution of his early years in Mexico to the entirety of his subsequent career.

It is well known that at the time of the movie's première in Mexico City on 9 November 1950, *Los olvidados* was mainly taken as an insult to Mexican sensibilities and to the Mexican nation. The stories of the film's original detractors are many and well documented.[1] Subject to the old Mexican "colonial complex," *Los olvidados* first had to gather prestige abroad before it could be welcomed in Mexico City.² After its triumph at the Cannes Film Festival (where Buñuel won the best director award) and other European festivals, *Los olvidados* enjoyed a successful first run. It was re-released in 1954 and acknowledged in Mexico, according to publicity materials, as both "a masterpiece" of Mexican cinema and as the "pinnacle" *(la obra cumbre)* of Buñuel's career.³

Luis Buñuel's relationship with Mexican cinema went through several different stages, and it is significant that *Los olvidados* was recognized both by international critics and Mexican film historians as the turning point in the director's career. *Los olvidados* was also the first film made during Buñuel's Mexican years in which the director specifically addressed issues related not only to Mexican cinema but more particularly to Mexican politics and society itself.

The small, yet significant amount of freedom that producer Óscar Dancigers allowed Buñuel in *Los olvidados* enabled the director to "return" formally and philosophically to his surrealist years. In particular, Buñuel returned to the violent visual and political style of *Las Hurdes*, his 1932 parody of John Grierson and Robert Flaherty's social and ethnographic documentary aesthetic. Nevertheless, as much as *Los olvidados* can arguably (and probably rightly so) be associated with the style and themes of *Las Hurdes*, the film also did something entirely new. It exposed and criticized the fissures, cracks and failures of classical Mexican cinema. In *Los olvidados* Buñuel directly addressed his expressed dislike for official folklore, for the image of Mexico as dictated by the visual style of classical cinema and revolutionary art, and of the social and political transition to modernization.

Los olvidados coincides with a current of critical intellectual thought about the Mexican revolution that was first articulated in Daniel Cosío Villegas's essay "La crisis de México." First published in the intellectual review *Cuadernos Americanos* in March 1947, the essay marked a turning point in Mexican intellectual debates about the Revolution.⁴ In the often-quoted opening paragraph, Cosío Villegas states, "The goals of the Revolution have been exhausted to the point that the very term revolution is already lacking any meaning."⁵ With this sentence (in both senses of the term), Cosío Villegas opens his critical review of the institutional Revolution's failure to achieve the utopian goals first expressed in 1910 and which seemed possible during the presidency of Lázaro Cárdenas. For Cosío Villegas, there were three goals of the Revolution that had not been achieved: first, to avoid the tenure of power by one person for indefinite periods of time, the most criticized political characteristic of *porfirismo;* second, to improve the conditions of the masses while avoiding the benefit of the small landed aristocracy composed of the so-called one-hundred families; and third, to acknowledge the demographic profile of the nation as mestizo, the brand of nationalism proper to the Mexican Revolution.[6] As noble as the original goals of the Revolution appeared to be in the 1920s and 1930s, Cosío Villegas argued that they were misconceived and that they were directed toward "destruction" rather than "construction."

> All the revolutionary men were inferior to the work the Revolution needed to do: Madero destroyed Porfirismo, but did not create democracy in Mexico; Calles and Cárdenas ended the large landed estates *(latifundia)*, but did not create the new Mexican agriculture.... Thus the work of the Revolution has always remained in the most vulnerable position: exposed to the fury of its enemies, and without generating in its followers the ... conviction of its achievements.[7]

Thus, in Cosío Villegas's view, not only was the Revolution a failure, but it was also unsuccessful in building up Mexicans' faith in national institutions. The crisis encompassed practical issues (no real improvement in the economic and social conditions of the lower classes, for example) as well as philosophical concerns. That lack of faith was turning "the crisis" of the Revolution into something of an emotional trauma, an "identity crisis," so to speak, at a national level.

Furthermore, by 1947, it was apparent that even the Revolution's true achievements were endangered in the face of economic policies that benefited only the traditional upper classes. In *Estado e ideología empresarial en el gobierno alemanista,* Mexican economic historian Felícitas López-Portillo Tostado analyzed the growth of the commercial/ industrial class, developmentalism, and the shift toward political conservatism in México under President Miguel Alemán.

History has branded President Alemán as a counterrevolutionary because of his government's pro-business, pro-industry economic policies. In a judgment that is common in Mexican history, López-Portillo Tostado negatively contrasts Alemán's six years in office to those of President Cárdenas, whose nationalist policies were "distorted by the Alemanista government in favor of private interests."[8] However, in López-Portillo's view, not all of Alemán's initiatives were ill conceived; they were more in tune with the original economic goals of the Revolution even though they contrasted with Cárdenas's utopian, romantic views about social problems. *Alemanismo* wanted to put Mexico in the course of modernization by "augmenting production, promoting agriculture, and promoting industrialization." These were all, says López-Portillo, legitimate revolutionary aspirations in the spirit of the 1917 Constitution.[9] Yet, according to López-Portillo, the president was not willing to acknowledge the crisis of the Revolution and its institutions, although he was aware of the pressing need to overhaul the economy, to make structural economic changes. In his inaugural address, Alemán invoked the Revolution's populist philosophy in the face of economic adversity and announced there was "consciousness that in ourselves—in our effort towards work and in our moral and spiritual convictions—lie the solution to our problems."[10]

Alemán's economic plan of "productivity" also imposed a political scheme, since the aid of the United States and other capitalist allies was necessary to ensure the growth of the economy and industry. Because of the "leftist" leanings of the nationalization policies of the previous decade, Mexico's political course had to turn right. After 1947, as the Mexican state embraced a more "Christian-Democratic" ideology, the most left wing factions of the [Institutional] Revolutionary Party were expelled.[11]

Such policy changes toward political conservatism, private interest, and industrial/capitalist development, inasmuch as López-Portillo writes that they did not contradict the 1917 Constitution, were precisely the kinds of reforms that Cosío Villegas predicted in 1947 and against which his essay spoke. They were signs of "the crisis," of the failure of the Revolution. In particular, the Revolution was seen as a failure, insofar that even such acts of bravura as President Cárdenas's nationalization of the railroads and oil resources seemed threatened. Cosío Villegas himself coined the term *neoporfiriato* to refer to the period's unwelcome ideological return to prerevolutionary times.[12]

Historians of the period agree about Alemán's achievements in matters of infrastructure. There was substantial improvement in railroads, the establishment of hydroelectrical and thermoelectrical plants (which is one of the subtopics of Buñuel's 1951 film, *Una mujer sin amor*), new housing projects, betterment of highways, and the development or revitalization of cultural institutions like the Instituto de Bellas Artes and the Instituto Indigenista.[13] Nevertheless, there is also consensus that the achievements of *alemanismo* improved neither the financial nor the social situation of the lower class. The turn of the decade of the 1950s, in fact, dramatized the gap between rich and poor that the first decades of revolutionary government had allegedly tried to close. Under President Alemán spending on social programs decreased steadily, to the point that in 1952 it represented 11.2 percent of the national budget, "the lowest since 1927."[14]

While there was real growth in production and manufacturing, income distribution became even more unequal than in previous decades. There was a decline in real per capita income between 1945 and 1950. Significantly, this was attributed in part to the rapid growth of urban population, as land reform laws proved ineffectual in keeping peasants away from the city (which was the immediate context surrounding the rise of the *cabaretera* subgenre of Mexican melodrama).

The critics of the Alemán administration thus saw the Revolution's failure on several fronts: social, economic, political, and even philosophical (the loss of "faith" in the Revolution and its "Mexicanness"). As the decade of the 1940s reached its end, "the crisis" was the topic of discussion in many intellectual forums. In the pages of *Cuadernos Americanos*, Jesús Silva Herzog declared the Revolution "dead" in 1949; "the crisis" was also discussed in *Revista Mexicana de Cultura* and *Filosofía y Letras*, among other publications.[15] A series of articles on "Mexico and Mexicanness" appeared from 1949 to 1953 in the intellectual reviews and took the shape of a philosophical debate on issues of national identity, with the Revolution providing historical background. "The crisis" also provided the immediate context for Octavio Paz's *The Labyrinth of Solitude*, the most influential cultural essay on Mexico in the second half of the last century.

"LOS OLVIDADOS" IN "THE LABYRINTH"

> Solitude, the source from which anguish springs, began the day in which we separated from the maternal dwelling and fell into a strange and hostile world.
> —Octavio Paz, *El laberinto de la soledad*

Mexico's revolutionary crisis under *alemanismo*, as well as the struggle with modernization (as seen in García-Canclini's *Hybrid Cultures*) serve as the background against which to understand the inherent "Mexicanness" of *Los olvidados* and its relevance within the context of 1950s Mexico. Perhaps not too coincidentally, the release of *Los olvidados* was also contemporary with the more direct and just as controversial questioning of Mexican society and culture in Octavio Paz's *El laberinto de la soledad*. Paz's book-length essay was a revisionist, provocative, and controversial look at the portrait of Mexico exemplified by revolutionary rhetoric and aesthetics. The book was the turning point for intellectual debates in Mexico about national identity, the Revolution, the role of the intellectual, and other themes.

Paz's controversial cultural essay can serve, like *Los olvidados*, as a marker of the crisis of Mexican culture in general at a time of accelerated urban development and the decay of "traditional" moral and revolutionary values. The same context characterizes the best *cabaretera* movies, which were associated with President Miguel Alemán's *sexenio*. A complete critical analysis of the chronological and formative coincidences between these two landmarks of Mexican cultural production remains to be done. I must, however, call attention to some of the contextual parallelism between the two works, since *Los olvidados* and *El laberinto de la soledad* both treat the "crisis" of Mexico as a form of psychosis in Mexican society and they are both based on the theoretical structure of "ethnographic surrealism."

At the time of the book's publication and the film's release, in 1950, *Los olvidados* and *El laberinto de la soledad* were both controversial and targets of cultural and intellectual criticism. But, in time, they both became seminal points of reference in film studies and Mexican cultural studies, respectively. Time and criticism may have been kinder to *Los olvidados* than to *El laberinto de la soledad*. Buñuel's film has no expressed pretensions of analyzing Mexican culture, Mexican cinema, Mexican art, or the Mexican nation. It does serve, however, as an example of the need to revise some of the representations of Mexico that were directly addressed, more deeply deconstructed, schematized, historicized, scrutinized, and set up for questioning in Paz's book.

El laberinto de la soledad has been called "a modern essay, itself a critical reflection on modernity. A cultural essay, an essay on cultural identity—Völkerpsychologie—[and] a moralist essay of historic interpretation."[16] Of all these characterizations, however, the book is considered especially relevant on the issue of "identity," and it is the inevitable reference, since its publication, in every scholarly debate about Mexico and "Mexicanness." "Within Mexican literature, in particular, writes Enrico Mario Santí, "the book occupies . . . a privileged space: it continues, summarizes, and closes the reflection about national identity."[17]

Paz's cultural formation and the intellectual trajectory that led to his writing of *The Labyrinth of Solitude* also shed light on the formal, psychological, methodological, and philosophical similarities between his book and *Los olvidados*. Paz's first publication, the poem "¡No pasarán!" which appeared in 1936, is said to be a reflection on the Spanish Civil War, sympathetic to the Republican cause. While in Paris in 1937, Paz befriended Alejo Carpentier and Robert Desnos, who "were by then part of the dissidents around the surrealist group," and Paz also met many Spanish Republican exiles in the Parisian political, cultural, and literary circles of the late 1930s.[18]

More significantly, Paz's flirtation with the surrealists of 1930s Paris also marks his initiation into the theories of "psychohistory," of interpreting history psychoanalytically, which Paz then used to rehearse an understanding of Mexican culture, which reached its final form in *El laberinto de la soledad*. Octavio Paz's "description" of Mexican identity, "supposes the Freudian model of neurosis: a reality which manifests a conflict whose symptoms point out another reality, distinct and latent, of which the patient is unconscious."[19] Luis Buñuel's original surrealist movies, *Un chien andalou*, *L'Age d'Or*, and even *Las Hurdes* are deeply grounded in the sort of orthodox Freudian exercises about dreams and the unconscious in which the surrealists were interested in the 1920s.[20]

The themes of *The Labyrinth of Solitude* and their treatment by Paz are also similar to those of *Los olvidados* and arguably to Buñuel's own working style. Santí writes that "the themes of *El laberinto de la soledad* are directed by a folkloric interest *(afán costumbrista)*, sometimes frankly and deliberately humorist, satirical, whose purpose is moral analysis."[21] Santí's judgment of *El laberinto de la soledad* is very much like that of the critics of *Los olvidados*. In one of the most famous reviews of the film, André Bazin calls the movie "the only contemporary aesthetic proof of Freudianism," and states that "Buñuel's surrealism is no more than a desire to reach the basis of reality. . . . The fantasy of *Un chien andalou* is a descent into the human soul, just as *Las Hurdes* and *Los olvidados* are explorations of man in society." Buñuel himself called *Los olvidados* a film "of social struggle."[22]

Like Luis Buñuel, Octavio Paz spent a formative period of his life in a diplomatic post, which took him to France and the United States. In his second long stay in France in 1946, Paz befriended the old surrealists of Buñuel's own generation, among them André Breton. "With them," says Santí, "he shared their interest in Mexico, whose 'strangeness' had fascinated other surrealists, like Breton and Artaud . . . [They also shared] their investigation of the poetic powers of the unconscious." Santí concludes that for these reasons "the influence of surrealism over . . . Paz [in] this period is very important."[23]

There is one more important issue that I have only hinted at here and that is most relevant to situate *Los olvidados* as a significant Mexican text that should have the place and importance in Mexican film that *El laberinto de la soledad* has in Mexican literature. The most important link between both texts is their common origin in ethnographic surrealism. Santí states that Octavio Paz's closest ties to surrealism came from his association with the "Collège de sociologie," founded in Paris in 1937 by surrealist dissidents Roger Caillois and Georges Bataille, who, like Buñuel, had departed the group proper in the mid-1930s. Like Buñuel, who chose the subtitle "An essay on human geography" for his documentary *Las Hurdes* in 1932,

Caillois and Bataille became interested in "human sciences," which prompted their exit from the group. From the surrealists Bataille, Caillois, and, of course, Buñuel, whom Santí does not mention, emerged "ethnographic surrealism," which "dissented from orthodox or academic anthropology by focusing its studies not on societies that were archaic or "primitive"—but on modern, current societies."[24] On this topic, Santí concludes:

> In *The Labyrinth of Solitude* we find in effect, what we could call, with the help of anthropologist James Clifford, an *ethnographic surrealism:* an ironic experience of culture which "attacks the familiar, provoking the irruption of otherness—the unexpected." Different from pure ethnography, whose efforts are to make the strange comprehensible, the surrealist tends to work backwards, making the familiar strange. Vanguard art in the XX century and the development of ethnography ... both achieve ... subversive cultural criticism.[25]

The critique of *The Labyrinth of Solitude* as surrealist ethnography proper both to Mexican cultural studies and surrealism could not be more germane. It helps us to frame *Los olvidados* in the same context. The well-documented links of Octavio Paz with surrealism do not deny but confirm the relationship of *Los olvidados* with debates about Mexico, the Revolution, and Mexican culture, which were by then a decade old. *The Labyrinth of Solitude* and *Los olvidados* both summarize and end the debate. After breaking with the surrealists, Buñuel's first film was indeed the ethnographic surrealist "essay on human geography," *Las Hurdes.*

In his book *Mists of Regret*, Dudley Andrew reaches practically the same conclusions about *Las Hurdes*, which critics generally agree is the formal parent of *Los olvidados*. This provides further evidence that Octavio Paz and Luis Buñuel were of a similar mind, along with a significant portion of the Mexican intelligentsia, when they produced their mid-century classics. Andrew writes:

> Buñuel's stark films help verify the link James Clifford has made between the surrealists and the founding of modern ethnography in Paris. Like Bataille, Leiris, and Roger Caillois, Buñuel learned to explore himself through the study of bizarre rites and foreign peoples. . . . Violence, the surrealists preached, can generate as well as destroy possibilities. If there exists any excuse for the cruelty that Buñuel so disturbingly displays in the manner in which he films the poor people of *Las Hurdes* it must stem from this need, this instinct, to make us shudder.[26]

Andrew's judgment on the origins, operations, meanings, and value of surrealist ethnography are as valid for understanding *Las Hurdes* as they are for understanding *The Labyrinth of Solitude*, and, of course, *Los olvidados*.

The surrealist pedigree of Buñuel's film is not in question. That has been established by fifty years of criticism about the movie and by every book about Buñuel. What remains to be seen is the film's real connection to Mexico, which is based on the movie's indisputable conjunction with what is an integral part of Mexican studies, however controversial. From Cosío Villegas, to the debates on "Mexicanness" of the 1940s, to Octavio Paz, "the crisis," surrealism, and ethnography, *Los olvidados* is a film that is meaningfully specific to its cultural and historical context.

In this sense, *Los olvidados* becomes the most critical link between surrealism and Mexico, and *The Labyrinth of Solitude* is the bridge that connects the film to the specificity of its Mexican context. From similar intellectual backgrounds and conforming to similar formal structures, *Los olvidados* and *The Labyrinth of Solitude* complement each other in their commentary about Mexico, the failure of the Revolution, and the crisis of the national in Mexican cinema. Like *El laberinto de la soledad*, *Los olvidados* does not just represent a "bizarre" culture drawn by a European surrealist, but it is what surrealism became in Mexico.

Like Buñuel, Paz had feared that the reception of his work could be negative.[27] This fear came in part because Paz's book was meant to be critical of Mexico's nationalist rhetoric, was meant to be yet another form of criticism of the "crisis" of the revolution as an ideological system. Paz's book specifically attempted to "treat" nationalism as a disease by "raising consciousness of its myths and mechanisms."[28] Paz thus turns the key issue of Mexican nationalism—the illicit, violent sexual exchange of Hernán Cortés with doña Marina (La Malinche)—into a "family romance" which includes "the violent father, the humiliated mother, the traumatized son."[29] This scenario is one of the key characteristics that makes Buñuel's Mexican melodramas *(Una mujer sin amor* and *El río y la muerte)* fit smoothly into the narrative conventions and ideological operations of classic Mexican melodrama. But this layout was first proposed in coherent theoretical terms in *El laberinto de la soledad*.

Los olvidados really begins by questioning the cinematic Mexico. But, unlike *The Labyrinth of Solitude*, *Los olvidados* is not much concerned with understanding the abstract psychoanalytic construction of Mexican national identity. That sort of analysis is present in Paz's book in the chapters on "La Malinche" and "El Pachuco," and in Paz's comments on "El Pelado" (all of whom are key figures of Mexican cinema: the virgin/whore, Tin-Tan, and Cantinflas, respectively). In Paz's essay, the "surrealist ethnographic" methodology of the book (making the familiar bizarre and drawing psychoanalytic conclusions based on the Freudian scenario of the "family

FIGURE 4. Roberto Cobo (as Jaibo), Alfonso Mejía (as Pedro, *center left*), and Javier Amezcua (as Julián) posing for *Los olvidados* (1950) in "the very real slums of Mexico City." In the film, the three characters die and are disposed of as garbage in locations similar to this one. Museum of Modern Art / Film Stills Archive.

romance") is employed to explain the "neurosis" of the Mexican national identity.

Buñuel's film shows the physical reality (notwithstanding its surreal elements) that may—in its modern and "modernizing" urban setting, in the very real slums of Mexico City—incarnate some of the issues brought up in Paz's book, as well as the "cracks" and "fissures" and "weaknesses" of classical cinema's anti-modernist utopia.[30] The characters that populate *Los olvidados* are, like Paz's Mexicans, traumatized and trapped in their own "drama of identification."[31]

In fact, Buñuel was openly opposed to the style, look, patriotic values, and rhetoric of classic Mexican cinema.[32] As one of the few true surrealists, Buñuel did not acknowledge "national" symbols as anything other than a political manipulation and a bourgeois aberration.[33] In *My Last Sigh* Buñuel tells Jean-Claude Carrière about his "profound horror" of "official folklore" and of his distrust and dislike of "organized" folklore and "patriotic" nationalism. For example, in recalling a meeting in Hollywood of Spanish Republicans and other Europeans, Buñuel wrote, "All patriotic displays make me nauseous."[34]

At face value, *Los olvidados* is an urban drama, an *arrabalera*, as Mexicans pejoratively called the realist movies set in the slums and back alleys of the city. Like Vittorio De Sica's *Sciuscia* (1946) and *Bicycle Thieves* (1948), both of which Buñuel admired, *Los olvidados* conforms to a picaresque structure.[35] Like its literary structural models, *Lazarillo de Tormes* and Francisco de Quevedo's *Historia de la vida del buscón*, *Los olvidados* follows its principal character, Pedro, through a series of adventures and encounters with a succession of formative figures. None of these individuals helps Pedro to accomplish anything. They only mistreat him, lie to him, take advantage of him, or, in their misdirected attempt to help (as in the episode with the farm-school director), lead him to his death. Unlike classic picaresque, which works as a rudimentary, primitive version of a Bildungsroman, there is no hope for the protagonist of *Los olvidados*.

Through hard knocks, Pedro "learns" what seems to be a life-lesson on self-preservation, which tragically fails him when he at last meets his nemesis, the evil Jaibo. The paradox lies in the impossibility of redemption for the protagonist. *Los olvidados*, like the Spanish picaresque novel, and the postwar film masterpieces of Italian neorealism, has often been recognized and interpreted as a social critique. With its realistic depiction of overcrowded slum shanties, domestic abuse, incest, child abuse, crime and punishment, poverty, and the ineptness of public social services, it is an indictment of contemporary urban society. Nevertheless, the real social and political context from which it sprang—the specific conditions of the Mexican "crisis" of the late 1940s—are all but ignored by film critics in favor of obvious comparisons with De Sica's work, which Buñuel did not welcome.

Los olvidados arguably rejects both the values put forward by some of the most important and popular genres of classical Mexican cinema and the stylistic conventions of the best examples of Mexican classical cinema from the 1930s to the 1950s. Certainly, *Los olvidados* was not the only movie set in the poor neighborhoods of Mexican cities. There were, of course, Alejandro Galindo's *arrabaleras*: *Campeón sin corona* (1945), *¡Esquina, bajan!* (1948), and *Espaldas mojadas* (1953), among others. But *Los olvidados* did go several steps further in its depressing pessimism and in displaying the city's sheer filthiness.[36] In that way, *Los olvidados* directly addresses and attacks the official idea of Mexican culture, the official shape of Mexican cinema that was part of the postrevolutionary cultural project which included the organization of national museums, the proliferation of murals, cultural publications, and, at the international level, the cinema. Where *Los olvidados* goes a little deeper than classic *arrabalera* is in its critical commentary on a specifically Mexican moment of "crisis" at so many different levels (economic, political, cultural, moral).

In accordance with its social "thesis" (or essay) façade, Buñuel and co-screenwriter Luis Alcoriza open the film with a disclaiming voice-over narration asserting that it is based on real-life events (the origins of which are unclear). This sets the tone and mood of the movie as one of skepticism and criticism, often taken, mistakenly, for "documentary." Like *Las Hurdes*, *Los olvidados* appears as "an essay," only this time one on Mexican society as well as "on human geography." The narrator states, "[The] film is based on real-life facts, is not optimistic, and leaves the solution to the problem to the progressive forces of society." It is relevant to note the similarity of these words to the inauguration address of Miguel Alemán, who stated precisely the need for a "progressive society," for the state, and for the people to find the solution to Mexico's social and economic problems. Indeed, Buñuel and Alcoriza acknowledge "the crisis" and the urge that it be addressed, that "a solution" be found, to use Alemán's words.

In his extensive interview about the film with José de la Colina and Tomás Pérez Turrent,[37] Buñuel tells of the research that went into the preparation for *Los olvidados*. Buñuel, co-screenwriter Luis Alcoriza, and production designer Edward Fitzgerald spent six months doing field research inside the Mexico City slums where the movie's action was to take place. They attempted to be particularly realist in their physical depiction of the environment—the interiors of shacks and shanties, the existence of animals, the number of people in each house, and so on. Buñuel and his team were concerned with being true to the "reality" that they found. "Reality," however, constituted a rejection of the dominant images, settings, and characters in classical cinema.

Los olvidados is populated by a cast of characters that represents the poorest of any society in situations that bring out only the worst in them: violence; murder; decrepit, filthy settings; overcrowding; lying; cheating; stealing; sickness; sexual abuse; domestic abuse; incest; abandonment; hopelessness. There are no noble Indian souls here, no "essence" of Mexican beauty (à la Dolores del Río in *María Candelaria* and María Félix in *Maclovia*): there is only the provocation that the only redeemable character in the movie is a naive country boy, "El Ojitos." He is the only one who wears a poncho and a sombrero, true markers of the folkloric Mexico for which Buñuel felt "profound horror."[38] There are neither gentle, manly revolutionary generals nor faithful *soldaderas* (as in Fernández's *Enamorada*):

there is only a mean blind man who speaks nostalgically of the times of Dictator Porfirio Díaz.

Significantly, El Ojitos is a country boy who is brought to the city and abandoned in one of the farmers' markets. Thus, El Ojitos is a product of the failure of the 1930s land reforms: he is left with no land, is displaced to the city, is unskilled, and must search for work. It seems rather calculating that this abandoned child, literally an "olvidado," ends up in the hands of the evil, "Porfirian" blind man, Don Carmelo, since this gives more relevancy to Daniel Cosío Villegas's judgment about the development of a *neoporfiriato* in the midst of the moral, political, and economic crisis.

Don Carmelo is first seen singing on the street and panhandling as a one-man band. He tells his audience:

> I'm going to sing you a song from the time of our great general Porfirio Díaz.... You may laugh, but in the time of our great general, people were more respectful. And women stayed at home instead of gadding around and deceiving their husbands like they do today.

Don Carmelo is thus introduced before he discovers El Ojitos, the abandoned Indian boy, who is then adopted by Don Carmelo as the blind man's own guide, or *lazarillo*.[39]

We may remember that, according to Cosío Villegas and López-Portillo Tostado, one of the Revolution's great failures by 1950 was the lack of improvement of the conditions of the Indians and Indian rural communities.[40] El Ojitos eloquently dramatizes that failure: he is lost and abandoned, he is taken for an Indian (the nickname "Ojitos" [Little Eyes] refers to his Indian facial features), and he is immediately adopted by a *neoporfirian* for exploitation. Don Carmelo soon decides that El Ojitos was abandoned because he represented a burden to his father, most likely a subsistence farmer from some rural community in the Valley of Mexico and possibly from a bankrupt agrarian cooperative *(ejido)*.

In *Los olvidados* no national landmarks in the backgrounds retell national history, as did Diego Rivera's murals in the National Palace prominently featured in Emilio Fernández's *Río Escondido*. There are no singular geographic landmarks, like the volcano Popocatépetl, shot against the background of "inevitably" white clouds. There are only the hills of a garbage dump where the body of the last victim, Pedro, is unloaded. There is the skeleton of a high-rise building under construction and the city smog, which effectively substitute for Popocatépetl and the "inevitable" white clouds and which are present in the background at both narrative turning points: the deaths of Julián and Jaibo.

The presence of the frame or skeleton of the high-rise building, to which Buñuel wanted to add the surreal touch of an orchestra of one hundred musicians, is also an important piece of "cine de arrabal." *Los olvidados* effectively comments on the conditions of the urban poor, but it also raises a key issue on Mexico's race toward modernization—the urban construction boom of the 1940s. The new city of the "developmentalist" 1950s was an urban nightmare because, just as the intellectual and cultural elite of the 1940s had feared, the changes in the city landscape also meant deep changes in the city's demographic profile. In *Los olvidados* the ever-present images of buildings under construction present a rare documentation of the actual construction boom at the turn of the decade, when thousands of rural Mexicans were relocating to the city every day, that was so characteristic of President Miguel Alemán's administration.

Finally, there are certainly no "traditional" family values in *Los olvidados*—no "God, nation, and home" in the fashion of the family melodramas of Juan Bustillo Oro, Fernando de Fuentes, and Julio Bracho. On the contrary, it is the absence of the Porfirian morals of the family melodrama that are more evident in *Los olvidados*. This, however, is surprisingly apropos to Don Carmelo's words at the beginning of the movie: "People were more respectful, and women stayed at home . . . in the time of our great general." Indeed, the moral decay of Mexico in the times of *alemanismo* was seen as a true sign of the Revolution's failure by intellectuals like Cosío Villegas, and a sign of the people's loss of "faith" in the Revolution. As stated in the narrator's opening remarks, the phenomena of both child neglect and child delinquency in Mexico City was no different than it was in big cities in developed countries, as the gender and class demographics of the industrial workforce expanded to include women. Thus, in Don Carmelo's "Porfirian" analysis, women's absence from the home, for whatever reason, was one of the causes of the moral decay of Mexican society.

Los olvidados can also be seen as a film that addresses the defining problem of the systematic but slow transition to modernity after the Revolution, and not just as it relates to the historical context of *alemanismo*, but as it relates to the discourse of classical cinema. The transition and negotiation of Mexican society into modernity was a deep concern of classical Mexican cinema that is especially treated in the canon-building 1940s films of Emilio Fernández.

Without referring directly to classical cinema, Néstor García Canclini has addressed the issue of "modernization" and its relationship to the defining postrevolutionary period in Mexico. García Canclini analyzes both the ill-fitting ideological position of classical cinema's resistance to "modernization" and the dramatic and thematic alliance of *Los olvidados* with "modernity" and the "new" nationalism of the 1950s. Mexico's cultural establishment, in coordination with the state, attempted to condense, to consolidate traditional arts and crafts with modern art (exemplified most dramatically in the projects undertaken by Diego Rivera, David Alfaro Siqueiros, and José Clemente Orozco, of course). The idea was to negotiate the paradox of modernization by incorporating modern and traditional tendencies under the signature of "the nation":

> Mexican cultural history of the 1930s through the 1950s demonstrates the fragility of that utopia and the attrition it was suffering as a result of intraartistic and socio-political conditions. The visual arts field, hegemonized by dogmatic realism, the dominance of content, and the subordination of arts to politics, loses its former vitality and produces few innovations. In addition, it was difficult to promote the social action of art when the revolutionary impulse was being "institutionalized."[41]

García Canclini's analysis of the failed "utopia" of the visual arts project in Mexico around 1950 can help us understand the rationale of the generally romanticized image of Mexico that was popularized by classical cinema. The films of Emilio Fernández were specifically concerned with the tensions of modernization, as some studies of his works demonstrate.

In his book *Cine y realidad social en México* Alejandro Rozado writes that the work of Emilio Fernández represented a sort of romantic, innocent resistance to Mexico's process of modernization.[42] In Fernández's imaginary, the paradoxical (hybrid, if you will) nature of modernization cannot be negotiated. Emilio Fernández's films, according to Rozado, fail to harmonize the romanticism of tradition with the pressing, unstoppable needs of modernization, thus failing, I may add, to conform to the "hybrid" social and cultural agenda of the Revolution, as Néstor García Canclini has concluded. "Hybridity," in the García Canclini sense of the word, refers to the negotiated coexistence in Latin American societies of "modern" technology, media, politics, and modes of production, with "traditional" values, the syncretism of religious cults, moral guidelines, and so on.

Appropriately, Fernández's anti-modernist position does not take the shape of any sort of anti-technological or anti-industrialist critique, but it becomes a moral position: it is the old Mexico's moral codes and values that are really opposed to and threatened by the decaying morals of the new, modernizing Mexico.

Of the entire panorama of Mexican film production in the 1940s, the work of Emilio Fernández stands out for the tragic resonance adopted in the filmic spirit by the conflict of modernization that [Mexico] has lived since the republican era. Fernández begins with melodramatic representation, whose tradition is extraordinarily vigorous in Hispanic America, and submerges in a space where the conflict of values generates a learning experience. From the beatified attitude that constitutes melodrama, which takes the side of "good" versus "evil" values, the visual tragedy of Indio Fernández develops in a reiterated reconsideration of the struggle between the traditional values of the "Mexican community" and the values of progress.[43]

Thus, according to Rozado, Mexico's precipitation into modernity under Presidents Ávila Camacho and Miguel Alemán was very traumatic and resulted in the kind of idealistic representation of Mexico ("nationalist rhetoric" and "physical formalism") that distinguished the cinema of Emilio Fernández. The classic images of Mexican cinema sprang from the Revolution's ambiguous position between traditional values and a modern economy. The films of Emilio Fernández, among the most illustrative of the country's cinema, fail to resolve that tension, either by simplifying (as in *Río Escondido*) or sometimes ignoring (as in *Pueblerina*), the impact of the economic changes of the 1940s and beyond. But Mexican cinema became known around the world as a result of Fernández's *Flor silvestre* and *María Candelaria*. Even Fernández's films *Río Escondido* (1947) and especially *Pueblerina* (1948), which now seem somewhat critical and more in agreement with the concerns of "the crisis," still impose a very romanticized version (a "foundational fiction," to borrow from Doris Sommer) of Mexico's state in the late 1940s.[44]

In clear contrast, *Los olvidados* presents Mexico at the threshold of modernization in a less melodramatic fashion than the contemporary *arrabal* films of Alejandro Galindo—which were also structured in the guise of moral predicaments—yet in a more realistic way than the films of Emilio Fernández.[45] If the image of classical Mexican cinema was one of moral resistance to modernization, then the image of Mexico's submission to modernization, which Buñuel dramatizes as one of hopelessness and a completely amoral existence in *Los olvidados*, would be the epitome of what was "anti-classical" in Mexican cinema.[46]

If there is anything that dramatically represents what "Mexico" is in *Los olvidados*, it is precisely moral and social decay as a sign of modernization. *Los olvidados*, unlike the imaginary world of Emilio Fernández, poses the problem of modernization in the shape of a moral dyad instead of a moral dilemma (which is more like the way Galindo's films present modernization). In *Los olvidados* Buñuel resists the temptation to "take sides," to judge in moral terms what Mexico *is* and what Mexico *is not*. In this sense, *Los olvidados* is, quite literally, an "amoral" tale: like Buñuel's *Las Hurdes*, it is emotionally detached from its subject(s).

In classical Mexican cinema being "amoral" could also be a way to be situated on the margins of the nation (no "God, nation, home"[47]) while at the same time participating in the "national" cultural debate on "the crisis," in which classical cinema represented the "traditionalist" position. Buñuel's *Los olvidados* inevitably placed the director in the middle of this debate, and it also situates itself as a commentary on the crisis of politics, economy, culture, and the nationalist rhetoric of Mexican cinema. In any case, Buñuel and Alcoriza's script, and Buñuel's aesthetic and thematic treatment of this "amoral" story, do attempt to negotiate the position of urban Mexico in the dyad of tradition and modernity. *Los olvidados* opposed the classic "Indianist" films of Emilio Fernández (which ignore modernization by placing characters in times and spaces where the Revolution seemed unambiguous) and the urban melodramas of Alejandro Galindo (which demonize modernization by turning it into a metaphor of Mexico's proximity to and relationship with the United States). *Los olvidados* comes closer to being a draft, a sketch, or an essay on Mexico City in the face of modernization. Consequently, *Los olvidados* can be taken as truly representative of this moment of crisis that is also a juncture of definition. If the negotiation of Mexico's "hybrid" cultural configuration in the revolutionary period is a marker of its national identification, as García Canclini points out, then *Los olvidados* can be seen as the quintessential "Mexican" movie of the late classical period.[48]

The only other films that in any way resemble the analysis of Mexican society proposed by *Los olvidados* are those in the *cabaretera* subgenre of Mexican melodrama of the late 1940s and 1950s—movies like Julio Bracho's *Distinto Amanecer* (1943), and Alberto Gout's *Aventurera* (1949) and *Sensualidad* (1950). *Los olvidados* evidently struck a cord in the classical cinema establishment, very much like the lurid *cabaretera* films initially did.

The original Mexican detractors of *Los olvidados* missed the key points of Buñuel's criticism. Distracted as they were by defending the "honor" of Mexico's institutions traditionally championed in national cinema ("God, nation, and home"), they were deeply wounded when the international festivals praised Buñuel's film. Like the European critics, they shifted their attention away from the film's primary target: "the crisis" of the turn of the decade.[49]

A few personalities involved in Mexican art, culture, and politics congratulated Buñuel on the film immediately upon its initial run in Mexico

City. Among them were Octavio Paz and the politically active muralist David Alfaro Siqueiros.[50] But most other celebrities and critics were originally negative, based on their belief that *Los olvidados* portrayed a viciously negative, false, and "dirty" image of Mexico. Even the film's producer, Oscar Dancigers, was afraid the film was too dangerous, that there was "too much filth" in it, not enough recognized talent, and that it was too much of a risk for his production company.[51] Significantly, when *Los olvidados* premiered at the Cannes Film Festival in 1951, Octavio Paz wrote what is still considered one of the most beautiful reviews of the film.[52] In it, Paz praised the film for "turning its back to the temptation of the impressive Mexican landscape" and referred to the film with direct references to *The Labyrinth of Solitude*. After acknowledging the film's debt to Spanish cultural and literary history, he wrote:

> And the children, their mythology, their passive rebelliousness, their suicidal loyalty, their thundering sweetness full of exquisite ferocity, their torn affirmation of themselves in and for death, their endless search for communion—even through crime—are nothing, nor can they be anything but Mexican. . . . Buñuel uncovers in the dream of his heroes the archetypal images of the Mexican people: Coatlicue and sacrifice.[53]

Paz's reference to Coatlicue is especially telling. She was the mythical Earth goddess of the Mexicas, and also the mother of Huitzilopocthli, one of the central deities of the ancient Mexicans, before the conquest. Paz here refers to the search for the mother in *Los olvidados* as "a Mexican obsession" and again makes a direct reference to *The Labyrinth of Solitude:* "The world of *Los olvidados* is populated by orphans in search of the 'others,' of their equals, [which is] the other face of the search for the mother. Or the acceptance of her definitive absence: knowing ourselves alone." These word echo those of Paz in the chapter on "The Pachuco and Other Extremes," where Paz writes, "The discovery of ourselves is manifest as the acknowledgment of ourselves alone."[54] Paz ultimately established the most direct and relevant connection between *Los olvidados* and *The Labyrinth of Solitude* by referring to the film by using the exact words from his essays on La Malinche and the Pachuco. He acknowledged more than anyone at the time the distinctly Mexican quality of the film. Solitude, violence, and being orphaned are definitive qualities of Mexicanness in Paz's imaginary, just as they are the defining qualities of the children of *Los olvidados*.

Although initial reactions to *Los olvidados* within Mexican critical circles were not just negative but almost visceral, it is significant that when it was released abroad the film encouraged comparisons (or rather, contrasts) with

FIGURE 5. Pedro's mother (Estela Inda) and Jaibo (Roberto Cobo) consummate the Oedipal narrative in *Los olvidados*. "The search for the mother," wrote Octavio Paz, is "a Mexican obsession." Museum of Modern Art / Film Stills Archive.

the classical style of Mexican cinema. Interestingly, the critics at *Cahiers du Cinéma* (particularly André Bazin) were the ones who originally shifted critical attention specifically away from Emilio Fernández and Gabriel Figueroa and toward Luis Buñuel in 1951, after the French release of *Los olvidados* and *Subida al cielo*.

Bazin, arguably the period's most influential film critic and a co-founder of *Cahiers du Cinéma*, expressed this change in the focus of attention from classical Mexican cinema to Buñuel's Mexican movies on the occasion of the French release of *Subida al cielo*:

> Juries seem to mistake cinema for photography. There was admittedly something more than beautiful photography in *María Candelaria* and even in *La Perla* (1945). But it is easy to see, year in and year out, that physical formalism and nationalist rhetoric have replaced realism and authentic poetry. With the exotic surprises gone, and [Gabriel] Figueroa's cinematographic feats reduced to fragments of technical bravura, Mexican cinema found itself crossed-off the critics' map.... It is entirely thanks to Luis Buñuel that we are talking about Mexican films again.[55]

Despite Bazin's hyperbolic style and judgmental claims, he often influenced the balance of criticism. Even Luis Buñuel, as apathetic as he was to the critics (and increasingly to *Cahiers du Cinéma*, later in the 1960s), sometimes listened and paid attention to Bazin's views about his films. In his book *André Bazin*, Dudley Andrew comments on the unlikely friendship that developed between the artist and the critic: "Buñuel, notorious for his cynicism and anger, found in Bazin a kind of depth and honesty of vision which set him aside from all other critics. Even before they had met, Buñuel had 'found in Bazin's essays truths about my films I had never thought of.'" Andrew went on, "Later, Buñuel would describe his projects to Bazin before final scripting."[56] According to Andrew, Bazin and Buñuel not only respected each other but Bazin's criticism may have even influenced Buñuel's later style in the 1950s, and consequently Bazin rediscovered Mexican cinema through Buñuel's lens.

What is most important about Bazin's criticism of Buñuel's Mexican films is that, as interested as Bazin was in technical and visual matters, he took up Buñuel over Fernández-Figueroa because neither he nor *Cahiers du Cinéma* was interested any longer in "the nationalist rhetoric" of Mexican cinema. Even though *Cahiers du Cinema*'s critics often praised the technical proficiency and artistic beauty of the Fernández–Figueroa movies exported to the European film festivals, and especially to Cannes, Bazin was no longer impressed with that "physical formalism." Instead, he detected that it was stalled, decadent, and in a creative decline. Classical Mexican cinema was no longer evolving, thought Bazin, and Buñuel appeared to him to dictate the future direction of Mexican cinema. It is most significant to note that for Bazin at *Cahiers* it was evident, visible, that Mexican cinema was going through a period of crisis, and that it needed some form of revision.

Buñuel's films, as demonstrated by André Bazin's prophetic review in *L'Observateur* in August 1952, replaced Mexican classical cinema both at the film festivals and in the critical circuits. In other words, *Los olvidados* exemplifies and represents a clear moment of transition, or crisis, in what constituted Mexican classical cinema. The classical period ended in 1950, in the eyes of festival juries and critics, and Mexican cinema became Luis Buñuel.

As Buñuel occupied the center of critical attention, his films began receiving the international festival awards previously presented to the predictable "nationalist" films of Emilio Fernández, Gabriel Figueroa, and their heirs.[57] Bazin's championing of Buñuel anticipates the clear transition of Mexican cinema's classic aesthetic to that of the New Cinema of the 1960s, which was more formally experimental and more critical of Mexican issues than classical cinema had been. As we shall see in the following chapter, after the impact of *Los olvidados* had secured his reputation Buñuel went through an experimental period with (and within) the styles, genres, and topics of classical Mexican cinema. Buñuel became one of the figures that helped to break the ground for the more open revision and experimentation with styles and genres that occurred in Mexican cinema in the 1960s.

The aesthetic crisis of Mexican cinema was closely related and rooted in the general political, economic, and cultural crisis of Mexico that was first articulated clearly by Daniel Cosío Villegas in his 1947 essay. Luis Buñuel's incorporation into the Mexican cinema industry at a time of crisis did not necessarily imply his "conversion" to the system of symbols and representations that classical cinema immortalized and that was best exemplified by *María Candelaria* and *Flor silvestre* (the "anti-modernist utopia" of classical cinema). Nevertheless, in spite of its critical aura, the resistance to the themes and visual conventions of classical cinema present in *Los olvidados* became a sign of the film's correspondence with the transitional juncture of the revolutionary crisis and modernization. The film thus initiated Buñuel's integration into the debates on Mexican politics and culture in the postrevolutionary period and thus corresponded with the processes of cultural negotiation about which Néstor García Canclini writes in *Hybrid Cultures*.

Interestingly, like García Canclini, although writing in a different context and nearly forty years apart, André Bazin, who did not know the first thing about Mexico but who did know about the cinema, also recognized the failure of Mexican cinema's "physical formalism and nationalist rhetoric [as they] replace[d] [the] realism and authentic poetry"[58] represented in the canonical works of Emilio Fernández. Thus, "the crisis" of Mexico may have had its original cinematic representation in the decaying aesthetics of the films of the 1940s and its transitional vision toward the New Cinema in Buñuel's *Los olvidados*.

Buñuel's arrival in Mexico in the "late Golden Age" coincided with the decline of the romantic aesthetic of Emilio Fernández and the rise of the psychoanalytic pessimism of Octavio Paz. But that juncture, that "crisis of nationalism" at the turn of the decade of the 1950s also helps us to contextualize and validate Luis Buñuel's inquiry into the idea of Mexico that was invented, codified, hierarchized, and divulged by the Revolution. For decades that image was conceived in the plastic arts and painting (as in the work of the muralists), in literature and philosophy (as in José Vasconcelos's *La raza cósmica* and Alfonso Reyes's *Última Tule*), and, of course, in national cinema.

Los olvidados, to some extent, represents the crisis of revolutionary

FIGURE 6. Pedro (Alfonso Mejía) is inevitably lost in the labyrinth of violence and solitude in *Los olvidados.* Museum of Modern Art/Film Stills Archive.

rhetoric in Mexican cinema and "the cultural nation"[59] at the juncture of the decline of the cinema's Golden Age, as well as an analogous comment on the discussions about "the crisis" of the Revolution of the turn of the decade. It also serves as a revisionist approach to the superficiality and weaknesses (the "masks," as Octavio Paz would call them) of Mexican revolutionary mythology and of "the myth of the revolution" as exemplified by the work of "the fourth muralist," as Emilio Fernández is said to have once called himself.[60]

The 1950s constitute the climactic moment of intellectual activity of the so-called "philosophy of Mexicanness" *(filosofía de lo mexicano)* in Mexico, a movement which recruited the musings of many an important figure in the arts, the letters, and the academy. From the works of José Vasconcelos in the 1920s to those of Leopoldo Zea in the 1930s, Alfonso Reyes in the 1940s, and ending with Paz in the 1950s, Mexican intellectuals had been "philosophizing" about the cultural, historical, and even spiritual characteristics that defined the nation's identity. Daniel Cosío Villegas's famous essay on "the crisis of Mexico" helped frame historically what Octavio Paz achieved culturally. In the manner of *The Wretched of the Earth, The Labyrinth of*

Solitude was an attempt at understanding the troubled postcolonial mind, and Paz's conclusions were a sign of the psychological and spiritual side of the failure of the Revolution. With *Los olvidados,* as Octavio Paz himself acknowledged in his writings, Luis Buñuel contributed to or became part of that debate. His groundbreaking film is a visual and poetic rendition of Mexico that was originally misunderstood as something foreign, or anti-Mexican, but that proved to be in close communication with the contemporary stream of Mexican intellectual activity.

4 Genre, Women, Narrative

> Melodrama was more important in Mexico than in the USA because, traditionally, Mexican popular culture is premised in the perennial confusion between life and melodrama.
> —Carlos Monsiváis, "Mythologies"

The commercial and critical success of *El gran calavera* and *Los olvidados* in 1949 and 1950 was something of a mixed blessing for Luis Buñuel. It meant that he never lacked work after that (in each year 1951 and 1952, he made three movies), but it also meant that he had become a participant in the workings of the Mexican film industry. Working as a director in Mexico implied a number of limitations in terms of topics and creativity since a strict censorship code, designed to protect the national image and morals, was still in place.¹ Yet Buñuel retained control in some minor ways as far as script approval and editing were concerned, and he was always actively involved in all stages of post-production.

The history of Buñuel's commercial projects in the Mexican film industry reveals some of the tensions of this period of his career. On the one hand, Buñuel was in command of genre conventions; on the other hand, he was a surrealist and a foreigner, and that meant that his approach to Mexican melodrama and comedy was somewhat mediated, cautious, self-conscious. To whit, Buñuel's most "generic" Mexican comedies and melodramas were made with a full awareness of their function as Mexican popular films, but they also seem to disclose the seams that hold them together. This is similar but less dramatic than the way in which *Los olvidados* unmasked the elaborate yet fragile façade of the best-known works of Emilio Fernández. This self-reflexive tendency in Buñuel's films is evident in the movies made in Mexico and for the Mexican public, such as *Susana, Una mujer sin amor,* and *El río y la muerte*. These films stand in clear stylistic and thematic contrast to the international co-productions that Buñuel was making for the film festival circuits and crossover markets—films such as *The Adventures of Robinson Crusoe* (Mexico/U.S., 1952), *Cela s'appelle l'aurore* (France/Italy, 1955), *La mort en ce jardin* (Mexico/France, 1956), *La fièvre monte à El Pao* (Mexico/France, 1959), *The Young One* (Mexico/U.S., 1960), and *Viridiana* (Mexico/Spain, 1961).

When Buñuel addressed the Mexican public, his films tended to communicate directly with Mexican issues and to be in dialogue with the functions and even the ideological positions of the Mexican variations of melodrama and comedy. These films even seem artificially aware of their "Mexicanness," which makes *Susana*, for instance, an exemplary self-parody.[2] Coming from Buñuel, however, it is not their parody elements that make these films extraordinary. The contributions of *Susana* (1950) and *La hija del engaño* (1951) rather lie in Buñuel's reflection on Mexico's cultural and economic processes in the 1950s, on the treatment of those issues in the nation's popular cinema, and on his connection to his Mexican audience.

In the late 1940s and 1950s marginal female characters *(cabareteras,* prostitutes, *femmes fatales)* gained ground in Mexican cinema, showing up in previously sacred spaces and settings, like the home, the ranch, and as participants in the Revolution. But such characters were also somewhat redeemed in modernizing Mexico, where the *cabaretera* films were exemplary of the country's transition to modernity, industrial development, and post-Porfirian morality.[3]

Buñuel's original venture into the cabaret setting, *Gran Casino*, rested largely on the star-discourse of Libertad Lamarque, who became something like the "Stella Dallas" of Mexican cinema.[4] Like the title character in that 1937 film by King Vidor, the characters played by Lamarque were often forced to give up everything, whether it be a career, a man, or a certain lifestyle, in order to accommodate the desires and needs of their children (or their lover).[5] In Mexican cinema, the *cabaretera* character was always a more complex one because her function was truly one of "mediation,"—of articulating the dilemma posed by the clash between (old) traditional moral values and (new) economic and industrial progress. The cabaret setting in these films guaranteed that the tensions between traditional (Porfirian) moral values and the urban economic demands of the Revolution would be "negotiated" in marginal spaces like the brothel and the cabaret.

MELODRAMA AND THE POLITICS OF GENRE: BUÑUEL'S "SUSANA" AND "LA HIJA DEL ENGAÑO"

In Mexican cinema the term "melodrama" generalizes several distinct subgenres, each a unique type with its own features, rules, and popular identity. These included: (1) the "musical" melodrama, exemplified by movies like *Nosotros los pobres (We, the Poor,* by Ismael Rodríguez, 1947); (2) the *cabaretera* films, of which *Aventurera* (Alberto Gout, 1949) and *Sensualidad* (Alberto Gout, 1950) are the most eloquent examples; (3) the "revolutionary" melodrama that set a romantic story against the backdrop of the revolutionary wars (e.g., Emilio Fernández's 1946 film, *Enamorada)*; and (4) the "family" melodrama which settled matters of nationalism, modernity, and post-revolutionary policy in a domestic setting. Examples of this latter genre include *Cuando los hijos se van (When the Children Leave)* by Juan Bustillo Oro, 1941; *Una familia de tantas (An Ordinary Family)* by Alejandro Galindo, 1948; and *No basta ser madre (It's Not Enough to Be a Mother)* by Ramón Peón, 1937. There were many variations of such titles incorporating the words "mother," "family," and "children.".

In his book *Mexican Cinema: Reflections of a Society,* Carl J. Mora characterizes Mexican melodrama as "attachment to [the] traditional values [of] 'God, Nation, and Home.'"[6] Loyalty to parents, respect for the home, and fear of God were signs of good citizenship and heroism. Several of Buñuel's films in the early to mid-1950s exemplify what was ideologically, narratively, and politically distinctive in Mexican melodrama.

Particularly in its thematic specificity, Mexican melodrama is different from Hollywood "classical" melodrama, which Linda Williams defines as "the foundation of the classical Hollywood movie."[7] Genre critics and theorists since the 1970s have been "revising" melodrama, redefining it, and also reevaluating the term to give political and theoretical currency to an otherwise unworthy, "feminine" genre. Nevertheless, as the work of Williams, Thomas Elsaesser, Christine Gledhill, E. Ann Kaplan and others suggests, the Hollywood melodrama seems more focused on gender issues (whether from a psychoanalytic, feminist, or semiotic perspective) than on the articulation of a coherent national imaginary, as is the Hollywood Western, arguably.[8] By contrast, in Mexico, melodrama was always popular; it was, and remains, the nationalist genre par excellence.

The many faces of melodrama in Mexico (revolutionary epic, family, *cabaretera*) make it the most popular of the country's film genres, and also the one that has undergone the most criticism, revisionism, and adaptation. Mexican film audiences' taste for melodrama, according to Jesús Martín-Barbero, comes from the genre's simplicity, its tendency to rely on an "absence of psychology," by virtue of which the plots, narratives, and characters of classic melodrama appeal to the public's "basic emotions: fear, enthusiasm, pity, and laughter."[9] These are certainly characteristics of classic melodrama in almost all its manifestations: from French Revolutionary theater to the *feuilleton,* or serial novel, from the American theatrical melodrama of Boucicault and Belasco to early American narrative film, from

Edwin S. Porter to D. W. Griffith. But it is through that tradition that melodrama is adapted into Mexican cinema, necessarily filtered via the classic Hollywood annals.[10]

In spite of its Hollywood-inspired origin, the musical variations of melodrama in the 1930s were the first to make a dent in Hollywood's domination of the Mexican film market. After the transition to sound (which happened in Mexico between 1929 and 1933), Mexican cinema developed its own musical form, the "revolutionary drama." These films demanded lots of vernacular music (sometimes up to twelve musical productions in a 100-minute movie), a dramatic plot involving some romantic situation, and a "historical" setting (usually the Revolution). But music was only one of the ways in which Mexican cinema "nationalized" Hollywood.

Mexican cultural critic Carlos Monsiváis has analyzed the appeal of different Mexican genres, and especially melodrama, in the Golden Age:

> The founding project of Mexican cinema was the nationalization of Hollywood.... [But] the Mexican film industry believed that mere imitation was suicidal, among other reasons because of the lack of financial resources.... It was preferable to have intensely local faces, landscapes, and ways of speaking and being, within Hollywood-derived cinematic structures. Once the familiar landscapes and sounds were recognized, the audience happily accepted the mechanics of emotional blackmail, the endlessly repeated formulas, and the lack of resources, which is a sign of poverty, as well as an invitation to fantasy.[11]

It is true that Monsiváis's general statements about the popularity of melodrama in Mexican cinema seem capricious. Yet, the theory that in Mexico melodrama played something of a "social" role is not arbitrary in Latin American film studies. In Mexican cinema, the "emotional," the "pathos," and the psychological roots of melodrama and the melodramatic formula take an ideological perspective that is rather foreign to Hollywood—"God, nation, and home"–but specific to Mexico, particularly in the critical nationalistic context of the late classical period (1946–55). This translation of the "emotional" and the "psychological" into the "national" was a correlation that the different subgenres of Mexican melodrama adopted in their narrative structures.

In her essay, "Tears and Desire: Women and Melodrama in the 'Old' Mexican Cinema," Ana López points out that in the case of classical Mexican cinema of the 1930s–1950s, "the revolutionary melodramas reworked national history... [and the] family melodramas focused on the problems of love, sexuality, and parenting."[12] López analyses the role of women in Mexican melodrama, based in part on a reading of Octavio Paz's

El laberinto de la soledad. She follows Jean Franco and others in arguing that women in Mexican cinema are often symbolic of the figure of "la chingada,"—La Malinche, the mythical traitor (and traumatic/psychological mother) of the Mexican nation. "The melodramatic became the privileged place for the symbolic reenactment of this drama of identification and the only place where female desire . . . could be glimpsed."[13] In other words, the foundational myth of the crisis of Mexican identity, the very psychoanalytical "essence" of "Mexicanness" (according to Octavio Paz), becomes one defining feature of Mexican melodrama.

In opposition to the "emotional and moral registers" that define classical melodrama of the Hollywood and European traditions, Mexican melodrama resorts not only to a metaphoric rendition of "the national" but also to the psychological links between nationalism, national identity, and the melodramatic form. Some "crisis of identity" is always one of the thematic features of Mexican cinema (and other Latin American and postcolonial cinemas, as well). Furthermore, as Monsiváis discusses, the Mexican practice of "nationalizing" Hollywood genres operates as a form of mediation through which popular cinemas help to link their audiences with contemporary politics and history. Doris Sommer writes that since the great nineteenth-century "foundational" novels of Latin American literature, melodrama has had a privileged space as a popular cohesive agent,[14] which was later extended to the consolidation of national film culture in the 1930s and 1940s. In his discussion of the functions of classical cinema in Mexico, Jesús Martín-Barbero adopts Monsiváis's argument to illustrate what "mediation" meant in the Golden Age:

> Melodrama made it possible for film to weave together national epics and intimate drama, display eroticism under the pretext of condemning incest, and dissolve tragedy in a pool of tears, de-politicizing the social contradictions of daily life.[15]

For Martín-Barbero, as for Monsiváis, the key to understanding the stubborn appeal of melodrama in Mexican cinema is the genre's ability to mediate between the popular classes, the nation, and the state. In its familiarity and repetition, and through the allure of gorgeous stars, bucolic settings, and rigid morals, melodrama gave "an image and a voice to national identity."[16] It is the specificity of these particular operations of genre in Mexico (some of which are stated in the "film laws" of the 1940s) and their correlation to political and historic contexts that truly makes Mexican cinema a national cinema. These films are in dialogue, so to speak, with their audience and with their social function.

Recently, critics have argued that Buñuel's parodic approach to Mexican melodrama somehow relieves his Mexican films of the burden of the term "national" as an adjective.[17] On the contrary, when we look at the movies Luis Buñuel, made for Mexican audiences and through the Mexican mode of production and genre systems, they become participants in this dialogue, even if they are filtered through Buñuel's peculiar humor and self-reflective consciousness. An analysis of Buñuel's strictly commercial Mexican movies points to a much more difficult question: What is the proper balance to allow for parody and criticism without totally disengaging from context, form, and generic function?

Susana

Buñuel's first film after *Los olvidados* was *Susana (The Devil and the Flesh)*. In spite of its (eventual) modest critical success, *Susana* remained one of the movies about which Buñuel said he had "nothing to say."[18] *Susana* appears to be a surprisingly conservative movie and, ideologically speaking, in spite of its evident spirit of parody, it seemingly reinforces the contemporary ideological framework of "God, nation, home" as effectively as any other Mexican melodrama of the period. *Susana* may turn out to be even less risqué than less-complex, moralistic movies like *Una mujer sin amor* (where the "treacherous," unfaithful wife is forgiven by her children), or *El río y la muerte* (where the machos show weakness in honor of their mothers).[19] After all, *Susana* repeats the patriarchal family/nation structure of Mexican cinema. It confirms and combines the traditional role(s) of the virgin/mother/whore that has been historically given to women in Mexican cinema, and it even participates in the "woman-as-traitor" national/mythological foundation that lies at the psychological core of Mexican nationality (according to Octavio Paz), and by extension at the mythological backbone of Mexican cinema.

Susana tells the story of a deceiving seductress who seeks to earn her place in bourgeois society with the sheer power of her sexual allure. She must fight against a number of specifically Mexican settings: the patriarchal home, the revolutionary progressivism of a son at the university (studying agronomy, Buñuel's initial university career), machismo, firearms, and violence. In the opening scene, Susana (Rosita Quintana) is seen in a state reformatory. She is being transferred to a solitary confinement cell, and she spits, kicks, and curses, resisting the guards' efforts. Once inside the cell, terrified of the bats, rats, and spiders there and in a furious storm, Susana invokes the "god of the prisons" to free her, asks for mercy, and, surprisingly, is granted her wish. She effortlessly pulls out the iron bars of her cell window (which distinctly project the image of a cross on the floor), props them against the wall, steps on the cross, and goes out into the storm. Soon she arrives at the hacienda of Don Guadalupe (Fernando Soler), where she lies her way into the protection of the family home.

Susana plays a different role with each of the principal characters of this skewed family melodrama. With doña Carmen, the mother, she is obedient, hardworking, and demure, "like a daughter." With don Guadalupe, the old patriarch, she is more like one of the mares in his stable: strong, powerful, and in a dangerously incestuous way, very seductive. Susana specifically tells don Guadalupe that she admires his position (as head of the family), that she needs the protection of his masculinity and power, and that she is ready to obey and please him. In their first scene alone together, don Guadalupe walks into his working quarters only to see Susana inside a large rifle case cleaning the glass panes, literally on display with the firearms that don Guadalupe is inspecting. There is no unambiguous message here: don Guadalupe looks inside the display case, looks at Susana, framed within the frame of the case and positioned at Guadalupe's eye level. Susana bends over to reach a low pane, and her cleavage (which she is plainly exposing) fills the smaller enclosure of the glass. In a medium shot, the two characters dramatize the woman's body as sexual spectacle: Susana "framed" yet inquisitively returning his gaze, don Guadalupe watching in fascination. They both seem aroused and embarrassed by the situation. Don Guadalupe then specifically asks Susana to dress more carefully, because the men in the ranch are going to be disturbed at the sight of such a voluptuous woman. Susana's sexual image, and especially her willingness to be on display, indeed disturb the peace of this bucolic setting.

When she is trying to seduce the son of the house, the university student Alberto (Luis López Somoza), Susana plays at being innocent, ignorant, clumsy, almost childish. She visits Alberto in his room where he is putting his books in order, climbs with him onto the bookcase ladder, and feigns curiosity about his studies. They both fall off the ladder, and Susana ends up on the floor with Alberto on top of her. The high-angle, medium shot of the two of them suggests Susana's vulnerability, as if she were waiting to be seduced, as opposed to her proactive provocation in front of don Guadalupe, the man of the house, where she actually bends over in the rifle case to attract his lustful gaze. Susana and Alberto kiss on the floor, sealing an unspoken love pact in Alberto's ingenuous, virginal mind.

In the presence of Jesús (Víctor Manuel Mendoza), the sombrero-wearing, horse-riding, pistol-packing overseer, Susana is what she is: a lying vixen, ready to work her way sexually into the home and away from the

FIGURE 7. Don Guadalupe (Fernando Soler) and Susana (Rosita Quintana) dramatize the nature of their initial relationship in Buñuel's *Susana* (1950). The tables are soon turned for the benevolent patriarch and his "adopted" daughter. Museum of Modern Art / Film Stills Archive.

failed social-services system (the state reformatory) from which she has escaped. During her seduction game with Jesús in the chicken barn, where she has come to collect fresh eggs, the two interact as equals. They are framed at the same level, Susana standing her ground opposite Jesús, to whom she refuses to yield, without giving up her titillating suggestiveness. In the mild skirmish that follows, the eggs Susana is carrying wrapped inside her apron and skirt get broken. The broken eggs suggest a surrogate sexual exchange, not only because the Spanish word for eggs *(huevos)* is customarily used to name testicles, but because of the way Susana secretly discards the apron with the yolky, slimy, semen-like remains of the encounter before casually returning to her chores. The episode also humorously suggests that Susana may be dangerous to men: indeed, she is a *rompe-huevos,* or a "ball-breaker."

Susana disturbs the balance of nature and of family life by being sexual, treacherous, deceiving, and even armed with her own pedestrian form of feminism. She manipulates those who do not contribute to her plans, allowing some space accordingly "for [her own] female desire to be glimpsed."[20]

What Susana wants is to be allowed to do what she wants, to be independent; as she tells Jesús when rejecting his advances, and in no uncertain terms, "I do not belong to the whims of any man!" Susana's sexual independence, which she uses as a tool of empowerment, is, of course, the most threatening thing in the lives of the men with whom she deals because she is focused, yet unpredictable, and because she will camouflage herself according to the expectations of each one of her "victims."

Interestingly, the only one of the major characters who is never deceived by Susana's mask is the housekeeper, Felisa, who foresees trouble during the stormy night when Susana escapes from the reformatory, even before Susana arrives at the house. "It seems like the devil is loose out there tonight," the housekeeper says. Felisa resists doña Carmen's decision to take Susana in, and later encourages doña Carmen to expel Susana. Felisa is armed with Catholic superstitions and always invokes some kind of religious parable to intercede with doña Carmen against Susana. Felisa is thus the person who more accurately understands Susana, since her religious/superstitious comments are indeed justified by Susana's story: from her invocation of God to be freed from prison, to her stepping over a cross to escape, and her "snake-in-paradise" disruption-through-temptation of the bucolic, Eden-like home setting.

In *Susana*, the forging forces of Mexican melodrama are dramatically brought into play and specifically exploited in the narrative. "God, nation, and home" serve as the very stages on which the adventures of Susana, *la perversa* ("the perverse one") will take place. In the movie, Susana, one of the most controversial female characters of Buñuel's career, as played by Rosita Quintana, could serve mainly as a "plot point," as a narrative excuse for Buñuel's parody of Mexican morals, politics, and patriarchy. However, that would only work if we were to recognize *Susana* as a parody of Mexican melodrama, a goal Buñuel fears was not achieved but that recent criticism supports. In her book *Mexican Cinema/Mexican Woman*, Joanne Hershfield defends *Susana* as participating in the critical portrayal of "postrevolutionary patriarchal discourses . . . with the father as the head of the household and the state as head of the national family." That structure, however, according to Hershfield, comes across as weak and failing, exposed by the "femmes fatales" *(devoradoras)* of Mexican cinema, particularly the title characters *Doña Barbara* (Fernando de Fuentes, 1943) and *Susana*, women who openly defy the "nation-as-home" allegory. Rosita Quintana, as Susana, is, indeed, a challenge to patriarchy, as Hershfield concludes, and as a femme fatale she embodies something of a counter-figure to the unambiguous character of the Mother in Mexican films.

Hershfield considers *Susana* a parody of melodrama, somewhat influenced by Buñuel's declared intentions and his surrealist background. *Susana* is certainly a form of parody, especially in its "Buñuelian" motifs and the opening scene of the film (when Susana escapes from the woman's prison). But the film's over-the-top flamboyance and aesthetic of excess, partly exemplified by Susana's own willingness to frame herself as spectacle, is perfectly acceptable in contemporary Mexican melodrama, especially of the *cabaretera* variety. Jesús Martín-Barbero in his hypothesis of melodrama in Latin America concludes that some of the reasons why the genre has been at the top of popular favor in different media throughout this century is its simplicity, and

> the rhetoric of excess . . . [in which] everything must be extravagantly stated, from the staging which exaggerates the audio and visual contrasts to the dramatic structure which openly exploits the pathos of quick and sentimental emotional reactions. The acting tries to provoke a constant response in raucous laughter, sobs, sweaty tension and gushy outbursts of identification with the protagonists.[21]

Susana is, indeed, baroque, openly excessive, and self-reflexively melodramatic. Those qualities confirm from a certain perspective its status as "classic" melodrama. Pedro Almodovar's *High Heels* (1991) and *All About My Mother* (1999), or Douglas Sirk's *Written on the Wind* (1957), despite their excess, self-parody, and humor, are no less "classic" melodrama than Griffith's *Broken Blossoms* (1919) or Carl Theodore Dreyer's *Gertrud* (1964).[22] *Susana*'s excess, while pointing toward a surrealist spirit (her escape from prison, with apparent aid from supernatural forces) and criticism of the Mexican family melodrama (the counterfeit happy ending, in which the family chooses to ignore Susana's brief stay in the house), is a lot more ambiguous. *Susana* resorts to a theatricality so evident (Susana on display; the prison cell that fails to contain anything; the weather's direct response to her presence) that it invalidates itself as parody, as opposed to the rather understated melodramatic quality of Buñuel's *Una mujer sin amor*. The implication that the aesthetics of excess in *Susana* is Buñuel's way of criticizing Mexican patriarchy is valid, but it also ignores the role played by parody and excess in Mexican film melodrama as a whole, which as Martín-Barbero and Monsiváis clearly state, is one of "mediation" and "identification."[23]

Susana's undeniable contribution is to take the sexual tensions from the *cabaretera* films and throw them right into the midst of a "family melodrama" and into the "ideal" Mexican family home: an old hacienda complete with a gentle patriarch, a submissive mother, a respectful son, faithful servants, and useful animals. Luis Buñuel's *Susana* is certainly not a *cabaretera* film, generically speaking, yet the protagonist is the kind of fatal, hypersexual, excessive anti-heroine found in the *cabaretera* films. Susana is both vixen and victim, serving to expose the weaknesses of Mexican rural patriarchy by taking the topical character of the *cabaretera* (the "fallen woman") and the *devoradora* (the femme fatale of Mexican cinema) and placing her within the sanctity of the patriarchal home.[24]

Hershfield treats Susana as one of the *devoradoras*, or femmes fatales, on the scale of a "Doña Bárbara,"[25] but not directly in relation to the functions of the *cabaretera*. Doña Bárbara, in the homonymous 1943 Fernando de Fuentes film, is a character who upsets the rural patriarchal order by being a woman who acts like a man (through her claims of power, land, guns, and independence). At the conclusion of *Doña Bárbara*, however, the *devoradora* meets her inevitable end, being herself "devoured" by the ranching land she has usurped from its rightful (male) owner, don Santos Luzardo. Ultimately, in *Doña Bárbara*, patriarchal rule is solidified. In opposition, the *cabaretera* is the kind of woman who threatens men and morals by being a seductive sign of Mexico's shift toward an urban-industrialized society. The *cabaretera* acts as a necessary evil, so to speak, as a sexual metaphor of Mexico's moral and social/economic changes. Susana is "femininity incarnate," as Joanne Hershfield concludes (unlike Doña Bárbara who is somewhat androgynous), yet Susana's power is ultimately dismantled by authority.

In *Susana*, Buñuel seems to be not only criticizing the façade of patriarchy, Catholicism, and the bourgeois lifestyle (as always), but also the quicksand foundation upon which Mexican cinema has structured the meanings of its characters, settings, and plots. *Susana* fails to satirize effectively the conventions of Mexican melodrama, in part because of its hybridity, with narrative characteristics of the "family" melodrama and the *cabaretera*, and in part because of its consolidation of key character types of Mexican cinema.

Susana interacts with three dominant versions of Mexican masculinity in classical cinema. There is the old, sanctified patriarch, don Guadalupe, who, as played by Fernando Soler, is a type borrowed from revolutionary melodramas like Fernando de Fuentes's 1934 film *El compadre Mendoza*. The brutal macho overseer Jesús, is the stock *charro* villain found in films like de Fuentes's *Allá en el Rancho Grande*. This is so apparent that in a scene in which Jesús is arguing with Susana through her window, Buñuel's framing is reminiscent of many similar courting and serenading scenes between *charros* and heroines in practically all the *comedias rancheras* with rural settings. Furthermore, Guadalupe and Jesús, of course, both bear critically Mexican-Catholic names. Finally, the educated, lay product of the postrevolutionary period, the son, Alberto, is a version of the many promising physicians, attorneys, and engineers of family melodramas. For a while, Susana succeeds in managing these men, in exercising her power. She states several times that she is "free to do whatever [she] wants," only to be reminded in the end that she, in fact, cannot succeed in permanently upsetting the rural patriarchal order.

Yet, in the conventional fashion of Mexican cinema, Susana, "the perverse one," called "a bitch of bad breeding," "a snake," a "bad woman," gets what is coming to her. In the dramatic climax of the movie, Susana seduces the old patriarch, the last "pillar" of traditional Mexican society. This short-lived triumph over the "nation-as-home" metaphor in turn creates problems with the patriarch and his young son, who is also chasing after Susana's sexual favors. Thus, Susana becomes the instrument of the confrontation between the "Old" and "New" Mexico, pre- versus post-revolutionary, triggered by the presence at home of the openly sexual woman, who would otherwise belong only in the nightclub.[26] This is where Susana takes on some of the symbolic responsibilities of the *cabaretera*, becoming a tool for negotiating the imbalance of tradition and modernity in turn-of-the-decade Mexico. To top things off, it is the (devoted) wife and mother of the household who, aided by Felisa, the housekeeper, saves the day and brings harmony back to the home. Doña Carmen prays for strength and asks God to help the family through the test it is facing. Yet, unlike Susana, who seems to receive divine intervention in her escape from the reformatory, when the bars in her cell magically yield, doña Carmen rests on the support of the superstitious Felisa. It is Felisa who hands doña Carmen the horse whip with which she chastises Susana. As doña Carmen beats the young woman, with a devilish, demented grin on her face, her position is emphasized in a low-angle, medium close-up in which she stares directly into the camera, giving the audience Susana's disempowered point of view. At the last moment, when doña Carmen is about to give up, in light of don Guadalupe's preference for Susana's favors, the police come in with Jesús, who has recognized where his loyalties should rest and alerted them. Two policemen brutally drag Susana away, back to the reformatory, as she kicks and screams, fighting to the end.

After Susana is properly punished and taken away, order is restored: don Guadalupe and doña Carmen reconcile, Alberto makes peace with his father, Jesús returns to his duties in the pastoral setting, and the final sequence reestablishes, albeit mockingly, the film's correspondence with the family melodrama. Invoking "God," doña Carmen prays for advice in the critical moment in front of a crucifix. Embodying the power of the "nation," the police take Susana away, and thus the state intervenes directly in the reconstitution of order. Finally, reconstituting the sanctity of "home," the family is last framed squeezed together to fit the window of their house, as they look out at the bucolic countryside, celebrating in a group hug their newly found peace.

The morning after Susana is taken away, doña Carmen, Felisa, and don Guadalupe—the three members of the older generation—comment that they seem to have come out of "a dream" or "a nightmare." In fact, the entire narrative of *Susana* can be compared to the surrealist interest in dreams and dream-works, since Susana really is like a dream: she awakens and tests the entire family's fears (in the women) and desires (in the men). She disrupts the apparently calm slumber of this traditional family in order to reconnect them with the kinds of basic instincts that they would repress in their conscious state.

The surrealists, as we know, were interested in dreams as an irrepressible, unconscious manifestation of fears and especially desires, and Buñuel had already established the paradigm of dream (narrative) filmic structure in *Un chien andalou*, and conveyed its symbolic power in the famous dream sequences of *Los olvidados*. Susana's presence within this family, which sparks sexual desires, insecurities, and transgressions, is like a dream. Susana's seductive path through the farmhouse operates in a similar form as the figuration of desire in *Un chien andalou*, which, as Linda Williams points out, "dissolves the constituted forms of social life [through transgression, violating] the established order."[27] Susana triggers the family's reconnection to unconscious states and uncovers the thin veil of their repressed personalities.

For instance, doña Carmen throughout the movie is a model of reason, decorum, and correctness, and yet is ultimately revealed as being on the border of insanity, out of control. There is a certain primal, almost frenzied joy on her face when she brutally beats Susana with a horsewhip in the climactic scene. The men respond openly to sexual impulses that also expose otherwise repressed feelings: Jesús has a clearly "animalistic," irrepressible attraction to Susana. He calls her "a snake," "a bitch," and states that she needs to be "tamed" before raping her in the barn amidst the hens and goats. Finally, don Guadalupe's fascination with Susana has an unambiguously incestuous side, not only because she is thirty years younger but because she has been explicitly adopted into the family "like a daughter." At the end, the family "awakens" to a beautiful morning-after to declare, in fact, that it has all been a bad dream.

What really seems like a dream, however, is the counterfeit restoration of patriarchal order in *Susana*. Doña Carmen fixes things up simply by pretending that nothing has happened, acting as the obedient wife, asking her son to acknowledge and respect his father, and even ignoring don Guadalupe's purpose of amendment. The entire family, and the adopted family members Felisa and Jesús, seem to erase from their memory Susana's intrusion, the way a bad dream is blocked from conscious memory. But it is evident that their seemingly firm order is all but fallacious, that they can only pretend that Susana's disturbance has left things untouched. In fact, patriarchal/Catholic morals come across as a rather conspicuous mask. Don Guadalupe's family's inability to absorb Susana into their static ways (they give up, turn her in, and pretend it never happened) symbolizes the ossified ways of the family melodrama, unable to evolve with modern Mexico.

Yet *Susana*'s undeniable connection to Buñuel's surrealist classics does not exclude the film from the tradition of Mexican cinema where it was produced. Not only is *Susana* mockingly concerned with the topics of "God, nation, and home" which Mexican film scholarship has established as instrumental for understanding classic cinema in Mexico, but Susana's character is a displaced variation of the *cabaretera*. Susana's excessive, flamboyant sexuality (her clingy, revealing costumes, her tendency to lower her blouse in the presence of a man, the freshness with which she uncovers her thighs at the slightest provocation) place her among contemporary *cabareteras*. This type of character, in words attributed to François Truffaut, is "an oblique challenge to bourgeois, Catholic, and all other moralities."[28]

Like the classic *cabaretera*, Susana incites the questioning of Mexico's contemporary economic and industrial changes through a sexual metaphor. Thus, Susana is a kind of character who belongs to Mexican cinema, but whose function within Mexican cinema—the dramatization of the threat woman's sexuality represents for Mexican patriarchy—also serves Luis Buñuel's lifelong commitment to exposing what he saw as the hypocrisy of Catholicism and the bourgeois lifestyle. With *Susana*, Buñuel not only consolidates his style, combining his mastery of melodrama, parody, and surrealism, but he does so by appropriating and reassembling meanings, characters, and settings that were already in place in Mexican cinema. Buñuel's *Susana* is a parodic regression to the rural settings of the old revolutionary melodramas. It is an amalgam of the topics, characters, and structure of the "family melodrama" and the *cabaretera* films, and it shows both the deceptive nature of Porfirian morals and the clashes between the "old" and the "new" Mexico of the 1950s. By testing the waters of these three subgenres of melodrama, *Susana* also shows the quickly changing faces of Mexican cinema in the decade.

La hija del engaño

Buñuel's follow-up film to *Susana*, *La hija del engaño* (*Daughter of Deceit*), is a remake of Filmófono's *Don Quintín el amargao*, re-titled for Mexican release. The timing of the two productions brings them rather close: *Susana* opened in Mexican theaters on 11 April 1951; *La hija del engaño*, on 29 August the same year. *La hija del engaño* brought Buñuel together for the third time in two years with actor/producer Fernando Soler *(El gran calavera, Susana)* and with producer Óscar Dancigers *(Gran Casino, El gran calavera, Los olvidados)*. Such minor details are important because in the Mexican mode of production genre and typecasting were ways of fulfilling the public's expectations. People went to the movies to see Fernando Soler play a certain kind of role (usually a benevolent, if confused patriarch), as was the case for every other major (or even minor) star in the system. This attraction has always been the basis of mass audience films in Mexico, Hollywood, and every major national film industry. And Soler played exactly this type of role in his three films with Buñuel. The two sister movies were each produced in twenty days *(Susana* in June 1950; *La hija del engaño* in January 1951) because cast and crew knew their roles and simply reproduced sets, shots, and performances in each movie. That is the principle behind the *churro,* the generic, assembly-line pictures that Buñuel was being offered.[29] But *Susana* and *La hija del engaño* complement each other by upsetting the roles that certain public and private spaces, specifically the home and the cabaret, play in Mexican cinema's conception of women and men.

In *La hija del engaño* Buñuel delves into the themes of the *cabaretera* once again. Only this time around it is the adopted setting of the cabaret that seems to be misplaced. Like Susana, who is a *cabaretera* forcibly jammed into a family melodrama, the female protagonists of *La hija del engaño* are combined to become a *cabaretera*. In the process, they both glorify prostitution as a suitable career for women who want to escape the home and the cabaret as an acceptable surrogate "home." Unlike *Susana* and the classic family melodrama, *La hija del engaño* allows the abject space of the cabaret (along with its significance in Mexican cinema of the period) to assume the moral weight of the home, which is depicted as a place of suffering and mistreatment.

The original version of *La hija del engaño,* the Spanish comedy/drama *Don Quintín, el amargao,* is rendered meaningless by the new Mexican setting given to Carlos Arniches's play. Despite the Spanish origin of the character don Quintin, he is quickly absorbed into Mexico, in part because of the star-persona of Fernando Soler, in part because the locations within which the story develops, the home and cabaret, are inevitably inscribed with fixed meanings. Ana López writes that the cabaret always represented "a place [for] men to escape from the burdens of home ... to engage in ... the ambivalent pleasures of the flesh."[30] "Home" was the place where saintly mothers lived and where there was a refuge for conservative Porfirian patriarchal values. This is why Susana's presence "at home" in the film by the same name is so provocative: it violates one of the last cinematic symbols of the "old Mexico." In *La hija del engaño*, there is no home other than don Quintín's casino/cabaret, the place where the characters' conflicts (parentage, coupling, machismo) get resolved.

The movie tells the story of Quintín, a man embittered (literally: *amargao*) by his wife's infidelity. Quintín comes home one night to find his wife in bed with his best friend. He throws his wife María out of the house and she spitefully responds that their baby daughter, Marta, is not his, that she is the "daughter of deceit." Quintín then abandons the daughter in the country, by placing her in the care of one Lencho, an abusive drunk, whose daughter, Jovita, is the same age as Quintín's daughter. For twenty years Quintín prospers in his casino/cabaret business, anonymously sending monthly payments to Lencho (now a widower) to keep his daughter. As the years go by, Quintín becomes increasingly volatile, violent, and of bad humor. His estranged wife is never allowed to know what has become of their daughter. When the wife becomes fatally ill, she asks Quintín to forgive her and confesses to him that, in fact, she has lied, and that Marta is his natural daughter. Thus begins Quintín's search for Marta (played as an adult by Alicia Caro) and for redemption.

The movie follows a series of unbelievable plot twists (not unlike the classic *cabaretera* excesses, however). These include Marta's escape from Lencho's abusive home, her marriage to a young mechanic she meets on the road, Quintín's unsuccessful search for Marta in Mexico City, and a restaurant brawl between don Quintín and Marta's husband (who do not know each other). Then the narrative of *La hija del engaño* adopts some classic *cabaretera* traits in its move toward resolution.

Quintín sends his tough guys, Angelito ("Little Angel," played by the famous comedian Fernando Soto "Mantequilla") and Jonrón (a Spanishism for "home run"), out to find Marta, who is known to be somewhere in Mexico City (which Carlos Monsiváis called "the endless city"[31]. The two characters are used for comic relief, as their buffoonish machismo puts in evidence their masculinity as a bluff. "¡Soy muy macho!" screams Jonrón, for example, in explaining his cheating at a card game, thus contesting the association of machismo with a certain code of gentlemen's honor. The stock machismo of Jonrón and Angelito is clearly a parody; they resort to showing off their pistols, repeatedly snorting and grunting their way out of arguments with the single line of reasoning, "¡Es que yo soy muy macho!" But Buñuel never allows them the chance to "prove" their masculinity, and each of their confrontations ends with a simple duel of bluffs. They sexually harass the cabaret dancers, who show no interest in them whatsoever, and they pretend to work hard for don Quintín, when it is evident that they spend most of their time eating and drinking.

It is Angelito, however, who comes up with a plan to find Marta. Using Lencho's daughter, Jovita (played by Lili Aclemar), who wants to be a cabaret singer, Angelito devises a plot to have Jovita debut at don Quintín's cabaret, which is called El Infierno. He surmises that if they advertise the show in every possible neighborhood they will ensure that Marta will hear about it, and she will not miss her sister's performance since they have not seen each other since Marta's escape from Lencho's house. By the time of Jovita's debut, El Infierno has developed into a full blown cabaret featuring live musical numbers, schmaltzy love songs, and scantily clad (but scarcely talented) women dancers. Both the Jovita and Marta characters are necessary, however, to complete the single character of the *cabaretera*. Marta brings to the characterization her past history of neglect, abuse, illegitimate conception (Marta's mother, because she was unfaithful, is compared to a prostitute), and escape from home. Jovita can sing, and she has the disposition (she tells Angelito, "I wanted to be *cinemática*, now I want to be *cabaretófila*), and the sexy, suggestive body and costumes of the *cabaretera*. In her saucy, "tropical" musical number, she sings a song full of sexual double entendres.

It is telling that Don Quintín, when he cannot find Marta, foresees and fears that she may in fact have fallen into the abject urban world of Mexico City's prostitutes and pimps. After three months go by with no sign of her, don Quintín tells Angelito and Jonrón that whoever Marta ran away with must have taken advantage of her and deserted her by now. He reasons that "she must have become a . . ." (Paradoxically, the word "prostitute" itself remains unspoken, despite the numerous plots surrounding prostitutes in Mexican cinema of the time.) He will not speak the word, yet don Quintín rationalizes Marta's experience according to the fatal destiny of the "fallen woman" in Mexican cinema narrative. Beginning with the original prostitute film, *Santa* (Antonio Moreno, 1931), the genre formulaically depicts escape from home, inevitably followed by seduction, abandonment, disgrace, and prostitution.

FIGURE 8. Nacho Contla (Jonrón, *left*) and Fernando Soto "Mantequilla" (Angelito) pose with Buñuel's counterfeit *cabareteras* in *The Daughter of Deceit* (1951). Museum of Modern Art / Film Stills Archive.

Marta's illegitimate lineage reinforces don Quintín's fears. As in Emilio Fernández's *María Candelaria*, the daughter of a prostitute is inevitably marked for such a fate. In a humorous coup de grâce to don Quintín's statement that Marta must have become a prostitute, Buñuel and editor Carlos Savage follow those last words with a slow dissolve to a shot of Marta standing alone in a dark streetcorner. This is the same pose that Emilio García Riera calls "typical of the prostitute in the manner of national cinema," and which is also parodied in Buñuel's *La ilusión viaja en tranvía* and Tito Davison's *Las tres alegres comadres* (1952).[32]

When Jovita is hired as bait to attract Marta, she becomes a singing artist who, in the fashion of the cabaret setting, literally "goes to hell" (since the cabaret's name is El Infierno). She quickly starts selling sexual favors for money—Angelito buys her kisses for a few pesos in exchange for allowing her the chance to become a cabaret star, or as she calls it, a *cabaretófila*. Still, Jovita's debut seems rather understated. She has the right tools to be a bona fide *cabaretera*: she is the main attraction, she wears a ridiculously low-cut and tight dress, she is properly harassed by the men, and she sings the right musical number, a mambo, with something of a Caribbean affectation in her delivery. She is, in fact, something like a "poor man's" Ninón Sevilla, the Cuban-born undisputed queen of the *cabareteras* of Mexican cinema and star of such genre classics as *Señora tentación* (*Madam Temptation*, José Díaz Morales, 1947), *Aventurera* (*Adventuress*, Alberto Gout, 1949),[33] and *Sensualidad* (*Sensuality*, Alberto Gout, 1950).

Yet Buñuel sets up the scene to make it look somewhat cheap: El Infierno is a "dive" and it lacks the excessive, tacky flashiness of the cabaret settings of Sevilla's best films. The El Infierno set looks counterfeit, although it was designed by Edward Fitzgerald (*Los olvidados*), one of the top set designers in Mexican cinema. Like everything else in *La hija del engaño*, El Infierno and its main attraction, Jovita, are make-believe yet stock features of the cinema of *alemanismo* that is filled with cabarets, prostitutes, and urban decay.

Buñuel's final provocation comes with the glorification of the cabaret, where peace is restored and the family reunited with the promise of further generations (Marta is pregnant; Jovita and Angelito fall in love). Yet, rather than emphasizing the marginality of the cabaret, Buñuel stresses the alienation of the idea of "home." It is in the home—whether don Quintín's or Lencho's—that abuse, infidelity, and illegitimacy take place, and it is in the cabaret where families are made and where family ties are solidified. Don Quintín's "Inferno," rather than being a place to contrast to "home," becomes the real home itself. Ultimately, the restoration of family relations in the cabaret setting of *La hija del engaño* makes more transparent what the classic cabaret films only obliquely suggest: a transition to modernity symbolized by the recognition of marginality. This comes about, however, at the expense of "home," as fantasized in classic melodrama, and at the expense of patriarchy. At the film's unbelievable conclusion, Quintín's efforts to reconcile with his estranged daughter lead him to turn around and ask to be kicked in the behind, which his new son-in-law does. Quintín and his anachronistic patriarchal style are effectively displaced by a new family configuration that ultimately reclaims the cabaret as its home. Jovita's decision to become a *cabaretera*, and her recognition of the conventions required to embody the *cabaretera* character, allow Buñuel to once again acknowledge while still satirizing (with transparent self-reflexivity) the cinema of *alemanismo*. *Susana* and *La hija del engaño* show sex and human relationships in contexts that acknowledge and upset Mexican cinema conventions about families, morals, and genre.

"MALINCHISMO" AS MELODRAMA

> In Buñuel's film, women are not born into the role of the Great Mother, it is thrust upon them. Their subordination is secured by rape, but it is rape that breeds a mute resentment expressed in gestures of rejection.
>
> —Jean Franco, *Plotting Women*

In *Los olvidados* Buñuel shaped a mother character who was selfish, unsympathetic, and, more dangerously yet, sexual. Actress Stella Inda's character in that film rejected, neglected, and ultimately renounced and abandoned her son Pedro for the sake of her immediate survival. In her discussion of *Los olvidados,* Jean Franco shows how the mother can spark a male-driven narrative (Pedro's aimless search for his mother's affection is what ultimately leads him to his tragic death) and, more importantly, how the mother can define a man's identity in crisis. Franco analyzes the function of the female characters in *Los olvidados* (the young girl Meche, and Pedro's mother) to demonstrate how they are deprived of narrative agency, yet by being both "objects of desire and . . . castrating woman" they represent the two major opposing forces in man's quest for identity: desire and death.[34] Franco thus "modernizes" the Oedipal narrative to conclude that in *Los olvidados* women provide the ground for men (young and old alike) to come to terms with the paternalistic authority of the state.

What at first scandalized the Mexican audience for *Los olvidados,* however, was not only the "filth" of the movie's look, but the violence inflicted upon the revered image of the mother. Pedro's mother character in *Los olvidados* got Buñuel in trouble: he received (unofficial) threats of deportation and disapproval from the actors' union[35]. In his subsequent Mexican films, Buñuel seems to have revised the place and meaning of the mother characters, at least in principle.

In *Susana,* as we have seen, Buñuel amended the mother figure of doña Carmen to make her asexual and thus a little more in tune with Mexican cinematic motherhood. Following the long tradition of self-abnegating mothers, initialed by the actress Sara García in 1935, doña Carmen's position eventually ensures everlasting patriarchy, in spite of the questions raised about her sanity. In *La hija del engaño* the unfaithful mother, María, is properly chastised for her violation of patriarchal law with twenty years of suffering, and can only be absolved by a priest and forgiven by her husband moments before her death, thus allowing her to be rescued from eternal damnation by patriarchy and religion. Therein lies the "classic" mother of Mexican cinema, if a bit overblown by Buñuel in a sort of self-reflexive critical gesture. In

Susana and *La hija del engaño* Buñuel adopted two extremes of the melodramatic mother, one saintly and one whorish, yet both of them, unbelievably, strengthen the position of patriarchy and are thus redeemed. Both gestures of "redemption" however, are suspiciously formulaic, and both movies end with self-reflexive, sardonic winks at the audience that suggest Buñuel's interest in unveiling the generic conventions rather than enforcing them.

In the classic Mexican family melodrama mothers indeed serve to reinforce patriarchal values and not to focus on maternal or women's issues, as does arguably the Hollywood woman's film or maternal melodrama (á la *Stella Dallas* or *Mildred Pierce*).[36] Luis Buñuel made two maternal melodramas in the 1950s, *Una mujer sin amor* (1951) and *El río y la muerte* (1954). The two films address the typical issues of mothers in Mexican cinema (prefigured even in Buñuel's earlier films): religion, nationalism, and, as Jean Franco has demonstrated, how, in Mexican narrative, mothers define a man's identity.[37] These questions of national identity with which Mexican popular literature and cinema were concerned provide a paradigm for analyzing Buñuel's maternal melodramas since they are condensed in a master narrative that has governed debates about national identity in Mexico since 1950—*malinchismo*.

The Mexican national/patriarchal myth is partially organized around the dichotomy of the good (virgin)/bad (whore) woman, with which men negotiate their troubled identity and sexuality. Certainly, the virgin/whore scenario is not a Mexican invention, but the mythological base of national identity issues in Mexico in relation to women has been much noted.[38] The Virgin of Guadalupe and La Malinche—the saintly virgin of the Catholic faith and the treacherous Indian whore of the Spanish conquest—are at the center of the national imaginary. According to historical accounts, legend, and the interpretations of codices and chronicles, in 1519 a Mayan woman named Malintzin (Malinal in Náhuatl; Marina in Spanish; La Malinche, popularly) served as Cortés's interpreter and later became his mistress, thereby facilitating the Spanish conquest of the Aztec Empire in 1521.[39] Furthermore, Malintzin and Cortés produced an offspring, Martín Cortés, regarded as the first Mexican mestizo. Therefore, Malintzin's relationship or betrayal with the conqueror is the origin of both the nation and the hybrid, mestizo national identity.

Octavio Paz and others have theorized a direct connection between the bastard-inferiority complex of *malinchismo* (stemming from the troubled circumstances of the conquest: military humiliation, sexual violation) and the traumatized identity of the Mexican man. "The question of origin," writes Paz, "is the secret center of our anxiety and anguish."[40] In other words, it is what governs the Mexican "drama of identification." The myth and trauma of origin (or, as it is popularly stated, of being *hijos de la chingada*—"children of the fucked one") is probably the most critical of Mexico's foundational myths; it is a myth around which national history is structured. It is relevant, then, to analyze how Buñuel's maternal melodramas, *Una mujer sin amor* and *El río y la muerte*, are inevitably inscribed within this cultural context, one just as important as the political and economic context of 1950s Mexico which Buñuel also addressed.

After *Susana*, Buñuel seems to have detoured back to his classic roots, apparently distancing himself from the popular surrealism of *El gran calavera* and *Susana*, following up these films with a Mexican adaptation of Guy de Maupassant's *Pierre et Jean* and an(other) look at Mexican life and customs, *El río y la muerte*. In these two movies, Buñuel scrutinizes Mexico's (and Mexican cinema's) fascination with the exploited topics of infidelity, violence, and loyalty to the mother. Those issues seemed more genuine, more attractive to Buñuel than the shameless interest in openly "folkloric" representations of Mexico, as in Eisenstein's *¡Que viva Mexico!* or Fernández's *María Candelaria* and *Pueblerina*, representations which he addressed in *Subida al cielo*.[41] As he did in *Los olvidados*, in *El río y la muerta* and *Una mujer sin amor*, along with the societal and moral crisis of the 1950s, Buñuel presents characters who are somewhat psychologically traumatized by their identity. Separated from their cultural context, the two films may seem inane and uninteresting, a point of view in which Buñuel and the critics agreed.[42] Yet, in relation to the Mexican maternal melodrama, they may be seen as new renditions of Mexico's metanarrative, of the "anxiety and anguish" of Mexico's origins, as represented by the violence done to or through the figure of the mother.

Una mujer sin amor

Una mujer sin amor (A Woman Without Love) was to have been a remake of the 1943 film by André Cayatte based on Guy de Maupassant's 1887 novel *Pierre et Jean*. Nevertheless, it was easily adapted into a Mexican contemporary urban, upper-middle-class setting, fitting comfortably into the generic form of the maternal (family) melodrama. *Una mujer sin amor* is admittedly Buñuel's most notorious creative disappointment, and he wrote in his autobiography that it was his worst movie. Interestingly, although it is one of the movies Buñuel disowned in his later years, it is also one of the most "Mexican" of his movies, in the sense that it is truly unrecognizable as a "Buñuel film." It lacks any of the markers of "Buñueliana" that critics like to gather and list. It includes some of the best-looking sets and highest production values of Buñuel's entire Mexican career, especially compared to *Los olvidados*, *Subida al cielo*, and even *Abismos de pasión*. The film features sets designed by the distinguished art director Gunther Gerszo (the Cedric Gibbons of the Mexican studios), original music by Raúl Lavista (who was imposed on Buñuel by labor union laws), and gorgeous, if uninspired black-and-white cinematography by Raúl Martínez Solares. A tragic love triangle, a "fallen woman," adultery, sibling rivalry, inheritance feuds, and a deceptively convincing happy ending characterize this technically flawless melodrama. All of which, however, dramatically make Buñuel invisible in this movie.

Una mujer sin amor tells the story of Rosario (Rosario Granados, of Buñuel's *El gran calavera*), an unhappily married woman who has a brief affair with a young engineer out of which a child is conceived. Twenty-five years later the former lover, who has been abroad in Brazil all those years, dies and leaves a small fortune to the illegitimate son who has been raised unsuspectingly by the (much older) husband of the woman. This sparks a series of controversies, most significantly the jealousy of the other child, that bring to the fore some of the defining characteristics of melodrama and their treatment in Mexican cinema. Rosario initially makes the most motherly, selfless decision for the sake of the sanctity of her home: she abandons her lover so that her sons can be brought up in a "traditional" bourgeois home. Yet, it is not just that she has been unfaithful, her infidelity (which is her only claim to sexuality, subjectivity, and desire) triggers a traumatic reaction in her sons. When it becomes apparent that his brother is the illegitimate product of his mother's affair, the eldest son, in particular, has to repress the intense frustration and psychological trauma brought about by the discovery of his mother's sexuality. The young man, a physician, is teased at work about his mother's illicit sexual past, which brands her inevitably as "one of those women." Sexual activity in almost any form marks a woman as a prostitute in Mexican cinema.

In a way, the process of recuperation that the sons go through because of the "treacherous" sexual activity of their mother is a version of the national identity myth, the traumatic heritage of the Mexican "children of *la chingada*." (One of Rosario's sons even calls her "an unworthy woman" and accuses her of "betraying my father," saying, "You covered us with shame.") Rosario's treachery of the family honor, which necessarily threatens the patriarchy, is symptomatic of the use of the domestic space as a national metaphor in Mexican cinema and of the portrayal of the stressful relationship between men and women as a form of negotiating identity issues. Rosario's sons are defined by her sexual affair (the older son actually states

Genre, Women, Narrative / 103

FIGURE 9. Rosario Granados in Buñuel's "classic" maternal melodrama, *A Woman Without Love* (1951). The mother's betrayal causes great pain and anxiety in her sons. Museum of Modern Art/Film Stills Archive.

that they are "sons of a bad woman"), and so these characters give literal meaning to the trauma of being Mexican, of being "hijos de la chingada," since it is through the mythical illicit sexual relation of Cortés and La Malinche that "Mexicanness" is instituted. Furthermore, the traumatic experience of learning of his mother's infidelity and unbecoming sexuality turns the older son into a self-declared misogynist. He has an argument with his brother's young wife and explains his confrontational attitude by saying, "It was my fault to think you were a different kind of woman. You are like all of them: vulgar, ambitious, and capable of selling yourself. I feel repulsion, contempt." The son's declaration of indiscriminate misogyny is perhaps another one of Buñuel's not-so-indirect references to Mexicanness and Mexican cinema. Misogyny emerges specifically as one of the expressions of the "*malinchismo* complex" in Mexican narrative, occurring often in Mexican literature and later in films. As Sandra Messinger Cypess writes, "The actions of woman as a category are identified as the origin of evil."[43]

For the sake of the family honor, their father's name, and the safekeeping of their fortune (which we can also call patrimony, of course), both sons cope with the trauma and, eventually, after much melodrama, forgive their mother. However, the conciliatory gesture of these "sons of la chingada" becomes a way to mediate the national myth. As Ana López puts it, "The melodramatic became the privileged place for the symbolic reenactment of [the Mexican] drama of identification, and the only place where female desire could be glimpsed."[44] Indeed, Rosario's desires, as problematic as they were for her sons, as repressed as they must remain, are finally allowed expression. At the very end of the film and after the death of her legitimate husband, the widow displays a photograph of her former lover on the mantelpiece with her sons' apparent approval. The gesture is significant in its understated revision of more classical similar narratives. The old patriarch's death and the acknowledgment of Rosario's desire is a way of granting her some narrative agency, customarily denied to women in Mexican cinema. Unlike Pedro's mother in *Los olvidados* for example, but like María (the unfaithful wife in *La hija del engaño*), Rosario is redeemed by her own suffering. Unlike those other mothers in Buñuel's Mexican imaginary, however, her redemption is signaled by some acknowledgement of her sexuality.

Nevertheless, it takes the death of both her lover and her husband for Rosario to find her own space (she sits knitting by the fire, in front of the lover's vigilant picture). The irony lies in the fact that what Rosario has really achieved is the passage of patriarchal power (symbolized by the family's patrimony) to her sons. Francisco Sánchez writes that a common maxim in Mexican cinema is: "Todas las mujeres son unas putas, menos mi madre, que es una santa" (All women are whores, except for my mother, who is a saint).[45] Rosario is, in fact, both saint and whore. Her sons' willingness to cope, to forgive, is a way for them to restate, along with every Mexican, that they are "hijos de la chingada." Yet, even on the fast track of modernization, nothing has really changed when it comes to what defines Mexican identity. The sons find an expression of identity through their mother's "betrayal" and sacrifice, but in the process they gain power by their access to property and wealth.

Una mujer sin amor, the story of an unfaithful mother whose acts define the identity crisis of her sons, is inscribed within the national allegorical paradigm of La Malinche. According to Sandra Messinger Cypess, La Malinche operates "as a subtext . . . when a woman is used as an object of exchange or is raped by an invading male figure, or *willingly consorts with newcomers and betrays her people* . . . or is blamed without reason for the evils that befall her people."[46] All these scenarios are stubbornly present in Mexican film history, and many of the nation's film genres seem to be organized around these themes.

Whatever Buñuel's intentions were in *Una mujer sin amor* (supporting his family is his most common explanation), he once again seems to emphasize the text's links to Mexican culture and, by extension, to the explicit issue of national identity. Plotwise, it is significant, for example, that Rosario's lover is an engineer who builds bridges and roads, a much appreciated profession in 1950s Mexico, and that he participates in the infrastructural improvement projects that President Alemán is pushing in that decade. The handsome young engineer (played by Tito Junco), who, as they say in the movie, "looks like a movie star," stands in stark contrast to the cold old patriarch who (of all things) is an antiques dealer (an occupation Buñuel symbolically depicts once again in *Archibaldo de la Cruz*). It is interesting that Buñuel and screenwriter Jaime Salvador chose occupations that clearly exemplify the contrast between two generations of Mexicans. The old wealthy aristocracy that more than metaphorically lives off the past is contrasted to the educated, postrevolutionary bourgeoisie that has toppled the landed elite and is attuned to the decade's technological infrastructural development.[47] Rosario's sons are products of that generational confrontation between the old and the new. The men of this younger generation (who are both physicians, the bourgeoisie's favorite profession) are greatly spoiled, troubled, even traumatized.

Buñuel may very well be exercising some understated form of parody in *Una mujer sin amor*. But, as in *Susana*, parody is lost in the blunt ways of Mexican melodrama, and this film, in particular, diverts in no visible ways from its generic format. Even the script's origins in foreign literature cannot help Buñuel reclaim *Una mujer sin amor* as anything other than an aptly executed Mexican melodrama. (In subsequent films based on foreign literature, such as *Wuthering Heights* and *Nazarín*, Buñuel would find a way to expressly detach the stories from their Mexican context.) The narrative and characters of *Una mujer sin amor* become Mexican by the strength of the mythical paradigm (bad Mother/La Malinche) and by their immediate context (Mexico in the 1950s). The movie ends up belonging less to Buñuel and more to Mexico, so much so that Buñuel eventually openly disowned the film in his autobiography.[48]

El río y la muerte

In *Una mujer sin amor*, Buñuel set out to adapt a classic story that context and tradition redefined as a Mexican text. *El río y la muerte (Death and the River)* was the only one of Buñuel's Mexican movies made with the intention of treating what he thought of as a specifically Mexican topic: violence. *El río y la muerte* was Buñuel's only assigned "social thesis" film, imposed on him by CLASA films and based on a novel by Miguel Álvarez Acosta.[49] It opened at the Venice Film Festival despite Buñuel's disapproval of its absurd social/moral thesis (education will eradicate violence). In his autobiography, Buñuel recalled some of the rationale that went into the making of *El río y la muerte*:

> Most of the events told in this movie are authentic and may also allow us to take an interesting look at this particular aspect of Mexican customs [namely, gun violence]. Someone can be killed over a "yes" or a "no," over an evil look, or simply because someone "felt like it." Every morning Mexican newspapers offer reports of some events that always amaze the Europeans.... The mayor of one town (in Guerrero) told me once, as if it was the most natural thing, "Every Sunday has its little dead."[50]

Most revealing is Buñuel's final editorial comment on the issue of violence in Mexico. After telling a story of random violence in which a man shoots another man in Mexico City for not knowing about the right bus stop, Buñuel adds, almost in admiration, "As Breton would have said: a pure surrealist act."[51] Buñuel's comments on violence in relation to *El río y la muerte* seem to justify the surrealist fascination with Mexico (and Buñuel reminds us of Breton's conviction that Mexico was the surrealist place par excellence), but the movie also reinforces Buñuel's ethnographic and psychological interest in Mexico.

Buñuel's look at "this ... aspect of Mexican customs" is relevant also if we think of the specific reflection on the absurd nature of violence in Mexican culture that had already been suggested in *The Labyrinth of Solitude*. For Octavio Paz, the violent nature of Mexican men has its origins in the psychologically traumatic experience of the conquest that defines Mexican nationality in relation to La Malinche. Paz states that Mexicans are solitary, violent, and traumatized because of the colonial experience (treachery, rape), and thus live to negate the possibility of "splitting open," or "cracking" *(rajarse)*, of showing any apparent sign of weakness, femininity. The aloofness of the Mexican man, writes Paz, is due to his intention of always hiding the "fissures" or "cracks" through which his fears and weaknesses may be verified or exposed. Public festivals and violence (both situations prominently displayed in *El río y la muerte*) are the only means of escape from the "labyrinth of solitude" and alienation of the Mexican people. The violence and the sexual nature of the fears of the Mexican man, according to Paz, find a fitting framework in Buñuel's *El río y la muerte*, making it a deeply "Mexican" movie.

The troubled characters of *El río y la muerte* are members of the Anguiano and Menchaca families of the fictional town of Santa Viviana, presumably in the state of Guerrero. They follow a one-hundred-year-old, senseless killing custom because one patriarch killed another in a barroom brawl stemming from an insult. In the opening scene Buñuel sets an alternately somber and ironic atmosphere. A voice-over narration introduces the setting over establishing shots of a lively, bucolic town: "Santa Viviana, one of many small Mexican towns on hot soil . . . pretty . . . with its weekly market where peasants come from surrounding towns." The establishing shots show peasants in the town market and banal street scenes, and then dissolve to a shot of a river across from which is the town cemetery. The narrator now takes on a severe tone, stating: "Anyone could think that peace reigns in Santa Viviana. . . . Nevertheless, the life of the town is ruled by death."

The peaceful images of the town are dramatically, yet comically juxtaposed, from a shot of a woman carrying a baby across a street to an extreme close-up of a skull, edited in consonance with the word "death" in the voice-over. The next shot, a medium close-up of the skull and torso, reveals the skull to be that of a traditional sugar skeleton-shaped candy, and then festive music suddenly comes up in the soundtrack. An anonymous hand puts the little sugar skeleton in the middle of dozens of others similar to it, and the shot tracks back and pans to show a table full of bottles and drinks and to reveal a joyous party with people dancing, drinking, and laughing. The scene is clearly reminiscent of Eisenstein's *¡Que Viva Mexico!*, in which a traditional Day of the Dead fiesta is presented as a cliché of Mexican culture. The sugar skulls and the fiesta setting introduce the first killing between the Menchacas and the Anguianos.

In the scene two *compadres* share a drink and make a toast to the health of a newborn Menchaca baby to whom the Anguiano has been named godfather. "We are soul brothers, compadre," says Menchaca, stressing the importance of the relationship of *compadrazgo*, customarily used to bring a friend closer into the family. As they lift their glasses, Anguiano suggests, jokingly, that "as the saying goes, now I have to court my comadre." Inevitably, the insult leads to an argument, and, within seconds, the insulted Menchaca kills his beloved *compadre* with a knife, thus starting the hundred-year feud.

Buñuel's play with the fortuitous, capricious nature of violence is doubly stated in the opening scene. The town of Santa Viviana is visually characterized as peaceful, while the narrator contradicts that impression and calls attention to its deceitful façade. The skull, for example, is at first a sign of "death," then it is sugar candy, and, finally, the two *compadres*, in the middle of a party, confess their brotherly love and immediately erupt in violence. This juxtaposition of images and sounds in the first two minutes of the movie downplays the "social thesis" of *El río y la muerte*, emphasizing in its playful contrasts the absurd nature of violence imposed by national tradition (as Paz predicted, the fiesta turns into a bloody fight).

Buñuel later recalled an anecdote that he included in the film to demonstrate Mexicans' generally violent nature. In one scene, several men are playing cards with the local priest. The topic of the town's violent history comes up and the protagonist's grandfather, a revered old man, tells the priest: "It seems as if you and I are the only ones here who don't carry a gun." The priest lifts his shirt and shows his gun, saying "Speak for yourself!" According to Buñuel, this exact conversation took place between the celebrated writer Alfonso Reyes and Minister of Education José Vasconcelos during a meeting about "Mexican traditions." Buñuel thought of it as a way to illustrate that Mexico's "gun cult" was something generalized even among educated, cultured men.[52] What is most interesting is how Buñuel's recollection of the episode puts in evidence the futile thesis of *El río y la muerte*, that culture and education will eradicate violence. The premise is indeed rendered powerless by the strength of tradition, because, as Octavio Paz would say, violence is inscribed in Mexican identity, a thesis to which Buñuel admittedly subscribed.

Throughout the movie, it is the strength of tradition (rather than evident danger) that drives the Anguianos to kill the Menchacas, and vice versa, because it is the "manly" thing to do, to take revenge, to *"chingar"* and not to be *"chingado."* The killings between the two families become, in fact, the norm. So quotidian are the killings that, upon seeing a funeral procession going down the street, a bystander remarks, "Every Sunday has its dead." The very Mexican fear of "opening up," of showing "weakness," gives narrative structure to the movie. There is no motive to these killings, except that if one does not kill one's assigned enemy one is not man enough, and perhaps also to keep up tradition.

One of the most interesting features of *El río y la muerte* is that the male protagonist (Joaquín Cordero, who played the older son in *Una mujer sin amor*), in spite of his mother's insistence, refuses to fulfill his duty of avenging his father's death . In *El río y la muerte*, oddly, it is a man who resists the violence. He is harassed by friends and peers, as his manhood is put into question. Meanwhile, his mother (Columba Domínguez) pressures the young man to continue the senseless killing. Interestingly, this mother, too,

FIGURE 10. Every Sunday brings a killing and all men have guns in Buñuel's *Death and the River* (1954). Museum of Modern Art/Film Stills Archive.

has conceived her child out of wedlock, which is the cause of further stress to the young man. It is ultimately the mother's duty to relieve her son of his "responsibility" (she says that "he no longer has to avenge his father's death" and that "the place of a man is with his mother"). It is the mother who allows peace to be restored by amending the patriarchal law that dictates what men do. Her son is almost about to give in to his tragic destiny when the mother yields and restores the peace among the quarreling families. After being vilified and ostracized in the town for having conceived her son outside of marriage, she becomes in the end the ultimate suffering mother. She redeems herself, the memory of her dead husband, and the life of her son out of her sense of duty and love: this mother was a whore, but she becomes a saint.

The portrait of the Mexican man in this movie directly contrasts with the macho *charro* of the *ranchera*, with the tough guys of the *cabaretera*, and with the venerable patriarchs of the family melodrama. Not only do the quarreling families make up, there is even a certain feminizing moment when the male protagonist and his former enemy actually embrace at the end of the film: they "weaken," they "open up." Now, such signs of weakness in Buñuel's Mexican leading men are not new. There is, after all, a conspicuous lack of positive patriarchal figures in *Los olvidados, Una mujer sin amor, Subida al cielo,* and *La ilusión viaja en tranvía,* as well as comically fraudulent signs of manhood and patriarchy in *El gran calavera* and *La hija del engaño.* But the hero's expressed objection to his manly duty in *El río y la muerte* makes him, on the one hand, an instrument Buñuel uses to reflect on the absurdity of violence in Mexico, and on the other hand, a parody of the virile-man tradition in Mexican cinema. This characterization is further stressed by the fact that the young man spends a large portion of the movie (during which he tells his story to a girlfriend, which is framed in an elaborate flashback) immobilized, locked inside an enormous artificial lung, where he is recovering from a respiratory illness. The narrative importance of this device is unclear, but the effect is comical, as the character's grave affectation seems ridiculously undermined by his immobile head sticking out of the machine. Even though his mother suffers greatly before reconciling the two families, she succeeds by ultimately disobeying the sacred cult of violence that has until then sealed the town's fate. As a traditional mother of Mexican cinema, she is both the cause and the arbiter of her son's identity issue. But she is ultimately the character who makes new law, reconstituting peace, feminizing and "weakening" patriarchy.

In three other films of the 1950s, *El Bruto, Él,* and *Ensayo de un crimen,* Buñuel delved even deeper into issues of manhood and troubled masculinity. In contrast to the films analyzed here, these films focus on motherless men, which further calls into question not only the validity of the macho image but also the propensity of Mexican cinema to rely on narratives of male-female relationships to settle matters of identity.

5 On the Road
Subida al Cielo *and* La Ilusión Viaja en Tranvía

> The government of Alemán was the dawn of a wordy age that made promises with no commitments, which was confused and oratorical, . . . demagogic. For years now, outside Mexico City men have also been breathing the asphyxiating air of verbose confusion, promises that cannot be kept.
> —Salvador Novo, *Nueva Grandeza Mexicana*

In the social and economic context of President Miguel Alemán's *sexenio* (1946–52), *Subida al cielo* and *La ilusión viaja en tranvía (Illusion Travels by Streetcar)* are two of Luis Buñuel's most "Mexican" movies. President Alemán's administration signaled a greater and more systematic governmental attention to industry, commerce, national infrastructure, and economic development than previous administrations since the Revolution.[1] It also represented a period in which the gap between the wealthy and the poor became much more evident than in the preceding administrations of Manuel Ávila Camacho and Lázaro Cárdenas. Buñuel's comedies of the decade, *Subida al cielo* (1951) and *La ilusión viaja en tranvía* (1953), take on the topics of developmentalism and modernization and their effects on the lives of the working class. Buñuel places these issues in the metaphoric setting of a rudimentary "road movie." These movies may very well correspond to the styles and themes of Buñuel's career outside of the Mexican film industry. They are full of "surrealist moments" and "Buñueliana," the search for which guides many a book on Buñuel. Yet, unlike the films of a decade later *(El ángel exterminador* and *Simón del desierto), Subida al cielo* and *La ilusión viaja en tranvía* specifically address Mexican topics with rich references to Mexican political processes, the state of the Revolution, and the economic and political context of *alemanismo*.

Buñuel does this in the form and style of classic Mexican comedy. Unlike the revolutionary epics and the family melodramas (which never denied their bourgeois setting), Mexican comedies operated under the presumption that they represented the interests and even worked as "defender of the poor."[2] Carlos Monsiváis has analyzed the function of Mexican comedy, arguing that it seeks to appeal to a popular, working-class audience while abstaining from actual social commentary. Monsiváis argues that in order to avoid political positions Mexican comedy centers around characters that pretend to "represent" the working class while exploiting their own limitations for comedic purposes. In other words, instead of taking on some social topic, the success of Mexican comedians like Cantinflas, Tin-Tán, and Mantequilla, lies in their ability to be cartoons of themselves. "The function of such comedy," writes Monsiváis, "is to make of social resentment a folklore of gratitude, and [to make] of humor a means of stifling all signs of rebellion."[3] Mexican classic comedy resorts to "sentimentalism," foregrounding a melodramatic plot (a love story, for example) whose resolution drives the narrative, which is only incidentally set in a working-class environment.

Subida al cielo and *La ilusión viaja en tranvía* mock these presumptions of Mexican classic comedy. On the one hand, both movies employ working-class characters as "types," who are involved in potentially dramatic circumstances (a mother's illness in *Subida al cielo* and unemployment in *La ilusión viaja en tranvía*). On the other hand, the public transportation settings of both movies downplay the role of the comic "star" in Mexican cinema. By adopting a "communal" protagonist, there are no characters like Cantinflas, Tin-Tán, or Mantequilla to speak for the collective.[4] Finally, Buñuel includes contextual information and allusions that allow for political/national allegorical interpretations, giving these films a social function that comedy rarely acquired in Mexican cinema.

Subida al cielo was co-written by Buñuel, Manuel Reachi (author of *Susana*), the Spanish poet Manuel Altolaguirre (of the "generation of '27"), Juan de la Cabada, and Lilia Solano Galeana. The movie is supposed to be based on actual observations made by Altolaguirre during a bus trip from Acapulco to Zihuatanejo.[5] In spite of its origin as a reflection on Mexico (which André Breton called "the surrealist place par excellence") through the eyes of an exile, *Subida al cielo* marks Buñuel's adaptation of his style of observation, distance, and surrealist wit (that which made *Las Hurdes* special) to Mexico's reality.

The narrative follows a "pilgrimage" structure: the protagonist is on his way to the city to meet with a lawyer who will legitimize his mother's last will. The "pilgrimage" structure of the film serves to weave Buñuel's observations on Mexico and link the different, not always logically associated narrative segments. The movie foresees Buñuel's *La voie lactée* (France, 1968), in which the road to Santiago de Compostela helps to frame a number of vignettes that comment on society, religion, politics, and history. In *La voie lactée*, the "Milky Way" to Santiago is present in the road itself, although it is rendered only vaguely in the symbolic title. Similarly, in the

Mexican film, the "Subida al Cielo" is the name of a steep mountain crossing that the bus traverses on its way to the city. The bus ride allows the film to introduce an inevitable amalgam of character types from diverse walks of life. There is the peasant protagonist, Oliverio, the seductress Raquel (another version of *Susana* and the *cabaretera*), the local politician don Eladio, plus an assortment of background characters. The film's plot thus brings together politicians, lawyers, peasants, drunks, American tourists, and other characters who would otherwise not mingle in any situation in the class-conscious Mexico of the 1950s. Within this frame, *Subida al cielo* calls attention to the demographic diversity of Mexico, to the problems of the land reform laws of the 1930s, and, specifically, to some of the frustrations brought about by President Alemán's economic and social policies of the time.

Miguel Alemán Valdés was Mexico's first civilian president since 1910, and he filled the government agencies with a new generation of university-educated liberals whose goals were to achieve social progress through development and a free-market economy. Alemán's goals, in part, were to continue the improvement of labor and peasant conditions started under President Lázaro Cárdenas in the 1930s and to legitimize the growth of the industrial-commercial class in the postwar era.[6] Attaining such a happy median between social goals and economic ambitions, however, proved difficult. Critics of Alemán's administration point out that the economic reforms he sought during his six-year term precipitated an internal migration and the unregulated expansion of Mexico City (soon to become one of the world's most populated urban centers), which resulted in economic crisis and the rise of an urban class of the underemployed. As we know, the *cabaretera* film genre boomed in this period (over a dozen movies were made in a few months between 1947 and 1948), which also coincided with production of *arrabaleras* like Ismael Rodríguez's *Nosotros los pobres (We the Poor)* and Alejandro Galindo's *¡Esquina, bajan! (Corner, Getting Off!)*,[7] movies that depicted the era's urban economic and moral dilemmas.

Buñuel's *Los olvidados, Susana,* and *La hija del engaño* affirmed and participated in these trends in the Mexican cinema. Like *Susana, Subida al cielo* mocks without really upsetting the symbolism of the key Mexican character types. In this instance, Buñuel turned his eye to new versions of these character types. The film showcases a *devoradora* (or femme fatale) character, Raquel (played by Lilia Prado); a *pelado*, Oliverio/Silvestre; a Mother; and two surrogate, over-the-hill patriarchs, one a former landowner, don Nemesio, and the other a candidate for Congress, don Eladio (played by Manuel Dondé). Yet these characters are only part of the scenery in a film that reexamines the contemporary state of politics, the economy, and "the road ahead" to modern Mexico.

Subida al cielo

Subida al cielo tells a very simple story. On his wedding night, Oliverio learns his mother is dying and he must postpone his honeymoon, go to the city of Petatlán (in the state of Guerrero), and find a lawyer who will notarize his mother's will. To reach the city, Oliverio must take the sole bus out of his hometown. Inevitably, on the bus and on the subsequent bus ride to Petatlán, Oliverio is brought together with a colorful assortment of characters: among them the local coquette, the drunk bus driver, a politician (and candidate for Congress), a pregnant woman, and an old, dispossessed landowner.

From the opening of the film, Buñuel and his collaborators set the stage for a satire of Mexico's institutions. For example, the name of Oliverio's hometown is San Jeronimito, which is a diminutive form of St. Hieronymous. This town, despite its Christian name, has no church, a telling reference to Mexico's experiment with secularization in the 1920s and 1930s. The reference is of no small import since the process of secularization in the 1920s led to the bloody Cristero Rebellion, the excommunication of Mexican government officials from the Catholic Church, the suspension of religious services, and even the persecution of priests and other church officials.[8] Although Buñuel seems to trivialize the context, it also serves as the narrative catalyst. Because there is no church, Oliverio must travel by boat to an island off the coast in order to be married, where his wedding night will then be postponed due to his mother's illness. In the opening voice-over narration, the church-less town of San Jeronimito is described humorously, as if it were one of the *ejidos*, or agricultural cooperatives, of the 1930s. The narration imitates the solemn style of the voice-over disclaimer in the introduction of *Los olvidados*, and mocks the promises of the failed oil and land-reform laws that made President Lázaro Cárdenas so popular. Over several establishing shots of the town, the narrator states:

> The only agricultural product of this town is the coconut palm tree. From the white core of the fruit, an oil is extracted that has multiple uses in industry. The inhabitants of these humble houses are almost all rich because they own hundreds of palm trees . . .

This promise of wealth just below the earth's surface was common during the ideological and political buildup that led to Mexico's nationalization of oil in 1938. Furthermore, the reference to "oil wealth" even seems to paraphrase or imitate some of President Cárdenas's speeches which promised that hard work and the nationalization of mineral and agricultural resources would inevitably lead to prosperity and economic growth.[9]

The town of San Jeronimito, with its laic but quiet life, its single-crop industry, and its peasant-owned economy, would appear to be stuck in the revolutionary reform era of the 1920s and 1930s. Yet, the film's time frame, the early 1950s, promises a period of new and different economic development, and the protagonist and supporting characters' "bus ride" almost literally takes them through that transition.

Thus, the metaphoric bus of Buñuel's "ascent to heaven" and the "pilgrimage" scenario seem quite significant. Although it denotes transition and forward motion, the bus itself, as a vehicle and as the site where dreams are forged but not quite realized, connotes possible associations to the PRI, the Revolution as an institution, and the state.

Oliverio's mother, who needs to legalize her modest estate so that she can leave it to a grandson on whom she has placed her hopes of a better life in the city, goes from being a dispossessed peasant to giving an inheritance to her orphaned grandson. Meanwhile, don Nemesio, an old, refined-looking passenger traveling with his granddaughter, claims to have spent twenty years or so trying to recover lands that were expropriated from him in the 1930s (illegally, according to him). Don Nemesio's worthless search for restitution of his expropriated lands is one of the film's references to government policies in the 1950s. Don Nemesio is insisting on financial indemnification or that his lands be returned to him (even though President Cárdenas had appealed to landlords, in a 20 November 1938 radio broadcast, to willingly give up the projected indemnification). This detail about don Nemesio foreshadows Buñuel's paranoid leading man in *Él*, don Francisco, who has also been struggling for reimbursement for lands expropriated from his family during the land reform.

In the film, Buñuel organizes his commentary on Mexican society and politics around a series of popular rituals, ceremonies, and rites of passage. First, there is the wedding of Oliverio and his bride Albina, and the postponed consummation of the marriage imposed by doña Ester's imminent death. The promise of life and reproduction suggested by the wedding is thus balanced by doña Ester's need to legalize her property before dying. Noticeably, it is a legal, bureaucratic transaction linked to Oliverio's mother which interferes with the completion of the couple's sexual union, and it is suggested that both Oliverio and Albina have remained virgins before their wedding. But the resolution of doña Ester's will, as well as the sexual coupling, is withheld until the end of the film. In between, Buñuel takes us on his "ride" through the Mexican countryside (it could be said that the "ride" is completed in Buñuel's 1953 urban counterpart to *Subida al cielo*, *La ilusión viaja en tranvía*).

Sexual desire and the son's duty must be negotiated in *Bus Ride* in a literal rendition of one of Buñuel's consistent themes: society and morality interfere with individual desires. As in *Los olvidados*, *Susana*, *El río y la muerte*, and *La hija del engaño*, *Subida al cielo* easily finds a way of joining Buñuel's observations of Mexico with the issues that permeated his films since *Un chien andalou*. In *Subida al cielo* Buñuel turns the outside interventions that would keep a couple from uniting or prevent a group of people from achieving a simple goal (as seen in *L'Age d'Or*, *El ángel exterminador*, and *Le charme discret de la bourgeoisie*) into specific references to Mexican politics, cinema, and culture.

The bus is itself a metaphoric rendition of the ineptitude of the state's institutions. Seconds after starting on its way, it blows a tire and has to be stopped so that Silvestre (the driver) and Oliverio can fix it. The sequence is deceptive: after building the viewer's anticipation of the bus ride in the first three scenes, the movie's introduction climaxes with the final departure of the bus, which is then abruptly brought to a halt. Until that moment, all the characters (who represent several sectors of Mexican society) have boarded the bus in good spirits (except for don Nemesio). They are thinking about their future and making plans for their earnings (many are farmers taking their produce to the city market) until their expectations and projections are frustrated when the tire blows. Yet, it is not simply a mechanical failure, but rather an outside influence (perhaps a nail or a broken bottle) that actually delays the beginning of the trip.

The vehicle's battered condition and its vulnerability becomes one of the recurring themes of the movie. Halfway through the film, the bus gets stuck trying to cross an overflowing river. (Noticeably, there is no bridge.) In this scene the bus as a metaphor of Mexican governmental institutions becomes most clear, almost literally specific. While the bus is stuck in the water, Silvestre calls on his *compadre*, who happens to be standing by, to help them pull the bus out with a oxen-powered cart. Don Eladio, the politician, in tune with developmentalist policy, objects to the use of such underdeveloped technology and calls upon a passing tractor to help them out, announcing:

> Animal traction is from the cavemen era, as if we were not industrialized. Bunch of retrogrades, enemies of progress . . . I'm going to get the tractor.

Don Eladio, likely a PRI politician, looks for the "progressive" way out, in what turns out to be a useless, patronizing effort. When both the bus and the tractor are immobilized under the water, the old cart, driven by a little girl, comes into action and saves the day. The push for modernization and machismo (a topic that Buñuel would further explore in *Él, El bruto,* and *Ensayo de un crimen*), as well as the paternalistic attitude of the state, are undermined by tradition and an unlikely heroine. Furthermore, don Eladio proves to be "a demagogue . . . [with] promises that cannot be kept."

In witnessing the failure of don Eladio's plan, one of the bus riders comments: "[Don Eladio] thought it was easy to whistle while eating cornmeal." The sarcastic remark is a commentary on Alemán's insistence that economic independence can be compatible with the Revolution's focus on social programs, nationalization of resources, and better conditions for workers, a program which resulted only in economic crisis.[10] The don Eladio character suggests that the economic focus of *alemanismo* was misdirected, and as we shall see below, Buñuel more clearly states the consequences of that misjudgment in *La ilusión viaja en tranvía*.

Don Eladio is the butt of many jokes in *Subida al cielo*. He is always seen as a demagogue whose thinking and strategies conflict with the logic and strength of tradition. The physical resemblance of actor Manuel Dondé with President Miguel Alemán has been noted, and Buñuel admitted it influenced his casting of Dondé.[11] Moreover, in one scene when the riders stop to celebrate Silvestre's mother's saint's day, someone asks don Eladio to give a speech and his ridiculously flowery, baroque, clumsy address presents a slightly overblown caricature of President Cárdenas's speaking style, which is known to be rather convoluted.[12] (The demagogue politician character was also adapted into a Mexican comedy character by Mario Moreno [Cantinflas] during the *alemanismo* era, however harmlessly, in his film *Si yo fuera diputado (If I Were Senator)*, also released in 1951.[13])

Don Eladio represents the look and even the politics of President Alemán (progress and technology versus backwardness and tradition), with something of the rhetoric of President Cárdenas thrown in. The candidate's efforts to lead his peers forward prove to be precipitous, misguided, a mistake. Similarly, Oliverio's mother's wishes for the promising young couple to move to the city in search of opportunity, presumably giving up their farming life in favor of industrial jobs, is another misconception, germane to Alemán's administration, that led in part to the uncontrollable urban demographic boom of the decade.

Silvestre's stop at home for his mother's saint's day and fiesta is presented as an unavoidable detour into Mexican cinema's themes of motherhood and national folklore. Silvestre, a pathetic drunk, weeps over being an unworthy son. Don Eladio, in his demagogue style, explains that "in the his-

FIGURE 11. In *Mexican Bus Ride* (1951) the locals put up a "traditional" fiesta to amuse foreign tourists. Raquel (Lilia Prado, *bottom left*) seems rather confused herself. Museum of Modern Art / Film Stills Archive.

tory of all nations mothers have always occupied the first place." Silvestre's drunkenness, however, only infuriates his embarrassed mother. Later, the melodramatic excuse of Oliverio's sick mother is subverted. Upon Oliverio's return home, he finds that his mother has died, and he proceeds to falsify the documents she was supposed to sign by stamping them with her fingerprints, making the trip to legitimize the property paradoxically end in forgery.

True to his statement that folkloric celebrations were a topic "for tourists and for Eisenstein"[14] and not for himself, Buñuel uses the fiesta in *Subida al cielo* as an opportunity to portray "folkloric" customs, especially as represented in Mexican classical cinema, as superficial, useless, and arbitrary. When the bus stops at doña Sixta's (Silvestre's mother's) house, the riders soon engage in drinking, dancing, and eating traditional dishes. In the middle of the party, a (modern) bus full of (presumably) American tourists inexplicably stops at the house and the tourists are immediately charmed by the local celebration. They take photographs, pretend to dance, and one even insists on buying Oliverio's hat. When some of the locals begin a fake "traditional" show only to please the tourists, Buñuel's criticism of organized superficial folklore (his "profound horror of Mexican sombreros") becomes most sarcastic.[15] In these scenes, Buñuel seems to be referring to the requisite show-stopping song-and-dance numbers of the classic *comedias rancheras*, which were appreciated by national audiences, but which Buñuel saw as "picturesque" exploitation for foreign critics and audiences.

Buñuel's *Subida al cielo* is a modestly ambitious microcosm of Mexican society that focuses alternately on diverse "types" rather than projecting all the problems of the working class on a single actor/character, as was usually the case in classic Mexican comedy. Even more than in *Los olvidados* or *Susana*, the movie comments on the impracticality of some of Alemán's policies, on the stubborn strength of popular tradition, and on the superficiality of the Mexican cinema's own cultural conventions. The "bus ride" allows for a free-flowing, episodic narrative. Each segment practically stands alone as commentary on any one character type's symbolic role. As in *Las Hurdes*, *La voie lactée*, and even *Le fantôme de la liberté*, Buñuel here seems more interested in social commentary than in narrative logic, a strategy that he developed further in his 1953 film, *La ilusión viaja en tranvía*.

La ilusión viaja en tranvía

In *La ilusión viaja en tranvía* Buñuel once again employs an arbitrary travel narrative through which he organizes his commentary on Mexican society. In this film, Buñuel discusses the economic and class crisis brought about in part by the developmentalist policies of *alemanismo*. *Ilusión* opens, too, with an ironic voice-over introduction, as in *Las Hurdes* and *Los olvidados*. This was a popular technique in other "social-thesis" dramas from the period, such as Alejandro Galindo's *Espaldas mojadas* (*Wetbacks*, 1953). Alfonso Cuarón returned to this same type of wry, ironic voice-over commentary, inspired by Buñuel, in his recently made social comedy, *Y tu Mamá también* (2001). As in the introduction to *Los olvidados* and *Subida al cielo*, the narrator of *Ilusión* establishes a casual, observational mood:

> Mexico, as many a great city, is the theater of varied and disconcerting events that are nothing but the throbbing of daily life, in spite of their apparent ordinariness. Every hour millions of men and women interchange their short-lived, simple stories. Their deeds and words are always bound toward the realization of a wish, a dream, an illusion. Together they all form the colossal swarm of city life.

These "simple stories" of people's "dreams and illusions" are, however, far from casual. *La ilusión viaja en tranvía* serves to frame Buñuel's view into the cityscape, as he poignantly observes the gap between the urban working and industrial classes. As economic historian Felícitas López-Portillo Tostado has observed, during the Alemán *sexenio*, this gap broadened dramatically in correspondence to the economic policies that favored the growth of private investment, which were intended to strengthen the administration's desired image of political moderation and a modernizing industry and economy.[16]

Like *Subida al cielo*, *La ilusión viaja en tranvía* has been the object of critical attention mainly for its surrealist elements (two trolley car attendants give free rides to the city poor, thus violating social, economic and company customs, etc.). Here, Buñuel's concerns with bourgeois society are focused on the specific juncture of the Mexican economy in the early 1950s. The story is, again, very simple and more a catalyst than a narrative: two trolley mechanics (Caireles and Tarrajas, played by comedians Carlos Navarro and Fernando Soto "Mantequilla") are frustrated by the company's decision to retire their car, "the 133," and by the subsequent possibility that their jobs will be terminated. They get drunk at a neighborhood party and decide to take the trolley for a last tour, offering people free rides since they have nothing to lose. The urban working class takes the economy into its own hands, which causes the admiration of their equals (butchers at the meat market, street vendors, school children) and the distress of the trolley company and the occasional capitalist clients (who insist in paying the fare).

As soon as Caireles and Tarrajas make their decision, they return to the neighborhood and pick up their first clients. Here, Buñuel introduces a brief narrative detour, offering a telling piece of contextual information. Without clear provocation, or narrative explanation, a professor explains to an uneducated trolley employee the meaning and mechanism of inflation:

> Inflation is the cause and the effect of the currency circulation being larger than the available goods that are for sale, thus prices rise continually. . . . And because the workers are paid the same salaries for a long time, this results in a de facto decrease in salaries. There you go, that's how inflation sparks misery among the people against the enrichment and luxury of industrialists and businessmen.

Such explicit references recur throughout the film, as Buñuel calls attention to the workers' marginal situation in the economy. But the function of comedy in Mexico was always to "mock" public characters, to take absurd situations literally, or to verbally exploit double entendres. Calling attention to a specific problem, referring to politics or unemployment, or explaining an economic technicality, was unheard of. Yet one of the great signs of the economic crisis that hit Mexico hard in the early 1950s was uncontrollable infla-

Subida al Cielo and *La Ilusión Viaja en Tranvía* / 121

FIGURE 12. The narrative detours of *Illusion Travels by Streetcar* (1954) stress the many financial difficulties that came with development and modernization under President Alemán. In this scene, the protagonist (Lilia Prado) and other women are unable to purchase goods because of price manipulations by distributors, as the store owner explains to them: "This is what free trade is." Museum of Modern Art/Film Stills Archive.

tion, and, here, Buñuel stalls the narrative to insert this textbook explanation between the taking of the trolley and the pickup of the first passengers.

In another scene, a group of women stand in line to buy dough. The shot slowly tracks down the line, showing the women's humble clothing and their dark skin. The shopkeeper posts the price and grudgingly announces that dough is now for sale. But the price he has posted is higher than the legal price cap, and the women voice their protests: "With these prices, I don't know where we are going to end." "This is an abuse." "Don't you know that there are price caps?" say the women. The shopkeeper replies: "And don't you know, Miss, what free trade is?" She replies: "You are free to sell the dough at up to 20 cents per kilo, earning almost double." "That's what people think," says the shopkeeper. "The wholesalers charge us more than you think." "Well, then, file a complaint, but don't rob people," she finally appeals. The shopkeeper, for spite, closes the store and refuses to sell anything, stirring more protest among the women. Later in the film, trying to stay off the streets (and avoid capture), Caireles and Tarrajas run into a group of corn smugglers. A skirmish ensues when the people on the back street try to steal the corn from them. Here, Buñuel is alluding to the illegal, marginal trade, which included the participation of foreign smugglers that flourished in the 1950s due to a negative balance of trade.[17]

Buñuel contrasts the resentment and difficult situation of the urban working class with the complex yet inefficient bureaucracy of the trolley company unable to even realize that a trolley is missing. The company's focus on "modernization" (the reason why the old, battered #133 is going to be retired) prevents it from properly overseeing its own operations, while the poor and the underemployed effectively maneuver to survive. Not only are Caireles and Tarrajas able to operate the trolley car, but we also see the urban workers trying to overturn the economic crisis (in the two separate scenes where they protest against both legal and illegal commerce practices). When Caireles and Tarrajas pick up the butchers at El Rastro, Mexico's major slaughterhouse, which also appears in *The Brute*, the butchers try to pay them back by giving them entrails and other take-home spoils in return. Their reasoning that "In these times, nobody gives something for nothing" renders a literal version of the popular saying that explains how the poor have to make do with spoils: "*Hacer de tripas corazón*" (Make hearts from tripe).

Almost every stop of the trolley car provides a new look into the economic crisis, into its consequences and even its cinematic treatment. Among the indirect signs of the crisis, Buñuel includes a small reference to the cinema of the era. When the trolley car stops near Churubusco Studios, one of the industry's largest, we see that some kind of "prostitute" movie is being made. The minimum signifiers are in place: a voluptuous, attractive woman wearing a tight black dress suggestively stands by the curb, fixing her stockings and showing her legs. Then we see and hear that she is part of a movie cast and crew that is filming there. Buñuel seems to be predicting in 1953 what Jorge Ayala Blanco wrote in 1968: that "movies about prostitutes are the cinema par excellence of *alemanismo*."[18] The moment is significant as a reference to the cinema of the time and even to Buñuel's own *cabaretera*. The mise-en-scène cleverly and self-reflexively repeats a scene from *La hija del engaño*, where the female protagonist stands similarly, as Emilio García Riera has observed, "in the typical attitude of the prostitute in national cinema."[19]

Both *Subida al cielo* and *La ilusión viaja en tranvía*, sometimes allegorically and sometimes literally, present the economic, cultural, and political problems of the modernization decade. In *La ilusión viaja en tranvía* Buñuel foresees Mexico's "bumpy ride" into a competitive economic international market. *Subida al cielo* delves into the same topic from the cultural and economic lens of tradition versus modernity, especially in its observation of folkloric rituals and the demagoguery of politicians.[20] The two movies resort to the loose structure of a voyage, which allows for acute yet unassuming commentary without the restraining demands of a logically interconnected narrative. By including accurate yet impertinent contextual information for comedy (what is inflation? what is free trade? what is the State's position on modernization?), these films usurp and subvert the social function of popular comedy in Mexican cinema. Their emphasis is on the communal rather than on individual plights, and by suggesting national allegorical readings they realize the presumption that comedy represents, speaks for, or mirrors the experience of the working class, a presumption that is customarily avoided in Mexican comedy. Furthermore, Buñuel avoids the sentimental pathos of classic Mexican comedy, which, like Chaplin's "Little Tramp" adventures, resorts to melodramatic detours (an orphaned child's search for parental figures, funding for a sick mother's operation) as narrative pretext. In these, his only openly comedic Mexican films, Buñuel once again addresses Mexican issues and Mexican cinema's simplification of those issues. Instead of using popular characters and working-class settings to "shy away from any idea of class conflict,"[21] as Monsiváis suggests has been the rule in Mexican comedy, *Subida al cielo* and *La ilusión viaja en tranvía* divert from their comic direction in order to emphasize social and economic adversity.

6 Masculinity and Class Conflict
Buñuel's Macho-Dramas

> I am pure Mexican, and I have made a pledge with the land where I was born, to be a *macho* among *machos*.
> —José Alfredo Jiménez, from the *corrido*, "Soy Puro Mexicano"

The critical portrayal of men in Buñuel's films *El Bruto (The Brute), Él (This Strange Passion),* and *Ensayo de un crimen (The Criminal Life of Archibaldo de la Cruz)* turns the instability of national politics and the economy into metaphoric renditions of troubled men. These three male protagonists engage respectively in homicidal, paranoid, and surrogate homosexual behavior: all clear violations of the Mexican patriarchal image of "wisdom, strength, courage, perseverance, self-control, dignified reserve, protection of the weak, punishment of wrongdoing."[1] Buñuel's leading men are evidently troubled in these movies, and because of an "agreement" that implicitly regulates the man's image vis-à-vis that of the state, the provocation of centering on male protagonists who are clearly "unstable" is another way of referring to the crisis of the 1950s. Not only is there an apparent crisis of the image of patriarchy in these films, but also and perhaps even more significant, there is a crisis of masculinity. Buñuel addresses these issues in his macho-dramas *El bruto* (1952), *Él* (1952), and *Ensayo de un crimen* (1955), emphasizing the correlations between his troubled men and the image of a state in crisis. Because the dramatic plight of these characters involves negotiations of masculinity, I have chosen the term *macho-dramas* to characterize the films in which they appear. One is a comedy *(Ensayo de un crimen),* and the others are melodramas, but they are all about men in crisis.

Scholars of the Mexican Revolution and Mexican culture have defined *machismo* as something that is closely associated with the nation's identity. From the misogynist implications inscribed in the nation's foundational myth of the treacherous mother, La Malinche, to the construction of a male-centered historical discourse around the heroes of the Revolution, Mexican culture and politics have granted to the macho male the banners of national stability and political power.[2] Ilene V. O'Malley has analyzed some of the workings of political propaganda around the heroes of the Revolution, particularly the "bandit," or outlaw, types exemplified by Emiliano Zapata and Pancho Villa. O'Malley writes: "The propagandists frequently praised the heroes for their manliness, attributed all the virtues of the ideal patriarch to them, and set them up as father figures.... This masculinization of the heroes of the regime encouraged a transference of the feelings they inspired to the government itself."[3] As long as patriarchy and machismo are put to work for the good of the nation (represented by a seemingly "stable" home where men, women, and servants—the latter often played by Indians—know and respect their place in the hierarchy), they are not only acceptable but beneficial practices. This is the case, for example, of the long line of actors who played the benevolent patriarchs of the family melodramas (where Buñuel's leading man Fernando Soler became iconic). Safekeeping the stability of the nation-home seems to be the key symbolism of men in power in Mexican cinema.[4] In his book, *Cinema of Solitude*, Charles Ramírez Berg characterizes machismo as one of the pillars that sustains Mexican society:

> *Machismo* is the name of the mutual agreement between the patriarchal state and the individual male in Mexico. Through it the individual acts out an implicit, socially understood role—*el macho*—which is empowered and supported by the state. The state in turn is made powerful by the male's identification with and allegiance to it.... More than a cultural tradition *machismo* is the ideological fuel driving Mexican society.... To speak of the male image in Mexico is to speak of the nation's self-image and ultimately to speak of the state itself.[5]

Not only is there an "agreement" between men and the state, according to Ramírez Berg, but the male image is a stand-in for that of the nation-state, and consequently we can say that what we do to a man, we do to the nation. It's up to women to provide the means, the locus for men to test and prove their status and thus legitimize the nation, whether they want to or not. The Macho is often tested through his exercise of power over the women in his life.

According to Jean Franco, La Malinche as a paradigm is "inevitable" in national culture because Mexican national identity and the colonial complex are structured around the mythical female character. This also provides the basis for the implied misogynist treatment of women (in history and fiction), as well as part of the rationalization for Mexican machismo. In her book, *Plotting Women*, Franco writes:

> The problem of national identity was presented primarily as the problem of *male* identity, and it was male authors who debated its defects and psychoanalyzed the nation. In national allegories, women

became the territory over which the quest for (male) national identity passed, or at best ... the space of loss and of all that lies outside the male games of rivalry and revenge.[6]

Thus, the violation of the male figure as symbolic of balance, justice, prosperity, and stability necessarily speaks about the nation, in the same way that female figures become the symbols of crisis and trauma. Berg also states that in Mexican cinema of the 1970s (the focus of his book) the male image was in crisis, in response to the political and economic instability that followed the (second) oil boom of the 1970s. Years earlier, however, Buñuel's macho-dramas were questioning the theme of male crisis as a form of national narrative.

El bruto

El bruto was written directly for the screen by Buñuel and Luis Alcoriza, who also co-wrote *El gran calavera*, *Los olvidados*, and *La hija del engaño*. Buñuel gave the title role to one of the major figures of classic Mexican cinema, Emilio Fernández's favorite leading man, Pedro Armendáriz (star of *I Am Pure Mexican*, the movie, as well as *Flor Silvestre*, *María Candelaria*, and many others). In this movie, however, Armendáriz played a villain from the slums. The decision to cast Armendáriz completely against type (and, uncharacteristically, without his mustache) was already a form of revision: he inevitably brought with him many years of stardom as the quintessential noble, manly, virtuous, handsome, almost picture-perfect, masculine hero in dozens of films. In *El bruto* (which in Spanish also means dumb, or slow-witted), by contrast, Armendáriz plays a slow-thinking thug who is hired by an evil landlord to bully his rebellious tenants, who are resisting his eviction orders.

In the tradition of the *arrabalera* melodramas of directors like Ismael Rodríguez *(Nosotros los pobres)* and Alejandro Galindo *(Campeón sin corona)*, Buñuel's *El bruto* explored a number of fashionable social topics. Like some of Galindo's movies, *El bruto* is about the impotence of the urban poor against the law and private interests, and the need for poor people to organize themselves to fight injustice. But what seems more provocative in this film is the tampering with the image of the male protagonist, both through Pedro Armendáriz's star-persona and through the character's relationship with women (significantly, the character's name is also Pedro).

In the movie, Pedro, "the Brute," is a butcher at Mexico City's major slaughterhouse, El Rastro. He is hired by the landlord Andrés (Andrés Soler, of *El gran calavera*) through the intervention of Andrés's young wife,

FIGURE 13. Class conflict and masculinity are fatally linked in *El Bruto* (1950). In this film Buñuel cast one of national cinema's secondary patriarchs, Andrés Soler *(left)* and one of Mexico's greatest unblemished movie stars of the 1940s, Pedro Armendáriz. Museum of Modern Art/Film Stills Archive.

Paloma (Katy Jurado, of Fred Zinnemann's *High Noon*), to scare off Andrés's rebellious tenants so that he can sell his property to urban developers. More than the obvious reflection on the problems of rapid urban growth in the early 1950s, a topic familiar to Buñuel, who lived in the city and who had already directed a number of films on this theme, *El bruto* seems to follow a similar type of gritty realism. However, *El bruto* is more clearly melodramatic and shows the protagonist in a slightly more positive light. (Unlike *Los olvidados*, there will be redemption for "The Brute," who dies repentant for his crimes trying to save the poor neighbors.)

The politics are not subtle in this movie: the landlord Andrés, upset and frustrated by the tenants' rebelliousness, blames "the Revolution" for his problems. Complaining about his tenants, he says: "It's the fault of the politicians. Now any bum thinks that he has rights. I wish I had the power to crush that bunch of revolutionaries." Don Andrés is only one in a long line of ambiguous leading men in Buñuel's Mexican movies who blame the Revolution or its aftermath (like the land reforms of the 1920s and 1930s that affected the upper classes) for their personal downfall. Like the old antiques dealer in *Una mujer sin amor*, like don Guadalupe in *Susana*, like don Eladio in *Subido al cielo*, and like the evil blind man don Carmelo in *Los olvidados*, don Andrés is a character who represents reaction, backwardness, and moral ambiguity. Also like his predecessors, Andrés faces some kind of sexual dysfunction that characterizes his frustration and triggers his actions. In this case, his young wife Paloma, probably half his age, denies him sexual favors while at the same time she tries to seduce the Brute.

In order to serve his boss properly and to be closer to Paloma, Pedro abandons his "family" in the poor neighborhood where he lives. His family is actually composed of a very young mistress, her bedridden, chain-smoking mother, her crippled uncle, her brother who is a bum, and some unidentified children, all of whom live off of the Brute. There is no sympathy for this family when Pedro picks up his things and leaves with no explanation. On the contrary, they are portrayed as parasites. The sickness and unemployment that surrounds them seems to be a matter of their own choice: as long as someone will keep them, there is no need for work. The interesting thing here is that, unlike the children in *Los olvidados*, the grownups in *El bruto* seem to have some options, like work and organization, as demonstrated by the tenants' alliance against don Andrés. The law protects the powerful, though, which makes the complaints of don Andrés somewhat moot. But don Andrés is old, weak, bitter, and attached to a young, unfaithful woman, all of which makes him an unlikely patriarchal figure. Furthermore, Andrés still lives with his father, a buffoonish character who is senile, silly, foul-mouthed, and childish all at the same time. The old man runs around in his pajamas and a beret, speaking with a thick peninsular Spanish accent. The father (played by the Spanish actor Paco Martínez) is clearly a caricature and his Iberian origin marks Andrés as a creole, a Mexican of direct Spanish descent (which was, indeed, the actor Andrés Soler's origin; he had been born in Mexico to Spanish immigrant parents). Andrés's lineage emphasizes his class difference with his tenants and the Brute. Andrés's patriarchal role is in crisis: his masculinity is in question, his property is endangered, his lineage is a joke. He needs Pedro to complement for his lack, especially since it is suggested that Pedro is actually Andrés's illegitimate son, the result of an illicit affair with a long-gone domestic servant.

Pedro supplies the sexual and physical power that Andrés is lacking. He intimidates the tenants with his brutal force and becomes Paloma's lover in the process. Making matters even more melodramatic, Pedro then falls in love with Meche, the daughter of the tenants' rebellious leader, whom he accidentally killed. ("Meche" and "Pedro" are the same names as the protagonists of *Los olvidados*.) Meche heals Pedro when he is stabbed after he is chased and attacked by the tenants. He is immediately attracted to her youth, sweetness, and motherly protection. He ultimately leaves Paloma and don Andrés to move in with Meche. Paloma catches the two of them together, and in the argument that follows, Pedro beats up Paloma. Paloma then accuses Pedro of having raped her, and when don Andrés confronts the Brute about the rape, Pedro kills him, crushing Andrés's head with his foot. (In the absence of legitimate heirs, Don Andrés's death could make the tenants' claims easier.) Paloma then leads the police to Pedro's hiding place. When the police encounter Pedro, he displays a gun, and he is killed at the end.

Pedro's relationships with don Andrés, Paloma, and Meche are all governed by illicit sexual liaisons: Andrés with Pedro's mother, Pedro with Paloma, Pedro with Meche. It is Pedro's sexual activity that places him in a weakened position when Paloma stakes her claim, and, once rejected, she turns him in to the police. Sexual prowess and physical force ultimately work against the macho Pedro. The Brute is a character that operates outside of both patriarchal and state law. But he is not an entirely villainous character: like the protagonist in *Susana*, he is properly punished for his crimes, yet unlike Susana, and unlike Jaibo in *Los olvidados*, Pedro does show remorse and the willingness to make amends for his actions.

Nevertheless, portraying Pedro as a tragic yet sympathetic antihero was not easy. While the character himself was ultimately redeemed by love, remorse, and ignorance, Buñuel had to deal with Pedro Armendáriz's star persona, which was complicated by the unwritten laws of star-discourse. "As a general rule," says Buñuel in *My Last Sigh*, "a Mexican actor would never do on the screen what he wouldn't do in real life." Armendáriz, remembers Buñuel, "refused to wear short-sleeved shirts . . . because this article of clothing was reserved for homosexuals." And another famous anecdote from the set of *El bruto* recounts how some lines of dialogue had to be changed because Armendáriz refused to say them as they were scripted, again because he thought they could be misconstrued as suggesting homosexuality. Eventually, Armendáriz agreed to wear the short-sleeved shirts, at least in the slaughterhouse scenes, and there were no major repercussions to his macho star-persona.[7]

This tension between actor and character was rare in Mexican cinema. A star's persona and typecasting were instrumental in the success of Mexico's genre system. Pedro Armendáriz, since Emilio Fernández cast him in his first feature film,[8] had come to symbolize "essential Mexicanness," either as an Indian or as a Revolutionary general. Allowing Buñuel to miscast him in a role Armendáriz thought might compromise his star-persona and male identity suggests two things: first, that with the foreign critical and commercial success of *Los olvidados* and *Subida al cielo,* Buñuel had achieved a comfortable position within Mexican cinema that allowed him to attract top talent (Armendáriz and Katy Jurado, for instance) and to take certain liberties; and second, that Buñuel was now less hesitant to articulate in his films his concerns about the image of the macho Mexican.

Before *El bruto* Buñuel had already depicted machismo, in a joking manner in *La hija del engaño* and as an irrational instinct in *Susana.* Furthermore, in his autobiographical account, *My Last Sigh,* he frames his discussion of *El río y la muerte* as well as his personal impressions of Emilio Fernández and Pedro Armendáriz by digressing on the subjects of Mexico's macho image and its "gun culture."[9] This character of "The Brute" was somewhat misleading when it came to his male personality: he was physically strong but slow-witted, "masculine" but easily manipulated by women, powerful yet only able to exert his strength on women and sick old men. Pedro fails in the role of the lower-class male who protects those who depend on him (his first concubine, the sick mother, the children), as he takes sides (temporarily) with the sexually disempowered petty bourgeois patriarch.

This attitude stands in opposition to the image of men of Pedro's own class seen in Mexican culture at the height of the Revolution. According to Ilene O'Malley, "Tales of class abuse were frequently portrayed as the usurpation of a man's patriarchal rights.... Lower-class men recovered their manhood during the Revolution by assaulting the socioeconomic structures that had oppressed them."[10] Masculinity and class conflict were closely associated issues during the Revolution. Don Andrés, the middle-class but disempowered patriarch, blames the Revolution specifically for giving the lower classes the impression that they had the right to question Porfirian patriarchal authority and class differences. Ultimately, however, don Andrés's defeat occurs in the sexual arena (Paloma denies him her sexual favors but grants them to the Brute) rather than as a result of his legal problems. Interestingly, O'Malley suggests that the Revolution allowed *all men* (rich and poor, creole and mestizo) to believe that they had the right to claim a place in the patriarchal structure. Thus, in a cynical way don Andrés is right about his class worries, as is Buñuel's interpretation of his fears.

Later, Pedro, in an attempt to redeem himself in the eyes of Meche, switches sides to help the tenants in their struggle to stay on the property. He is inevitably led to his death, betrayed by Paloma and ungratefully forgotten by the people that he tried to protect. It is relevant to note that Pedro's change of heart is not a response to any sudden awakening of class consciousness, as would be more acceptable in Mexican cinema, but is strictly the result of his interest in a woman, which confirms O'Malley's perception that "class conflict received a . . . sexual expression"[11] in revolutionary times. Buñuel's cynical choice for an ending (Pedro is killed by the police, and in don Andrés's absence the tenants are probably free to stay in the property) clearly distances this movie from its closer generic relatives, Ismael Rodríguez's *arrabaleras*. Buñuel denies us even the possibility of a happy ending, and also the film is not very sympathetic to the poor as a class. Redemption is as useless for this Pedro as it was for the homonymous character in *Los olvidados*. Interestingly, producer Sergio Kogan reportedly asked screenwriter Luis Alcoriza to tone down the conflict between Pedro and the neighborhood people. According to Ávila Dueñas, they feared that Mexican audiences would not tolerate a working-class character that betrayed his own people.[12] The film's intriguing final images show Paloma running away from the dying Pedro and coming face to face with a rooster standing on a fence. The image is a return to a Buñuelian motif seen in *Los olvidados* and other films, a "nightmarish vision," says Buñuel, which in this case suggests Paloma's own punishment for her selfish, destructive actions. Like the blind man don Carmelo, who ends up in a similar situation in *Los olvidados*, Paloma is left alone to face her own nightmare.[13]

In *El bruto*, Buñuel uncovers a social, patriarchal, and masculinity crisis that is made explicit by the miscasting of Pedro Armendáriz, by the lack of positive patriarchal figures, and by the inability of the law (that is, the Revolution) to protect the poor, the dispossessed. Yet, Buñuel's misuse of Armendáriz was not limited to the actor's character; it also addressed Armendáriz's symbolic status in the nation's cinema. Buñuel deliberately uses self-reflexive irony in a scene when Pedro goes looking for Meche to make her his live-in companion. Pedro sweet-talks the newly orphaned Meche, who is destitute and only in her late teens, convincing her to move in with him, in part for protection, in part as his concubine. She accepts (she really is out of options) and Pedro, overtaken by joy, smiles broadly, stands up triumphantly, and utters in celebration the unbelievable line, "*¡Qué chulo es México!*" (How lovely is Mexico!). Pedro is strategically and ironically standing on a pile of rubble, surrounded by dirt, garbage, and (as the homonymous character in *Los olvidados*) half-demolished buildings. In its visual context the line of dialogue acquires a doubly insulting meaning. On the one hand, the mise-en-scène is unambiguously unattractive (as are many similar locations in *Los olvidados* and *El bruto*). On the other hand, coming from the lips of Pedro Armendáriz, the iconic, untarnished, symbolic star of such emblematic films as *I Am Pure Mexican* (Emilio Fernández, 1942), *María Candelaria* (Fernández, 1943) and *Juan Charrasqueado*

(Ernesto Cortázar, 1947), it is aggressively incompatible with his role as a star-persona in the nation's cinema.

Moreover, by 1952, Buñuel was starting to work his way around censorship with apparent ease. The censorship laws of 1949 made it illegal in Mexican films to portray national institutions as ineffective, to celebrate illicit sexual affairs, or to use profane language in film. All of these forbidden topics are thinly disguised in *El bruto*. Pedro, for example, abandons what seem to be his illegitimate children and lives out of wedlock with two women. The police arbitrarily serve the needs of a "villain" in this film, at the expense of the dispossessed. And don Andres's father, the buffoonish old Spaniard, is constantly cursing. His words are doctored with slight syllabic variations that turn *puñeta*, or "jerk-off" (a common Spanish curse word) into *puñales*, or "knives" (which has no meaning as a curse word). These deceptive pleasures, along with the specific and implied references to class conflict and revolutionary politics, situate *El bruto* as a turning point in Buñuel's Mexican career.

Buñuel's next project was *The Adventures of Robinson Crusoe* (1952), a U.S.–Mexico co-production in which Buñuel, for the first time since *Gran Casino*, departed from the genre models of Mexican cinema. With the biggest budget and the longest production schedule of his entire career, *The Adventures of Robinson Crusoe* became Buñuel's first color film, his biggest commercial success to date, and his first movie since 1946 that was not limited by the genres of Mexican cinema.[14] *Robinson Crusoe* was a clear departure, and one of the films that Buñuel clearly did not make specifically for the domestic market.

Él

Upon returning to Mexican cinema after *The Adventures of Robinson Crusoe*, Buñuel made *Él*, one of his own favorite films, and one in which he retook the issues of masculinity and class conflict dramatized in *El bruto*. Like *Una mujer sin amor*, *Él* was based on foreign literature, the semi-autobiographical novel of the same title by Spanish author Mercedes Pinto. Yet, Buñuel's interest in the crisis of Mexican male identity in *Los olvidados* and *Una mujer sin amor*, his commentary on machismo and class in *El bruto*, along with inevitable questions of context, make *Él* a careful look at machismo and patriarchy, this time as a psychological ailment, as paranoia. Because of the implied weight of machismo and patriarchy in Mexican politics and identity, *Él* becomes a very critical look at those issues, since, paraphrasing Charles Ramírez Berg, what Buñuel did to the male image in Mexican cinema, he also did to the nation's image.

Many interesting things have been written about Francisco Galván de Montemayor, the pathetic, insanely jealous husband in *Él*, played by Arturo de Córdova, a distinguished Mexican leading man. Francisco's psychological profile has been the subject of criticism, praise, and speculation from sources as diverse as Max Aub, who interviewed Buñuel about his interest in psychoanalysis, to Jacques Lacan, who discussed Francisco as a faithful portrait of a paranoiac, to Charles Tesson of *Cahiers du Cinéma*, to Linda Williams.[15]

Fernando Césarman, a psychologist at the National Autonomous University in Mexico, provides one of the most rigorous analyses in his book, *L'oeil de Buñuel*, in which he concludes that Francisco "suffers a progressive psychological disintegration as his heterosexual relationship intensifies." Francisco's potential homosexuality is presented as a symptom of his paranoid delusions that lead him to imagine all sorts of infidelities by his wife. Most tellingly, Césarman states that Francisco suffers from "a chronic homosexual problem. . . . His relationships with women are reduced, whereas they are more stable with men."[16] Buñuel's portrait of a paranoid is, in fact, faithful to the case of Dr. Schreber, which Freud made famous in his treatise "Psychoanalytic Notes . . . of a Case of Paranoia,"[17] particularly in the associations drawn by Freud between paranoia, homosexuality, and delusions of grandeur. Like Dr. Schreber, Francisco is a classic paranoid whose neurosis is manifested in his belief that everybody is out to get him, and who exists in a realm of moral superiority (in Francisco's case, transformed into Catholicism and patriarchy), and who has difficulty relating to women. Gripped by fears of his wife's infidelity, Francisco forges a rather intimate relationship with his valet (played by Manuel Dondé of *Subida al cielo*) and confesses to him that he was happier before ever having had relations with a woman. He physically and psychologically abuses his wife, Gloria (played by Argentine émigré actress Delia Garcés), which constitutes the clearest instance of faithfulness to Mercedes Pinto's novel. Francisco is, however, commended for his righteous ways by his priest, his valet, his male friends, and even his mother-in-law, who refuses to believe her daughter's complaints. By the time it is clear that Francisco has crossed over the threshold of sanity, which comes only after he attacks his priest in church, his only refuge is a monastery abroad, where Francisco finally "confirms" (upon meeting his ex-wife's new husband) that he was right about her infidelity all along. Thus, Francisco is a faithful rendition of a paranoiac, at least in the Freudian sense of the word, and in any case, Freud's case was Buñuel's model. Yet, to look at Francisco also as a Mexican man does not invalidate the psychological profile of the character; it just gives it some added relevancy in the light of Buñuel's specific views about men and machismo in Mexico.

Interestingly, in what seems like a trend in Buñuel's Mexican movies of the 1950s, the paranoid don Francisco in *Él* is something of an old Porfirista": he is a devout Catholic, a "Knight of the Sacred Sacrament," and the wealthy, conservative, tradition-minded heir of an "old" family fortune.[18] Yet, Francisco, who seems too mature to be a bachelor, soon shows signs of an arbitrary character flaw: in discovering an affair between his valet and a maid, he fires the maid. Francisco is further emotionally distressed by an old lawsuit that his lawyers tell him he is going to lose. The lawsuit, which we learn Francisco has been fighting for years, concerns the restitution of lands expropriated from his family in the city of Guanajuato. Indeed, our first glimpse of Francisco's erratic temperament comes in the second scene of the movie, when his lawyer tells him that the documents upon which Francisco is basing his claim are "too old" and that the lawyer fears there is no way they can win. Francisco fires the lawyer on the spot. The choice of Guanajuato as the site of Francisco's claims is also significant: since the 1700s the city has been an enclave of silver mining and had also served as the administrative and economic center of the Bajío region, both of which accounted for the aristocratic aura and enormous wealth of the city's "old" families . Therefore, Francisco's origins certainly mark him as someone from a privileged background, and consequently as someone who sees the Revolution as a threat. It is implicit that his lawsuit concerns lands expropriated by the government, especially in light of Buñuel's use of characters with similar social concerns in *El bruto*, *Una mujer sin amor*, and *Subida al cielo*. Francisco is one of the wealthy landed elite directly and adversely affected by the Revolution's land reforms of the 1930s.

Francisco's family home—a baroque-styled mansion with a taste of Antonio Gaudí, that gives the decor an expressionist function,[19] seems to reflect his skewed perception of reality. But the house, designed by his grandfather and decorated with objects purchased at the Paris exposition of 1900, like Francisco's moot lawsuit and his nostalgic honeymoon trip to Guanajuato, also signifies his propensity toward living in the past. By contrast, Francisco's romantic rival, Gloria's former fiancé Raúl, is a young engineer who builds bridges and dams out in the country. These distinctions between "old guard" and "modern" Mexican men are not only common in Buñuel's movies, but they are also surprisingly consistent. As we saw earlier in *Susana*, *La hija del engaño*, *Una mujer sin amor*, *Él*, *El río y la muerte*, and *Ensayo de un crimen*, the younger heroes of Buñuel's films are men educated in implicitly progressive occupations, like agronomy, mechanics, and engineering, especially significant in the decade of modernization. Furthermore, don Guadalupe in *Susana*, Quintín in *La hija del engaño*,

FIGURE 14. Patriarchy, masculinity, and insanity are the same thing in Buñuel's *Él* (1952). Francisco Galván de Montemayor (Arturo de Córdova) is symbolically trapped by his past, his present, and by the schizophrenic architecture of his own home. Museum of Modern Art / Film Stills Archive.

Rosario's husband in *Una mujer sin amor*, and Francisco in *Él* all try stubbornly to hold on to their moral positions and the mode of production prevalent before the Revolution. By contrast, the younger men who threaten the old ways and the old masculinity are all immersed in the wave of progress and modernization. This is most clearly suggested by the choice of two bridge-building engineers of the same age group to meddle with the marriages of young women to older men in the similarly structured melodramas *Una mujer sin amor* and *Él*.

Francisco's diagnosis of paranoia is well founded and documented, according to the analyses essayed by critics such as Fernando Césarman and Charles Tesson. But, whereas in Mercedes Pinto's novel the anonymous married couple's crisis seems to take place in a time and place vacuum, giving it a strictly psychological angle, in Buñuel's film Francisco and Gloria are unmistakably placed in a Mexican context in the 1950s. Francisco is still a man going insane, but as written by Buñuel and his collaborator Luis Alcoriza, he is also a man whose masculinity is threatened, both by women and by the presence of younger men (to whom Francisco seems attracted). He is, moreover, a failed Mexican patriarch who has lost his land and (also in contrast to Pinto's novel, in which the couple has a child) who does not produce an heir.

Francisco is implicitly feminized by impotence, and he is disempowered by the loss of his property and the end of his family name. He also represents the crisis of machismo: he is written as an unmistakably Mexican man (from an old, Catholic, landed Guanajuato family) and, by extension, he dramatizes the crisis of the Mexican state. Indeed, the suggestion in *Él* of Francisco's homosexual inclinations (which are confirmed by Freud's own study on paranoia),[20] along with the brief family history that the movie supplies, portrays the psychological crisis of one Mexican man as the trauma of the entire Mexican patriarchy.

By the time he directed *Él*, Buñuel's inclination to treat Mexican issues or crises metaphorically as personal traumas had become a pattern in his Mexican films. We see it in the relationship of Pedro and Jaibo in *Los olvidados*, in doña Carmen and the aging patriarch don Guadalupe in *Susana*, in Rosario's traumatized older son in *Una mujer sin amor*, and in Pedro's homicidal impulses in *El bruto*. In 1954 Buñuel utilized this national crisis/male trauma scenario in depicting the mother/son relationship in *El río y la muerte*. A year later, Buñuel would give us the amusing portrayal of the decadent aristocrat Archibaldo de la Cruz, played by Ernesto Alonso, in a version of Rodolfo Usigli's elegant novel, *Ensayo de un crimen*.

Ensayo de un crimen

Rodolfo Usigli's novel—in which the main character is actually named Roberto de la Cruz—was published in 1944, and the author intended it to be a profile of a gratuitous, brilliant murderer set in the "real" Mexico City of gentlemen, well-dressed ladies, and tea rooms of the 1940s. That is, the location was to have been a "more European" Mexico City—the city as it was before the urban boom of the 1950s brought the poor to the city from the hinterlands, before the advent of *Los olvidados*.[21] In spite of its snobbish tone, the novel has been praised for its remarkable re-creation of Mexico City landmarks and of upper-class genteel customs. Usigli describes in painstaking detail many of the daily traditions of the Mexico City of the 1940s—like breakfasting at the Casa de los Azulejos, and leisurely afternoon walks from the Alameda Central along Paseo de la Reforma to the Chapultepec forest. The author even sometimes used the real names and addresses of people and places from the period, describing the particularities of a restaurant's menu or the doings of crowds and people with journalistic accuracy.

In Usigli's novel, Roberto de la Cruz is the wearied son of a fine (but now destitute) Cuernavaca family, who lives off of gambling and a small trust allowance. Purely out of boredom, and convinced that he is an intellectually superior person, Roberto decides that there are people who do not deserve to live, and that, as a greater being, he is allowed to kill them. Roberto thinks of himself as something of an aesthete. In his mind, his crimes really have no need for motive. On the contrary, they must be executed coldly and cleanly, and with no moral qualms whatsoever.

In Buñuel's film, the main character has been re-named Archibaldo de la Cruz, in part because of a dispute with Usigli, who was unhappy with Buñuel's adaptation of his novel. Instead of being "based on" Rodolfo Usigli's novel, the movie is credited as having been "inspired by" the novel. Moreover, its title was changed to *La vida criminal de Archibaldo de la Cruz* for the purposes of foreign exhibition. Buñuel later clearly stated that he was not familiar with the setting and lifestyle described in Usigli's novel, and that, for his film, he had been solely interested in the obsessions of the book's main character.[22]

Yet, as Buñuel had done in adapting the paranoid hero of Spanish author Mercedes Pinto's novel, so, too, for *Ensayo de un crimen*, Buñuel gives us a great deal more information about the main character's history than ever appeared in the novel. In the novel, Roberto de la Cruz's story is loosely based on a real homicide case in Mexico City in the 1940s, and his character is modeled after the infamous American murderers, Leopold and Loeb. In the film, Buñuel suggests that Archibaldo de la Cruz's homicidal impulses originated in a traumatic childhood experience. In the film's opening scene, original to the adaptation, Archibaldo narrates his background and family history over a flashback of his childhood, which includes a specific reference to the Revolution. The reference is much less precise in the novel. All Usigli wrote about the Revolution in the novel is one sentence: "He remembered his childhood in the quiet provincial city, with the exception of the slow and at the same time vertiginous years of the revolution."[23] Screenwriters Buñuel and Eduardo Ugarte, by contrast, open their film with a shot of pictures from a book about the Revolution, where, over images of numerous corpses and general chaos, the narrator tells us: "We were going through one of many violent moments of the Revolution. Throughout the country parties were rising up in support of one side or the other. The provincial capital where I used to live with my parents was one of the few places where there was still some peace."

This disjuncture between Archibaldo's description of his childhood town and the photographs in the book suggests the same kind of narration/image juxtaposition that Buñuel exploited in *Las Hurdes* and *El río y la muerte*. Unlike Roberto de la Cruz in the novel, in Buñuel's film Archibaldo's homicidal desires are specifically linked to the Revolution. Archibaldo's governess finds him hidden inside an armoire, wearing his mother's clothes and shoes. At the same moment, an armed skirmish between indistinct factions in the war is occurring on the street outside. A stray bullet comes in through the window and accidentally kills the pretty young governess. Archi's nanny dies right in his presence. She falls dead on the floor, displaying her legs and thighs, which attract Archi's attention even more than the bleeding bullet wound on her neck. Seconds before, the governess had been telling Archibaldo a made-up story about a king who killed people with the sheer force of his desire, and now Archi is convinced that he caused the nanny's death because the thought crossed his mind.

In this original introduction, Buñuel has given Archibaldo a psychological history that includes an aristocratic family that "benefited from the Porfiriato and was made destitute by the Revolution,"[24] an early propensity for cross-dressing, and the impressive memory of a woman's death that takes place under erotic circumstances. The result is that Archi will forever connect, or confuse, sexual desire with death and vice versa. Out of this first scene comes the association between the political turmoil of the 1910s, Archi's latent homosexuality, and his desire to kill women (as well as the comical impossibility that he will ever realize that desire). Here, Buñuel seems to be completing the picture of the Mexican male crisis begun in *Susana*, *A Woman Without Love*, and *Él*, but now with a more systematic feminization of the leading man. Like Francisco in *Él*, Archibaldo is portrayed as someone with a disturbed personality, but whereas Francisco's character is understood through a serious clinical study on paranoia, Archibaldo's is more of a cartoon: effeminate, frustrated, impotent.

None of this is explicit in Usigli's novel. Roberto de la Cruz is certainly egomaniacal and narcissistic, but he is not completely sexually dysfunctional with women. In fact, in the novel, Roberto occasionally relates with women, and he also wants to kill men, specifically, the old count Schwartzemberg, who Roberto suspects to be a homosexual. Therefore, in the movie, Archibaldo de la Cruz's one-sided fixation against women makes the character somewhat less complex, his trauma more explicit, and the diagnosis more certain. Archibaldo is most likely a repressed homosexual, the antithesis of the masculine hero demanded by Mexican machismo. We know that Buñuel did not have very kind words for homosexuals, and he often used the term *pédéraste* in his writings, which implies he found a direct connection between homosexuality and pedophilia.[25] Thus, the choice of Archibaldo as a parody of Mexican machismo is as prejudiced as it is straightforward.

Archibaldo is single, a dilettante who passes his time between leisurely courting the young Miss Cervantes, gambling in secret gaming houses, and making ceramic vases—a "feminine" hobby. He drinks milk, not alcohol; he likes music boxes, not guns; and his thin mustache, silk robes, fine suits, and elegant manners also characterize him as effeminate, or at least as a counter-figure to the manly images predominant in Mexican cinema. Furthermore, the choice of the actor Ernesto Alonso, a soap opera star who never married, added a dandy bachelor star-persona to Archibaldo's profile. In his floating narration Archibaldo states that he wants to marry Miss Cervantes, not because he loves her, but because he knows that marriage will "cure him." He tells Miss Cervantes when proposing marriage: "I am not a man like other men. I know my inclinations, and they scare me."

Archibaldo's homosexual/homicidal "inclinations" are frustrated constantly by external circumstances. Archibaldo can never fulfill his destiny as a great killer of women because his chosen victims always die due to external causes never directly related to his acts. A nun accidentally falls down a broken elevator shaft while he chases her; another woman commits suicide; and Archibaldo's fiancée, Miss Cervantes, is herself shot by her lover (an architect!) in the middle of her wedding to Archi (which interferes with Archibaldo's plan to kill her on their wedding night).

Implicitly, the impulse to kill women is sublimated by Archibaldo's homosexual inclinations, since his misogynist attitudes are a projection of his homoerotic desires. Like Francisco in *Él*, Archibaldo also conforms to specific descriptions of neuroses in Freud's writings. Freud specifically characterized neurotics as showing "inverted impulses, fixation of their libido upon persons of their own sex," as well as displaying "active and passive forms of the instinct for cruelty. . . . It is also through the connection between libido and cruelty that the transformation of love into hate takes place."[26] Thus, in Buñuel's (arbitrary) historically specific Freudian discourse, Archibaldo is typically a neurotic paranoid who constantly battles his "inverted" impulses by imagining violent scenarios. Archibaldo believes that forced heterosexuality through marriage to Miss Cervantes will have the reverse result and "cure" him.

Archibaldo channels his frustrations by picking visible fetishes, such as a music box, and a mannequin that resembles Lavinia, one of his potential victims. His plans to strangle Lavinia (played by the actress Miroslava Stern) are interrupted by the arrival of a group of American tourists who have come to see his ceramic vases. Archi instead burns the mannequin in his kiln and watches in ecstatic fascination as it melts in the flames. The mannequin and its obvious fetishistic value is probably the most-talked-about aspect of *Ensayo de un crimen*. More than a fetish, however, the mannequin is an actual "dead" version of the desired woman, and Archibaldo's "healing" process begins with the elaborate ritual of seeing her burn in the kiln. This is, indeed, as close as Archibaldo gets to fulfilling his desire. In a way, he succeeds in "killing" Lavinia, and the next time he meets with her, he is in fact "cured." The meeting occurs at the end of the film, after he has tossed his music box into the lake at Chapultepec forest, and Archibaldo and Lavinia walk away together. Unlike Francisco's famous lonely zigzagging walk at the end of *Él*, Archi walks away "straight" and in the company of a woman, showing that he is in fact "cured."

Archibaldo conforms to a psychological profile that seems to be resolved with the negotiation of his homicidal and homosexual leanings through the cleansing ritual of burning the mannequin. Nevertheless, Buñuel and Ugarte also emphasize the context of the Mexican Revolution in giving Archibaldo a psychological history. Archi's desire to kill and his homosexuality are linked to the death of the governess in the middle of a revolutionary battle. So, we also have to see this character as a version of Mexican masculinity in crisis. The first images shown in the film are photographs of the carnage of the Revolution as little Archi thumbs through a history book, and those are the images that frame Archibaldo's confession of his awakening as a killer. The editing of the film takes us from seeing the pictures of dead soldiers, to hearing the tune from the music box, to seeing the governess killed by a revolutionary's bullet. The final shot in the sequence is of Archi's morbid arousal, triggered by the sight of the dead woman's exposed legs. That sequence of events inevitably provides the explanation for Archibaldo's neurosis: sex and death, sure, but first of all, the Mexican Revolution.

In their film, Buñuel and Ugarte effectively heightened the specific historical context. They gave Archibaldo an added dimension: his neurosis may be drawn from a Freudian textbook, but he is also, unmistakably, a former Mexican aristocrat whose family was deprived of its wealth, position, and title by the Mexican Revolution. Ultimately, the traumatic experiences of the Revolution are at the root of Archi's problems. Like Pedro in *El bruto* and Francisco in *Él*, Archibaldo is a type of male leading character who is somewhat emasculated by the turn of events against his family and social class in the years since the Mexican Revolution. It is significant that Buñuel created these characters only after his immersion in the Mexican film industry had been solidified by the foreign success of *Los olvidados*, *Subida*

FIGURE 15. Ernesto Alonso as the troubled title character in *The Criminal Life of Archibaldo de la Cruz* (1955). Miroslava Stern *(right)* ultimately makes him walk "straight," although it takes sacrificing her own image to do so. Museum of Modern Art/Film Stills Archive.

al cielo, and *The Adventures of Robinson Crusoe*. The emphasis on the characters' histories in specific Mexican contexts, such as the urban boom of the 1950s and the slow-moving lawsuits against the government's land reform policies, gives these films a peculiarly Mexican relevance that strict psychological studies (such as Aranda's) do not address. By subverting traditional male character types, Buñuel was holding up to the light his eternally favorite topics (violence, obsession) as well as his increased understanding of Mexico. These characters are machos in crisis, and they suggest the inability of the Mexican male to fulfill his "manly" responsibilities (or murder), as well as showing homosexuality or potential homosexuality as a sign of the weakening of patriarchy in the 1950s, and by extension, the crisis of the nation. Buñuel may have very well opened a revisionist trend in the nation's cinema with these films. Classical cinema had long before reached its peak: the cinematic image of the nation had already been put in question by Buñuel's own *Los olvidados*, and the state was facing its biggest economic and philosophical crisis since the 1930s.[27] Buñuel's films seem more

Mexican than ever, equating as they do the national crisis with masculinity. As Charles Ramírez Berg points out, in the two decades following the filming of Buñuel's macho-dramas *Él* and *Ensayo de un crimen*, the subsequent generation of Mexican filmmakers was even more open to using images of "weak," "soft" or openly homosexual men to refer allegorically to national crises.[28]

Buñuel had been in Mexico since 1946 and had evidently observed not only the meaning of machismo for the nation but also the customary reverential treatment given to patriarchal figures and leading men in the nation's cinema. As we saw in *Susana* and *La hija del engaño*, Buñuel had already explored the topic, using in both instances one of Mexico's favorite icons of patriarchy, the actor Fernando Soler. By mocking, deconstructing, and violating the male image, the macho-dramas make Buñuel's revisionism even more evident. Revisionism was also one way of revising the image of the nation and national cinema itself.

Conclusion
From Buñuel to "Nuevo Cine"

> In a way, Buñuel was the antipode of Emilio Fernández.
> —Alberto Isaac, in *Conversaciones con Gabriel Figueroa*

BUÑUEL AT THE MARGINS OF THE NATION

With *The Adventures of Robinson Crusoe* in 1952, Luis Buñuel broke new ground. By experimenting with a movie that was formally unlike anything in classic Mexican cinema, he earned respect for the adventure genre which belonged to the realm of B-type swashbucklers. *The Adventures of Robinson Crusoe*, co-produced by Producciones Tepeyac (Óscar Dancigers) and United Artists (USA) opened the way for a number of international co-productions in the following decade. These, Buñuel made with foreign talent and usually released abroad, or they went directly to film festivals before being released in Mexico.

In 1952, for example, the original version of *The Adventures of Robinson Crusoe* was filmed in English and released in Paris, New York, London, Rio de Janeiro, and other major cities before it was dubbed into Spanish and released in Mexico in 1955. The Spanish version went on to achieve great recognition in Mexico, winning "Ariel" awards for best picture, director, screenplay adaptation (by Buñuel and Phillip Ansel Roll), production design, film editing, and supporting actor.[1]

After *The Adventures of Robinson Crusoe*, Buñuel made three Mexican–French collaborations, *Cela s'appelle l'aurore (That Is Called Dawn)* in 1955, immediately followed by *La mort en ce jardin (Death in the Garden)* in 1956 and *La fièvre monte à El Pão (Fever Mounts at El Pão)* in 1959, and another Mexico–U.S. co-production, *The Young One*, in 1960, in which he collaborated with Hugo Butler. The critical and commercial success of *The Adventures of Robinson Crusoe* and *Viridiana* (which won the Palme d'Or at the Cannes Film Festival in 1961) allowed Buñuel to confirm the viability and marketability of his style in the international film market. Thus, the work phase that began with *The Adventures of Robinson Crusoe* can be characterized as Buñuel's search for a springboard back into the international film scene and away from the constrictions of the national film market. Although *Robinson Crusoe* and *La ilusión viaja en tranvía* coincide chronologically, for example, there is a distinct departure from Mexican context and Mexican topics in the "international" films of the 1950s and 1960s.[2] In his Mexican films Buñuel is concerned with issues that are relevant to Mexico and with the representation of those issues in Mexican cinema. The films that started with *Robinson Crusoe* and continued until *Simón del desierto*, and which include *Abismos de pasión* and *Cela s'appelle l'Aurore*, are deliberately absent from the Mexican context.

The co-productions of the period 1952–65 gave Buñuel the opportunity to make movies with characters and themes far removed from the implied, sometimes imposed Mexican context of the movies made, for example, for CLASA *(El río y la muerte, La ilusión viaja en tranvía)* and Internacional Cinematográfica *(Una mujer sin amor, El bruto)*. In spite of the limitations imposed on him by the demands of the Mexican film industry, the Mexican films were useful as a training ground for Buñuel. At the same time, Buñuel's work with independent and foreign producers gave him the freedom to put aside the Mexican context, to address a different audience.

When he was constrained by the generic and popular demands of the commercial Mexican film industry, Buñuel complied, addressed his Mexican audience, and even enriched the Mexicanness of his characters, such as Francisco in *Él*, Rosario's sons in *Una mujer sin amor*, and Archibaldo de la Cruz. Given the opportunity, however, in independent or co-produced films like *Abismos de pasión*, *Nazarín*, and *Viridiana*, Buñuel was able to set aside the impositions of Mexico's censorship and labor laws and position himself and his films at the margins of national cinema.

Through the decade of the 1950s Buñuel continued to work with those Mexican producers who allowed him a greater degree of independence. Consequently, he made some of his best movies with them. First, Buñuel worked with Óscar Dancigers, who produced *Los olvidados*, *Él*, and *Robinson Crusoe*, along with *Gran Casino*, *El gran calavera*, and *La hija del engaño*. In the mid- to late 1950s Dáncigers also produced *Abismos de pasión* and *La mort en ce jardin*. Later, in 1958, Buñuel teamed up with legendary independent producer Manuel Barbachano Ponce,[3] who produced *Nazarín*, one of Buñuel's own favorite films. In his final Mexican phase, Buñuel worked with Gustavo Alatriste, an ambitious producer who sought out prestige products as vehicles for his wife, the actress Silvia Pinal, and

FIGURE 16. Buñuel directing *Nazarín* (ca. 1958), one of his independent films produced by Manuel Barbachano Ponce. Museum of Modern Art / Film Stills Archive.

who gave Buñuel complete creative control for *Viridiana, El ángel exterminador,* and *Simón del desierto*.[4]

The more independent films of Buñuel's Mexican period, such as *Robinson Crusoe, Abismos de pasión,* and *Nazarín,* are distinguished from the typical Mexican movies in terms of their popular (or populist) appeal. As opposed to films like *Susana, Abismos de pasión* and *Nazarín* were "prestige" projects, part of a tradition in Mexican cinema that included harmless (and usually inane) costume dramas and adaptations of classic literature. With these adaptations of non-Mexican literature, Buñuel was effectively distancing himself from the popular contexts and genres of Mexican cinema.

Buñuel did not adapt these novels to specifically Mexican contexts in a spirit of criticism and parody, as he had done with his version of Maupassant's *Pierre et Jean (Una mujer sin amor)* and Arniches's *Don Quintín, el amargao (La hija del engaño)*. Instead, with these films Buñuel was unequivocally reclaiming his own style of filmmaking, putting his emphasis on atmosphere and employing the stylistic economy of his old surrealist

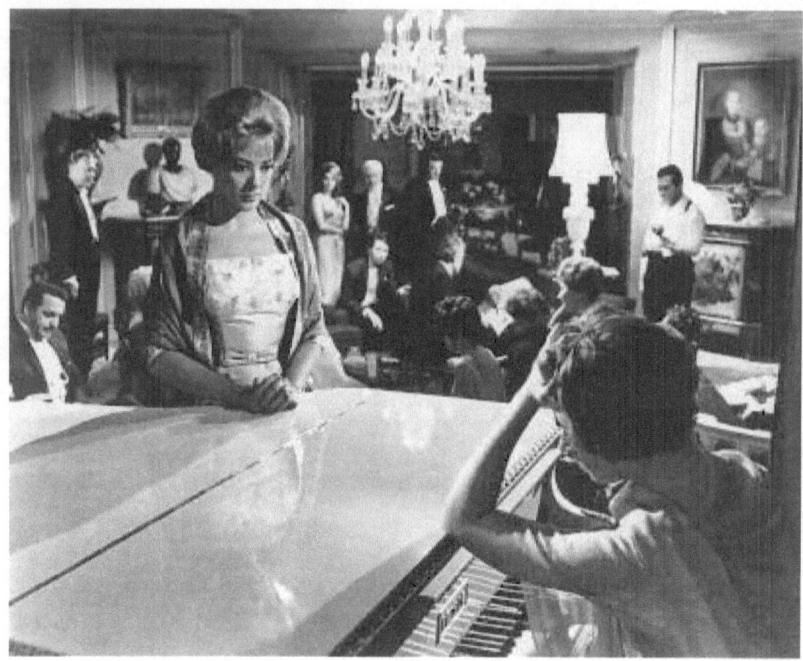

FIGURE 17. Silvia Pinal in *The Exterminating Angel* (1962). Buñuel's long-desired independence was aided in part by his association with Pinal and her husband, producer Gustavo Alatriste, in this film, as well as in *Viridiana* (1961) and *Simon of the Desert* (1965). Museum of Modern Art / Film Stills Archive.

classics. *Abismos de pasión* brought Buñuel back to an earlier, abandoned project, bringing to film Emily Brontë's *Wuthering Heights,* something he had attempted with Pierre Unik in the 1930s. Buñuel's interest in recreating "the spirit" of the 1847 novel (as the opening titles of the film clarify) translated into a condensation of what is really about a third of Brontë's novel, specifically the affair of Heathcliff (renamed Alejandro) and Catherine (Catalina) as adults. Buñuel's movie starts abruptly with Heathcliff's return to Yorkshire. It freely follows the couple's brief encounters there, and then moves forward to Catherine's death. In an improvised ending, Hindley Earnshaw, Catherine's estranged brother, shoots Heathcliff as he watches her body in the grave, so the two end up together in death.[5] Instead of emphasizing the family feud and exploiting the melodramatic possibilities of Brontë's novel (which is what William Wyler's 1939 version does), that is, instead of turning the story into a Mexican family melodrama, in *Abismos de pasión* Buñuel focused on the surrealist appeal for *amour fou* and on the external obstacles to the couple's union, thus making the film a closer relative of *L'Age d'Or*. Furthermore, Buñuel declared his dissatisfaction with the movie, precisely because the largely Mexican cast seemed to him inappropriate for the Gothic spirit of the tale. As Buñuel told his interviewers José de la Colina and Tomás Pérez Turrent, he had wanted to make *Abismos de pasión* in Europe with European actors. He was concerned that the Mexican accent of Ernesto Alonso (Edgar Linton), the sexualized star-persona of Lilia Prado (Isabella Linton), and the physical aspect of Luis Aceves Castañeda (Hindley Earnsaw) were not right for his concept of *Wuthering Heights*.[6] This, even though physique, star-discourse, and speech were instrumental in effectively casting his Mexican films *Subida al cielo* and *El bruto*, for example.

Likewise, *Viridiana*, a movie made in Spain with Mexican capital (producer Gustavo Alatriste), and employing a Mexican female lead (Silvia Pinal) with a Spanish supporting cast (Fernando Rey and Francisco Rabal), dramatizes the complexity of Buñuel in the 1960s: independent, subtle, "speaking" a more universal film language. Buñuel's latter works with Dáncigers (specifically, *Abismos de pasión*), Alatriste, and Manuel Barbachano Ponce *(Nazarín)* are the key bridging films of this period, the last movies in which Buñuel addressed his position as an exile, as a stranger in Mexican cinema.

BUÑUEL WITHIN MEXICAN CINEMA

At the height of his Mexican period, in the early 1950s, from *Los olvidados* to *Él* to *El río y la muerte* Buñuel observed Mexican society and Mexican customs with a critical eye, with the fascination of a stranger witnessing some exotic, incomprehensible culture. But, more importantly, Buñuel also observed and analyzed the face of Mexican cinema, criticizing what was founded on the implied false façade of organized culture and folklore.

Buñuel's ironic, sardonic take on the face of Mexican film was often stated by carefully re-staging, so to speak, the imaging of national culture and by contrasting the cinematic view of Mexico to reality. As Carlos Monsiváis, Ana López, and Jesús Martín-Barbero have argued, in the classic era of Mexican cinema, movies, genres, and movie stars served as a "mediating" force that the everyday moviegoer could look up to in order to find an image with which to identify. According to Martín-Barbero, in the heyday of the Mexican Revolution (the favorite topic of classic cinema), "going to the movies ... was the point of encounter between the collective lived experience generated by the Revolution and the mediation which, even though it deformed this experience, gave it social legitimacy." Mexico's was "a cinema in the image of the people."[7]

By thinking about Mexico through its cinematic image, by intermittently re-creating, perhaps deconstructing, Mexican cinema's topics, images, stars, settings, and characters, Buñuel was, in a projected or displaced fashion, if you will, also re-inventing the nation. He was digging out the conventions of Mexico's image and exposing their weaknesses, their prefabricated quality and their voids. We see Buñuel's critique in the forced artificiality of *Gran Casino*'s musical numbers and in the violent reactions provoked by *Los olvidados* because of its "filthy" image of Mexico. It is evident in the macho-threatening and genre-bending provocation of *Susana* and *La hija del engaño,* and in the contextual specificity of social and political satire in *Subida al cielo* and *La ilusión viaja en tranvía.* It is in the irreverent dissection of the "agreement" between the state and the Mexican male, known as machismo, which Buñuel exercised in almost all of his Mexican films, but particularly in *Los olvidados, Él, El bruto, El río y la muerte,* and *Ensayo de un crimen.* And, finally, it is also in the violation of the psychological structure of the national identity in *Una mujer sin amor.* In his Mexican films Buñuel was always aware of Mexican cinema's operating conventions, and he used his knowledge of the codes and conventions of Mexican cinema to exercise his surrealist critique of the political and social institutions that governed the nation.

By deceptively framing his criticism within Mexican cinema's recognizable formats, like family melodrama *(Susana, Una mujer sin amor, Él)*, the arrabalera *(Los olvidados, El bruto)*, comedy *(Subida al cielo, La ilusión viaja en tranvía)*, and melodramatic comedies *(La hija del engaño, Ensayo de un crimen)*, Buñuel was doubly effective. He was able to get his criticism through to his Mexican audience without alienating them (as the success of *El gran calavera, Los olvidados,* and *Subida al cielo* suggest), and without violating his surrealist, anti-nationalist convictions, as he stated in his memoirs.

Buñuel entered Mexican cinema as a reluctant participant, wary of "violating his personal morality." Yet, he found ways to stay true to his style and convictions through parody and allusion. Buñuel found a middle ground in his Mexican movies where he could defend his position as a surrealist on the margins of the nation while also gaining access to a national film industry that was regulated by laws and censorship and was dependent on governmental funding. The key distinction between Buñuel's truly Mexican movies (those made primarily for the domestic commercial film industry and analyzed here) and his festival-bound international projects lies in the articulation of Buñuel's perennial ideological positions about desire, bourgeois society, and Catholic morality. Those themes appear alternately in either Mexican (or "Mexicanized") contexts *(Los olvidados, Él)* or in non-nationally specific contexts *(Abismos de pasión, Nazarín, El ángel exterminador)*.

MEXICAN CINEMA AFTER BUÑUEL

The emergence of the "Nuevo Cine" generation in Mexico in the late 1960s, and the group's experimentation and interest in revitalizing the regretful condition of national cinema, was a result of the general crisis of the film industry through the decade. In the early 1960s Mexican and exiled young writers, cinephiles, and intellectuals, among them Carlos Monsiváis, Emilio García Riera, Jomí García Ascot, and Gabriel García Márquez, along with established cultural figures, such as Carlos Fuentes and Buñuel himself, swarmed around the self-proclaimed group, "Nuevo Cine." In the group's manifesto, published in the first number of their official publication—the *Cahiers*-inspired journal *Nuevo Cine* (published from November 1961 to August 1962)—they called for the improvement of the national cinema's quality. Specifically, they demanded an opening up of the closed ranks of the filmmaking establishment (which greatly opposed the influx of new talent), greater freedom of expression, and the suppression of censorship. They even demanded the institution of a national film school to train new filmmakers. *Nuevo Cine* also attempted to initiate a tradition of serious film criticism in Mexico. It rehearsed that concept in the seven numbers that were published, with critical articles on Eisenstein, Buñuel, Von Stroheim, Roberto Rossellini, Cyd Charisse, and Gary Cooper, and with an abridged synthesis explaining the critical and philosophical style of André Bazin, whom the group embraced as an inspiration.[8]

Nuevo Cine later dedicated a special double issue entirely to Buñuel (November 1961), significantly, in celebration of the first anniversary of the founding of the group. In that issue they included new and previously published special reviews, essays, and criticism by such noteworthy critics as Henry Miller and Octavio Paz, regular staff writers García Riera and Salvador Elizondo, and future Nuevo Cine filmmakers Alberto Isaac and Jomí García Ascot. Furthermore, in their editorial, the writers acknowledged that "an homage to Buñuel was predictable since the foundation of our group ... (an homage) justified by the existence of films like *Los olvidados, Él, Nazarín,* [and] *Viridiana*. Each one of these films is in and of itself irrefutable proof that the cinema usually made in Mexico is not the only cinema that could and should be made."[9] *Nuevo Cine* correctly predicted that Buñuel would be the figure to look to in Mexican cinema's search for groundbreaking, original directions, and it embraced his work as exemplary of what the "new cinema" should become.

The collapse of the Banco Nacional Cinematográfico and of major studios such as Churubusco, as well as the perennial dependence of independent producers on formulaic *churros* that were quickly and cheaply made and returned good profits, condemned Mexican cinema to a creative slump. The repressive social and economic policies of President Gustavo Díaz Ordaz (1963–69) sparked an atmosphere of unrest that reached a sad climax on 2 October 1968, when police repressed demonstrating students and workers and hundreds of them were reportedly killed, wounded, and imprisoned. Through the 1960s the critical state of national cinema was a reflection of the status of national politics.

By that time, Buñuel was already disengaged from national cinema, thanks to his association with independent and foreign producers beginning with the release of *El ángel exterminador* (*The Exterminating Angel*, 1962) and *Simón del desierto* (*Simon of the Desert*, 1965). Yet these were his most experimental films of the early 1960s, and they coincide chronologically with the emergence in Mexico of the "new cinema" of the decade. The films were subsequently appropriated by a later generation, if not as part of "the movement," then certainly as decidedly inspirational films.[10]

Buñuel critics have been reluctant to recognize his Mexican period as anything other than a fluke, an accident, as if he had magically remained untouched by his time in Mexico. But Buñuel's greater contribution to Mexican cinema is perhaps to have initiated an articulate, critical strand, a new tradition in Mexican cinema. After the crisis of the classical era in the 1950s, and the symbolic collapse of the Revolution's mythical image dramatized by the violent political turmoil during Díaz Ordaz's administration, the new cinema movement re-conceptualized Mexico's image in film, and in doing so "redefined Mexicanidad."[11] Buñuel's immersion in Mexican cinema arguably served as an indispensable link between two distinct eras of the nation's film history. The classic era of revolutionary optimism and positive images of Mexican institutions was nearing its end when Buñuel arrived in Mexico. And the "New Cinema" period after 1967 saw a new generation of filmmakers whom Buñuel admittedly did inspire. Directors like Alberto Isaac (*En este pueblo no hay ladrones*, 1964), Rubén Gámez (*La fórmula secreta*, 1964), Alejandro Jodorowski (*El topo*, 1969), Paul Leduc (*Reed: México insurgente*, 1970), Felipe Cazals (*El apando*, 1976), Jaime Humberto Hermosillo (*María de mi corazón*, 1979), and Arturo Ripstein (*El lugar sin límites*, 1977) broke with the conventions of classical cinema. Berg

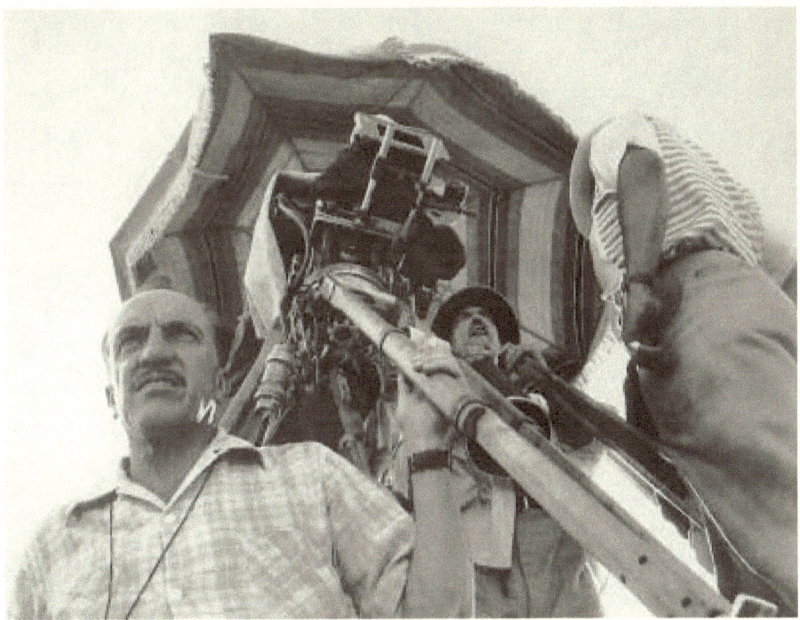

FIGURE 18. Gabriel Figueroa *(bottom left)* and Buñuel (with hat and megaphone) on the set of *Nazarín*. Museum of Modern Art / Film Stills Archive.

writes that they "[made] films that dealt frankly with social issues, and that were more politically daring, more sexually explicit, and to a degree narratively and aesthetically experimental."[12]

Some of the new filmmakers were largely influenced and inspired by Buñuel, as *Nuevo Cine* accurately predicted and others have acknowledged.[13] In every "new cinema" movement, from Italian Neorealism to Brazilian Cinema Nôvo, from the French *nouvelle vague,* to the New Latin American cinema, there is a moment of rupture, when something old is rejected in order to open the way for new forms of expression. Classic cinema in Mexico was that "something" against which the new filmmakers had to rebel. Because Buñuel entered Mexican cinema as the classic era was beginning its decline, his films of the 1950s served as a buffer that eased the rupture between what were destined to be two conflicting generations of Mexican filmmakers. The new generation embraced Buñuel as an inspirational figure. They admired him because of the striking originality of his work and because in his Mexican films Buñuel, "the antipode of Emilio Fernández,"[14] had experimented from within, beginning a decade too early to rework the style, ideology, and image of the old cinema.

Filmography of Luis Buñuel

NOTE: Many of Buñuel's films are available through American distributors in 16mm prints. Connaisseur Video, LAVA, and Facets Video now have many of the Mexican titles for sale. For video purchases, access the Latin American Video Archives website at www.lavavideo.org, or Facets Video at www.facets.org.

Abismos de pasión. 1953. Producer: Óscar Dancigers and Abelardo Rodríguez (Mexico); director Luis Buñuel; screenplay: Luis Buñuel, Pierre Unik, Julio Alejandro, and Arduino Mauvrí, based on the novel *Wuthering Heights* by Emily Brontë; photography: Agustín Jiménez and Sergio Véjar; editor: Carlos Savage; talent: Jorge Mistral, Irasema Dilián, Ernesto Alonso, Lilia Prado, Luis Aceves Castañeda. Black and white, 91 minutes. (Connaisseur)

The Adventures of Robinson Crusoe. 1952. Producer: Ultramar Films and United Artists (Óscar Dancigers and Henry Ehrlich, Mexico/USA); director: Luis Buñuel; screenplay: Luis Buñuel and Hugo Butler, based on the novel by Daniel Defoe; photography: Alex Phillips; editors: Carlos Savage, Alberto Valenzuela; talent: Dan O'Herlihy, Jaime Fernández. Color (Pathécolor), 89 minutes.

L'Age d'Or. 1929. Producer: Vicomte de Noailles (France); director: Luis Buñuel; screenplay: Buñuel and Salvador Dalí; photography: Albert Duverger; editor: Buñuel; talent: Gaston Modot, Lya Lys, Max Ernst, Pierre Prévert, José Artigas, Jacques Brunius. Black and white, 63 minutes.

The Andalusian Dog. See *Un chien andalou.*

El ángel exterminador. 1962. Producer: UNINCI, S.A., and Films 59 (Gustavo Alatriste, Mexico/Spain); director: Luis Buñuel; screenplay: Luis Buñuel and Luis Alcoriza; photography: Gabriel Figueroa; editor: Carlos Savage; talent: Silvia Pinal, José Baviera, Luis Beristain, Claudio Brook, Tito Junco. Black and white, 93 minutes.

Belle de jour. 1966. Producer: Paris Film Production (Robert Hakim and Raymond Hakim, France); director: Luis Buñuel; screenplay: Luis Buñuel and

Jean-Claude Carrière, based on the novel by Joseph Kessel; photography: Sacha Vierny; editor: Loissette Taverna; talent: Catherine Deneuve, Jean Sorel, Michel Piccoli, Francisco Rabal, Pierre Clementi, Geneviève Page. Color (Eastman color), 100 minutes.

The Bitterness of Don Quintín. See *Don Quintín, el amargao.*

El bruto. 1952. Producer: Internacional Cinematográfica (Óscar Dancigers, Mexico); director: Luis Buñuel; screenplay: Luis Buñuel and Luis Alcoriza; photography: Agustín Jiménez; editor: Jorge Bustos; talent: Pedro Armendáriz, Katy Jurado, Andrés Soler, Rosita Arenas. Black and white, 83 minutes. (Connaisseur, LAVA)

The Brute. See *El bruto.*

Cela s'appelle l'Aurore. 1955. Producer: Film Marceu, Laetitia Films, and Insignia Films (France/Italy); director: Luis Buñuel; screenplay: Luis Buñuel and Jean Ferry, based on the novel by Emmanuel Robles; photography: Robert Le Febvre; editor: Marguerite Renoir; talent: Georges Marchal, Lucía Bosé, Gianni Esposito, Gaston Modot. Black and white, 102 minutes.

¡Centinela alerta! 1936. Producer: Filmófono (Ricardo Urgoiti and Luis Buñuel, Spain); directors: Jean Grémillon and Luis Buñuel (both uncredited), Eduardo Ugarte; screenplay: Eduardo Ugarte and Luis Buñuel, based on the play *La alegría del batallón* by Carlos Arniches; photography: José María Beltrán; editor: Jean Grémillon; talent: Angelillo, Ana María Custodio, Luis Heredia. Black and white, 90 minutes.

Cet obscur objet du désir. 1977. Producer: Greenwich Films, Les Films Galaxie, Incine (Serge Silberman, France/Spain); director: Luis Buñuel; screenplay: Luis Buñuel and Jean-Claude Carrière, based on the novel *La Femme et le pantin* by Pierre Louÿs; photography: Edmond Richard; editors: Luis Buñuel and Hélène Plemiannikov; talent: Fernando Rey, Angela Molina, Carole Bouquet, Julien Bertheau. Color, 103 minutes.

Le charme discret de la bourgeoisie. 1972. Producer: Greenwich Productions (Serge Silberman, France); director: Luis Buñuel; screenplay: Luis Buñuel and Jean-Claude Carrière; photography: Edmond Richard; editor: Hélène Plemiannikov; talent: Fernando Rey, Delphine Seyrig, Michel Piccoli, Jean-Pierre Cassel. Color (Eastman color), 100 minutes.

Un chien andalou. 1928–1929. Producer: Luis Buñuel (France); director: Luis Buñuel; screenplay: Buñuel and Salvador Dalí; photography: Albert Duverger; editor: Buñuel; talent: Pierre Batcheff, Simone Mareuil, Salvador Dalí, Luis Buñuel, Xaume Miratvilles. Black and white, 17 minutes.

The Criminal Life of Archibaldo de la Cruz. See *Ensayo de un crimen.*

Daughter of Deceit. See *La hija del engaño.*

Death and the River. See *El río y la muerte.*

Death in the Garden. See *La mort en ce jardin.*

The Devil and the Flesh. See *Susana.*

Diary of a Chambermaid. See *Le journal d'une femme de chambre.*

The Discreet Charm of the Bourgeoisie. See *La charme discret de la bourgeoisie.*

Don Quintín, el amargao. 1935. Producer: Filmófono (Ricardo Urgoiti and Luis

Buñuel, Spain); director: Luis Marquina; screenplay: Eduardo Ugarte and Luis Buñuel, based on the play by Carlos Arniches; photography: José María Beltrán; editors: Buñuel and Eduardo Maroto; talent: Alfonso Muñoz, Ana María Custodio, Porfiria Sanchíz, Luis de Heredia. Black and white, 85 minutes.

Él. 1952. Producer: Nacional Films (Óscar Dancigers, Mexico); director: Luis Buñuel; screenplay: Luis Buñuel and Luis Alcoriza, based on the novel by Mercedes Pinto; photography: Gabriel Figueroa; editors: Carlos Savage and Alberto Valenzuela; talent: Arturo de Córdova, Delia Garcés, Luis Beristáin, Manuel Dondé. Black and white, 91 minutes. (Omni Films, LAVA)

Ensayo de un crimen. 1955. Producer: Alianza Cinematográfica (Alfonso Patiño Gómez, Mexico); director: Luis Buñuel; screenplay: Luis Buñuel and Eduardo Ugarte, based on the novel by Rodolfo Usigli; photography: Agustín Jiménez; editor: Jorge Bustos; talent: Ernesto Alonso, Miroslava Stern, Ariadna Welter, Rita Macedo, Andrea Palma. Black and white, 91 minutes. (New Yorker Films, LAVA)

¡España leal en armas! 1937. Producer: Ciné-Liberté (Paris); supervision: Luis Buñuel; narration: Pierre Unik and Luis Buñuel; photography: Roman Karmen, Manuel Villegas López; editor: Jean Paul Dreyfus; narrator: Gaston Modot. Black and white, 40 minutes.

The Exterminating Angel. See *El angel exterminador.*

Le fantôme de la liberté. 1974. Producer: Greenwich Films, 20th Century Fox (Serge Silberman, France); director: Luis Buñuel; screenplay: Luis Buñuel and Jean-Claude Carrière; photography: Edmond Richard; editor: Hélène Plemiannikov; talent: Adriana Asti, Michel Piccoli, Monica Vitti, Michael Lonsdale. Color (Eastman color), 103 minutes.

Fever Mounts at El Pão. See *La fièvre monte à El Pao.*

La fièvre monte à El Pao. 1959. Producer: Groupe des Quatres, Filmex (Raymond Borderie, Mexico/France); director: Luis Buñuel; screenplay: Luis Buñuel, Luis Alcoriza, Charles Dorat, Louis Sapin, Henri Castillou, José L. González de León, based on the novel by Henri Castillou; photography: Gabriel Figueroa; editors: James Cuenet, Rafael López Ceballos; talent: María Félix, Gérard Phillipe, Jean Servais, Domingo Soler, Tito Junco. Black and white, 97 minutes.

The Golden Age. See *L'Age d'Or.*

The Great Madcap. See *El gran calavera.*

El gran calavera. 1949. Producer: Ultramar Films (Fernando Soler and Óscar Dancigers, Mexico); director: Luis Buñuel; screenplay: Luis Alcoriza and Raquel Rojas, based on the play by Adolfo Torrado; photography: Ezequiel Carrasco; editor: Carlos Savage; talent: Fernando Soler, Rosario Granados, Ruben Rojo, Andrés Soler. Black and white, 90 minutes. (KINO, LAVA)

Gran Casino. 1946. Producer: Ultramar Films, Películas Anáhuac (Óscar Dancigers, Mexico); director: Luis Buñuel; screenplay: Mauricio Magdaleno, Edmundo Báez, based on the novel by Michel Weber; photography: Jack Draper; editor: Gloria Schoemann; talent: Libertad Lamarque, Jorge Negrete,

Mercedes Barba, Charles Rooner, Trío Calaveras. Black and white, 85 minutes. (LAVA)

La hija del engaño. 1951. Producer: Ultramar Films (Óscar Dancigers, Mexico); director: Luis Buñuel; screenplay: Raquel Rojas, Luis Alcoriza, based on the play *Don Quintín, el amargao* by Carlos Arniches; photography: José Ortiz Ramos; editor: Carlos Savage; talent: Fernando Soler, Alicia Caro, Rubén Rojo, Lili Aclemar, Fernando Soto "Mantequilla." Black and white, 80 minutes. (LAVA)

Las Hurdes. 1932. Producer: Ramón Acín (Spain); director: Luis Buñuel; photography: Eli Lotar; editor: Buñuel; narration: Buñuel and Pierre Unik. Black and white, 27 minutes.

La ilusión viaja en tranvía. 1953. Producer: CLASA Films (Armando Oribe Alba, Mexico); director: Luis Buñuel; screenplay: Luis Buñuel, Luis Alcoriza, José Revueltas, Mauricio de la Serna, based on a story by Mauricio de la Serna; photography: Raúl Martínez Solares; editor: Jorge Bustos; talent: Lilia Prado, Carlos Navarro, Fernando Soto "Mantequilla," Agustín Isunza. Black and white, 82 minutes. (Connaisseur, LAVA)

Illusion Travels by Streetcar. See *La ilusión viaja en tranvía.*

In Old Tampico. See *Gran Casino.*

Le journal d'une femme de chambre. 1964. Producer: Speva Films, Cine Alliance, Filmsonor, Dear Film Produzione (Serge Silberman and Michel Safra, France/Italy); director: Luis Buñuel; screenplay: Luis Buñuel and Jean-Claude Carrièrre, based on the novel by Octave Mirbeau; photography: Roger Fellous; editor: Louissette Hautecoeur; talent: Jeanne Moreau, Michel Piccoli, George Géret, Françoise Lugagne. Black and white, 98 minutes.

Land Without Bread. See *Las Hurdes.*

Mexican Bus Ride. See *Subida al cielo.*

The Milky Way. See *La voie lactée.*

La mort en ce jardin. 1956. Producer: Producciones Tepeyac and Dismage (Óscar Dancigers and David Mage, Mexico/France); director: Luis Buñuel; screenplay: Luis Buñuel, Luis Alcoriza, and Raymond Queneau, based on the novel by José-André Lacour; photography: Jorge Stahl, Jr.; editor: Marguerite Renoir; talent: Georges Marchal, Simone Signoret, Charles Vanel, Michel Piccoli. Color (Eastman color), 97 minutes.

Una mujer sin amor. 1951. Producer: Internacional Cinematográfica (Sergio Kogan and Óscar Dancigers, Mexico); director: Luis Buñuel; screenplay: Jaime Salvador, based on the novel *Pierre et Jean* by Guy de Maupassant; photography: Raúl Martínez Solares; editor: Jorge Bustos; talent: Rosario Granados; Tito Junco; Julio Villarreal, Joaquín Cordero, Xavier Loyá. Black and white, 90 minutes. (Connaisseur, Kino, LAVA)

Nazarín. 1958. Producer: Manuel Barbachano Ponce (Mexico); director: Luis Buñuel; screenplay: Luis Buñuel, Julio Alejandro, and Emilio Carballido, based on the novel by Benito Pérez Galdós; photography: Gabriel Figueroa; editor: Carlos Savage; talent: Francisco Rabal, Marga López, Rita Macedo,

Ignacio López Tarso, Jesús Fernández, Luis Aceves Castañeda. Black and white, 97 minutes.

Los olvidados. 1950. Producer: Ultramar Films (Óscar Dancigers, Mexico); director: Luis Buñuel; screenplay: Luis Buñuel and Luis Alcoriza; photography: Gabriel Figueroa; editor: Carlos Savage; talent: Stella Inda, Alfonso Mejía, Roberto Cobo, Miguel Inclán, Alma Delia Fuentes. Black and white, 88 minutes. (LAVA)

¿Quién me quiere a mí? 1936. Producer: Filmófono (Ricardo Urgoiti and Luis Buñuel, Spain); director: José Luis Sáenz de Heredia; screenplay: Eduardo Ugarte, Enrique Horta, and Luis Buñuel; photography: José María Beltrán; editor: Luis Buñuel; talent: Lina Yegros, Mari-Tere, José Baviera. Black and white, 80 minutes.

El río y la muerte. 1954. Producer: Clasa Films (Armando Oribe Alba, Mexico); director: Luis Buñuel; screenplay: Luis Buñuel and Luis Alcoriza, based on the novel *Muro blanco sobre roca negra* by Miguel Álvarez Acosta; photography: Raúl Martínez Solares; editor: Jorge Bustos; talent: Columba Domínguez, Joaquín Cordero, Miguel Torruco. Black and white, 93 minutes. (LAVA)

Sentinel Alert! See *¡Centinela alerta!*

Simón del desierto. 1965. Producer: Gustavo Alatriste (Mexico); director: Luis Buñuel; screenplay: Luis Buñuel and Julio Alejandro; photography: Gabriel Figueroa; editor: Carlos Savage, Jr.; talent: Silvia Pinal, Claudio Brook, Luis Aceves Castañeda, Jesús Fernández. Black and white, 42 minutes.

Simon of the Desert. See *Simón del desierto.*

Subida al cielo. 1951. Producer: Isla Films (Manuel Altolaguirre and María Gómez Mena, Mexico); director: Luis Buñuel; screenplay: Luis Buñuel, Manuel Altolaguirre, and Juan de la Cabada; photography: Alex Phillips; editor: Rafael Portillo; talent: Lilia Prado, Esteban Márquez, Luis Aceves Castañeda; Manuel Dondé, Carmen González. Black and white, 85 minutes. (LAVA)

Susana. 1951. Producer: Internacional Cinematográfica (Sergio Kogan and Manuel Reachi, Mexico); director: Luis Buñuel; screenplay: Luis Buñuel, Jaime Salvador, and Rodolfo Usigli, based on a story by Manuel Reachi; photography: José Ortiz Ramos; editor: Jorge Bustos; talent: Rosita Quintana, Fernando Soler, Víctor Manuel Mendoza, Luis López Somoza, Matilde Palau. Black and white, 80 minutes. (Connaisseur Video, LAVA)

That Is Called Dawn. See *Cela s'appelle l'Aurore.*

This Strange Passion. See *Él.*

Tristana. 1970. Producer: Epoca Films, S.A., Taliá, S.A., Films Corona, Selenia Cinematográfica (Spain/France/Italy); director: Luis Buñuel; screenplay: Luis Buñuel and Jean-Claude Carrière, based on the novel by Benito Pérez Galdós; photography: José Aguayo; editor: Pedro del Rey; talent: Catherine Deneuve, Fernando Rey, Franco Nero, Lola Gaos, Jesús Fernández. Color (Eastman color), 100 minutes.

Viridiana. 1961. Producer: UNINCI, S.A., and Films 59 (Gustavo Alatriste,

Spain); director: Luis Buñuel; screenplay: Luis Buñuel and Julio Alejandro; photography: José F. Aguayo; editor: Pedro del Rey; talent: Silvia Pinal, Fernando Rey, Francisco Rabal, Margarita Lozano, Lola Gaos. Black and white, 90 minutes.

La voie lactée. 1969. Producer: Greenwich Films and Fraia Films (Serge Silberman, France/Italy); director: Luis Buñuel; screenplay: Luis Buñuel and Jean-Claude Carrière; photography: Christian Matras; editor: Louissette Hautecouer; talent: Paul Frankeur; Lauren Terzieff, Alain Cuny, Michel Piccoli, Pierre Clementi, Delphine Seyrig. Color (Eastman color), 98 minutes.

Who's in Love with Me? See *¿Quién me quiere a mi?*

A Woman Without Love. See *Una mujer sin amor.*

The Young and the Damned. See *Los olvidados.*

The Young One. 1960. Producer: Producciones Olmec and George P. Werker (Mexico/USA); director: Luis Buñuel; screenplay: Luis Buñuel and Hugo Butler, based on the novel *Travellin' Man* by Peter Mathieson; photography: Gabriel Figueroa; editor: Carlos Savage; talent: Zachary Scott, Bernie Hamilton, Kay Meersman, Claudio Brook. Black and white, 95 minutes.

Notes

INTRODUCTION

1. Williams, *Figures of Desire*, 151 (my emphasis).
2. Higginbotham, *Luis Buñuel*, 63.
3. Buñuel, de la Colina, and Perez Turrent, *Conversations avec Luis Buñuel*, 62–67.
4. See King, *Magical Reels;* Armes, *Third World Filmmaking and the West;* and Pick, *The New Latin American Cinema.*
5. Bazin, *The Cinema of Cruelty*, 51–58.
6. In *André Bazin*, Dudley Andrew sheds some light on the personal relationship between the artist and the critic, suggesting that, when writing screenplays, Buñuel even thought about what Bazin would think about the completed films (213–14).
7. Perhaps the definitive classification of Mexican film genres is Carlos Monsiváis's essay, "Mythologies" (quote is from p. 118).
8. See Monsiváis, "Mythologies"; see also Monsiváis, "Mexican Cinema"; López, "Tears and Desire"; and Martín-Barbero, *Communication, Culture, and Hegemony*, 112–68.
9. Interestingly, it is in non-U.S. sources that some critical interest has recently been given to Buñuel's Mexican period. Besides Lillo's book, published in France in 1993, other recent works are Cañizal, *Um jato na contramão;* and Fuentes, *Buñuel en México.*
10. Evans, *The Films of Luis Buñuel.* Evans's approach to *Los olvidados,* for example, is comparable to Jean Franco's, who also covers the themes of Oedipality and motherhood in her book, *Plotting Women.*
11. Berg, *Cinema of Solitude*, 121–25.
12. A classic example of this is Michael Wood's essay, "Buñuel in Mexico," in which Wood deliberately ignores context and dismisses most of the Mexican movies in favor of the usual auteurist perspective. Wood writes that the "lesser" movies "almost all have *flickers of interest, flashes of Buñuel's cinematic signature*" (42, my emphasis). As is the case with most Buñuel scholar-

ship, from Freddy Bauche to Fernando Césarman, from Gwynne Edwards to Paul Sandro, from Virginia Higginbotham to Linda Williams, for Wood the idea of accepting these movies as "Mexican" seems unimaginable. Critics make these movies fit the category of "Buñuelian," in spite of their signs of "Mexicanness."

13. Mayne, *Directed By Dorothy Arzner*.

CHAPTER 1: MEXICAN CINEMA IN THE TIME OF LUIS BUÑUEL

1. López, "Celluloid Tears," 32.
2. In Mexican Film Studies the family melodrama is often thought of in terms of its allegorical structure. The familial setting stands in as a metaphorical rendition of the patriarchal state's relationship to the Mexican people, where even in the midst of difficulty "the father" is always right and able to defend his children and dependents (see Ayala Blanco, *Aventura del cine mexicano*).
3. "Ley de la Industria Cinematográfica" (1941, amended 1947, 1949), reprinted in its entirety in García Riera, *Historia documental del cine mexicano*, 4:11. In 1952 Cantinflas was censored by the Mexican Congress for his versions of *Romeo and Juliet* and *The Three Musketeers*, thought to compromise the image of quality that Mexican cinema was expected to project internationally. In fact, a senator named Lauro Caloca said he was "embarrassed" by the popularity of Cantinflas in Europe (Ibid., 4:15).
4. Several versions of the "film industry law" (Ley de la Industria Cinematográfica), in 1941, 1947, and 1949, were imposed during the tenures of Presidents Ávila Camacho (1940–46) and Alemán (1946–52) (see García Riera, *Historia documental del cine mexicano*, 4:11–15).
5. See Mora, *Mexican Cinema*; Ayala Blanco, *Aventura del cine mexicano*; Sánchez, *Crónica antisoleme del cine mexicano*; and García Riera, *Historia documental del cine mexicano*. More recent works on specific topics include Hershfield, *Mexican Cinema/Mexican Woman*; and Ramírez Berg, *Cinema of Solitude*.
6. Hayward, *French National Cinema*. Hayward credits Benedict Anderson's *Imagined Communities* and Homi Bhabha's *Nation and Narration* for the main theoretical framework of her "national cinema" model (5).
7. Hayward, *French National Cinema*, 5.
8. Ibid., 6 (emphasis in original).
9. Ibid., 8–16.
10. Ibid., 15.
11. Anderson, *Imagined Communities*, 192–206.
12. Ibid., 163–64.
13. For example, anthropologist Néstor García Canclini has analyzed the organization of the National Museum of Anthropology. He argues that the exhibit displays and the architectural design of the museum's buildings are intended to "centralize" the Mexicas and Aztecs, who resided in the Valley of Mexico, where the Mexican capital is located today. The design, says García

Canclini, emphasizes "the triumph of the centralist project," that is, the revolution's nationalist agenda (see García Canclini, *Hybrid Cultures,* 118–23).

14. García Canclini, *Hybrid Cultures,* 118.

15. I should clarify here that the "institutionalization" and diffusion of cultural products was, in fact, a governmental initiative. The "Ley Cinematográfica" that regulated production, exhibition, and the content of motion pictures was meant to ensure national cinema's participation in the cultural project (see García Canclini, *Hybrid Cultures,* 117; García Riera, *Historia documental del cine mexicano,* 4:11).

16. García Canclini, *Hybrid Cultures,* 117.

17. For more on the ideological debt of the Mexican Revolution to the independence movement, see Florescano, *Memoria mexicana,* 462–522.

18. See Hayes, "Touching the Sentiments of Everyone," for an analysis of radio broadcasting and nationalism in Mexico in the 1930s.

19. O'Malley, *The Myth of the Revolution,* 3.

20. Ibid., 113–14.

21. See Joseph and Nugent, "Popular Culture and State Formation in Revolutionary Mexico."

22. Ibid., 4–5.

23. Martín-Barbero, *Communication, Culture, and Hegemony,* 155–56.

24. Hayes, "Touching the Sentiments of Everyone," 411.

25. Martín-Barbero, *Communication, Culture, and Hegemony,* 166.

26. Vaughan, *Cultural Politics in Revolution.* Vaughan writes: "Since 1921, when José Vasconcelos as the first minister of education had launched the cultural nationalist movement, the SEP had championed the aesthetics of Mexican culture. The mural movement redefined the Mexican as Indian, brown, mestizo, mulatto. . . . This coloring of the Mexican took hold as the state-building phase of the revolution progressed in the 1920s and 1930s" (44–46).

27. Knight, "Popular Culture and the Revolutionary State in Mexico."

28. Ley de la Industria Cinematográfica, Article 2, Section VIII, reproduced in García Riera, *Historia documental del Cine Mexican,* 4:11 (my translation).

29. See Alberto Isaac's interviews with Gabriel Figueroa in Figueroa and Isaac, *Conversaciones con Gabriel Figueroa,* 107–10.

30. Vaughan, *Cultural Politics in Revolution,* 46.

31. Ibid., 19.

32. Ibid., 20.

33. Martín-Barbero, *Communication, Culture, and Hegemony,* 166.

34. See Wolfe, *The Fabulous Life of Diego Rivera,* 345. Wolfe quotes the painter's own words in describing this particular mural so prominently featured in Emilio Fernández's last great epic. According to Wolfe, Rivera said that it was "the only plastic poem I know which embodies the whole history of a people." Describing the mural, Wolfe writes: "For all its propagandistic and legendary distortion and fantasy, it is the most ample, complete and wide ranging plastic expression and portrait ever done of Mexico, or indeed, of any country by any painter. Only a giant of physical strength, plastic fecundity, large talent, auda-

cious imagination, and limitless ambition would ever have undertaken to capture thus on three giant walls the entire history of his country. In a riot of color and a marvel of organization, what lives on the stairway walls, is not a painting but a world, full of life of its own, intellectually, emotionally, plastically" (345–46). It is also relevant that Rivera's first "epic" murals were painted in the Ministry of Education building starting in 1923 (p. 167). It is most interesting to note the correspondence between the content of the mural, as described by Wolfe, its significant, if admittedly false, condensation of Mexican history, and its temporal concurrence with the mythologizing of the Mexican revolution. Furthermore, in Wolfe's judgment, the men of the cultural establishment seem to have been clearly absorbed into the historical myth, as if they were part of the "historical continuum" of the Revolution. Wolfe describes Rivera's work with clearly virile, even phallic adjectives and nouns: "giant," "strong," "fecund," "large," and "ambitious," all of which are consistent with the "machismo" that informs the myth of the Revolution and the revolutionary hero (see O'Malley, *The Myth of the Revolution*).

35. Vaughan, *Cultural Politics in Revolution*, 11.

36. Fernández drew comparisons between his work and that of the muralists in numerous interviews and writings (see García Riera's critical biography, *Emilio Fernández*, 45–62).

37. Knight, "Popular Culture and the Revolutionary State in Mexico," 419–35.

38. Vaughan, *Cultural Politics in Revolution*, 163–88.

39. García Canclini, *Hybrid Cultures*, 52.

40. Vaughan, *Cultural Politics in Revolution*, 49–54.

41. The classic examples are, of course, Fernando de Fuentes's *El compadre Mendoza* (1933), *Vámonos con Pancho Villa* (1935), and *Allá en el Rancho Grande* (1936).

42. Some of these include the previously cited works by García Canclini *(Hybrid Cultures)*, Vaughan *(Cultural Politics in Revolution)*, and Knight ("Popular Culture and the Revolutionary State in Mexico"), as well as recent works by historians Adolfo Gilly *(El cardenismo)* and Felícitas López-Portillo Tostado *(Estado e ideología empresarial en el gobierno alemanista)*.

43. One of the key readings on this topic is the groundbreaking essay by Daniel Cosío Villegas, "La crisis de México."

44. Bhabha, *Nation and Narration*, 1.

45. Sommer, "Irresistible Romance."

46. See Gilly, *El cardenismo*, 189–219.

47. See Monsiváis, "Mexican Cinema." See also Sánchez, *Crónica antisolemne del cine mexicano*, 35–48.

48. Carl J. Mora told me that after shooting in Mexico Eisenstein was detained by U.S. immigration authorities in Texas. He returned to the USSR, leaving his footage behind. The footage ended up in Hollywood, where it was used in other films. Upton Sinclair eventually turned over the footage to the Museum of Modern Art, which made it available to Grigori Alexandrov and

Edward Tissé. Alexandrov and Tissé eventually edited a version of the film, based on Eisenstein's notes, which was released in 1979.

49. García Riera, *Emilio Fernández*, 15, 12–17.

50. The links between the Bolshevik and the Mexican revolutions were many at this time, and of course, Eisenstein was a sort of linking figure (see Karetnikova and Steinmentz, *Mexico According to Eisenstein*, 3–32).

51. World War II had inevitably affected the flow of films between European nations and Latin America. Mexico joined the allied forces in 1942, which is the reason why it was not until after the end of the war that Fernández's films, released in Mexico in 1943, were finally seen in Europe.

52. I base my time frame of the "classical era" of Mexican cinema on the work of Mexican film historians Carl J. Mora *(Mexican Cinema)*, Jorge Ayala Blanco *(Aventura del cine mexicano)*, and Francisco Sánchez *(Crónica antisolemne del cine mexicano)*.

53. Sánchez, *Crónica antisolemne del cine mexicano*, 43–44 (my translation).

54. Ayala Blanco, *Aventura del cine mexicano*, 193–94 (my translation).

55. An informative review of this debate appears in the erudite Cátedra edition of Octavio Paz's *El laberinto de la soledad* (18–65). The preliminary study, notes, and edition of the text is by noted Paz scholar Enrico Mario Santí.

56. Paradoxically, *María Candelaria* raised some controversy upon its initial release precisely because it focused on an indigenist theme. The movie was boycotted by a theater owner and was premiered in a theater rented by the producer, but critical acclaim soon opened the doors for wider distribution (see Mora, *Mexican Cinema*, 66).

57. The identity crisis of Mexican society, according to Octavio Paz, is partly organized around rituals of violence and public displays of manly behavior, consistent with the revolutionary hero as seen in the classic films of Fernando de Fuentes and Emilio Fernández. In *El laberinto de la soledad* and from a psychoanalytic perspective, Octavio Paz analyzes the trauma of the "rape" of Mexico by the Spanish conquerors and turns it into an interpretation of Mexican national identity. Paz describes the character of Mexican men as solitary, violent, and traumatized. According to Paz's interpretation, Mexican men live in constant denial of the possibility of "splitting open," or "cracking" *(rajarse)*, of "opening" to anyone in a passive (that is, feminine) attitude, as was the case with the Indian women whose sexual encounters with the Spaniards triggered the demise of the Aztec Empire.

58. See Berg, *A Cinema of Solitude*.

59. Buñuel said that he told his friends, "Should I suddenly drop out of sight one day, I might be anywhere—except there" (Buñuel, *My Last Sigh*, 197).

CHAPTER 2: BUÑUEL AND MEXICO

1. Bazin, *The Cinema of Cruelty*, 52.
2. Mahieu, "El período mexicano de Luis Buñuel."
3. I am referring here to *Le journal d'une femme de chambre* from the novel

by Octave Mirbeau; *Belle de jour* from the novel by Joseph Kessel; *Tristana*, his second adaptation of a minor work by Benito Pérez-Galdós; and even *Cet obscur objet du désir*, based on, and surprisingly faithful to, Pierre Louÿs's *La femme et le pantin*. Most of these are based on turn-of-the-century melodramatic literature.

4. Buñuel, *My Last Sigh*, 30.
5. Ibid., 58–59.
6. See González Dueñas, *Luis Buñuel*, 106; and Buñuel, *My Last Sigh*, 75–77, 87.
7. See Gómez Mesa, "La generación cinematográfica del '27," 54.
8. See Fuentes, *Buñuel*, 9–28.
9. Gómez Mesa, "La generación cinematográfica del '27," 52–58.
10. Buñuel, *My Last Sigh*, 57, 77.
11. Ibid., 88.
12. Ibid., 89.
13. Buñuel, de la Colina, and Pérez Turrent, *Conversations avec Luis Buñuel*, 27–29; Buñuel, *My Last Sigh*, 89–91.
14. See Kyrou, *Luis Bunuel*, 107–9.
15. Buñuel, *My Last Sigh*, 91. See also Avrich, *Sacco and Vanzetti*. The episode is also retold in John Baxter's biography (*Buñuel*, 61–62).
16. Kyrou, *Luis Bunuel*, 9–10. See also Buñuel, *My Last Sigh*, 105–7; Tesson, *Luis Buñuel*, 13–16.
17. Buñuel, *My Last Sigh*, 107.
18. Tesson, *Luis Buñuel*, 13 (my translation of "Buñuel n'a pas fait du cinéma pour être surréaliste mais il a été surréaliste pour faire du cinéma").
19. See Williams, *Figures of Desire*, 106–10.
20. Buñuel, *My Last Sigh*, 122–24; Buñuel, de la Colina, and Pérez Turrent, *Conversations avec Luis Buñuel*, 50–51.
21. Williams, *Figures of Desire*, 112–50.
22. Buñuel, *My Last Sigh*, 117, 139–40.
23. Ibid., 131. John Baxter, in his *Buñuel*, has some doubts about the identity of the director described in this anecdote, but the spirit of the story, whether it describes Von Sternberg or not, is the same.
24. Buñuel's system for deciphering the workings of Hollywood melodrama, its predictability, and its faithfulness to formula, are mentioned in *My Last Sigh* (131–33); the memoir also shows Buñuel's deep familiarity with the genre in literature, theater, and cinema.
25. Buñuel, *My Last Sigh*, 123.
26. Buñuel, de la Colina, and Pérez Turrent, *Conversations avec Luis Buñuel*, 50–51.
27. Rotellar, "Luis Buñuel en Filmófono."
28. Buñuel's *Las Hurdes* was immediately banned after its private première in Madrid in 1932, and his work remained prohibited under strict censorship laws until the 1960s (see Higginbotham, *Spanish Film under Franco*, 7–18).

29. Rotellar, "Luis Buñuel en Filmófono," 37.

30. Ibid., 39.

31. Ibid., 38.

32. Arniches was one of the most popular of Spanish authors when it came to film adaptations, and Buñuel made one of his most famous plays, *Don Quintín, el amargao*, twice in fifteen years (see Higginbotham, *Spanish Film under Franco*, 1–6; see also Kinder, *Blood Cinema*, 292–300).

33. Ávila Dueñas, *El cine mexicano de Luis Buñuel*, 83.

34. See Rucar de Buñuel and Martín del Campo, *Memorias de una mujer sin piano*. Recently published, Rucar de Buñuel's memoir presents a rather human account of the life of Luis Buñuel. The book's contribution is that it shows a side of Buñuel that seems incompatible with his public persona. From Buñuel's abusive, dictatorial ways of running the household, to the arbitrary curfews imposed on his teenaged sons, to his intransigent opposition to his wife's pursuit of any kind of personal career (he made her give up teaching gymnastics because the clothing made her show her legs; he sold her piano for three bottles of champagne), the Luis Buñuel portrayed in *Memorias de una mujer sin piano* is a conservative, if benevolent tyrant, often insanely jealous, who kept his wife and kids locked up and subdued at home (49–78).

35. See Kinder, *Blood Cinema*, 298–99.

36. Manuel Rotellar insists that from early in his career Buñuel wanted to be more accessible, that he abhorred the surrealists' contempt for "common people," and that he wanted to find a larger audience: "[Buñuel] had received offers in France to make commercial films after *L'Age d'Or*, but had refused them because he did not like the stories. [At Filmófono] he had the opportunity to improve the level of production in Spain, and to reach a popular audience, although he feared that his name in the credits would be a risk for the films' popular success" ("Luis Buñuel en Filmófono," 39).

37. Indeed, we know that in 1930 Buñuel had been in trouble with the "hard-liners" of the surrealist movement, for "selling" the screenplay of *Un chien andalou* for publication in *La Revue du Cinéma*. Furthermore, by 1933–34 the exhibitionism of Dalí, Breton, and Eluard, and the snobbish character of *Minotaure*, had all contributed to alienating Buñuel from surrealism as a "movement" (see Buñuel, de la Colina, and Perez Turrent, *Conversations avec Luis Buñuel*, 34, 51).

38. Buñuel, *My Last Sigh*, 138–39.

39. Buñuel, de la Colina, and Perez Turrent, *Conversations avec Luis Buñuel*, 57.

40. See Aranda, *Luis Buñuel*, 118–22.

41. See Rucar de Buñuel and Martín del Campo, *Memorias de una mujer sin piano*, 63–64 (my translation).

42. Buñuel, de la Colina, and Perez Turrent, *Conversations avec Luis Buñuel*, 57.

43. Higginbotham, *Luis Buñuel*, 57; Aranda, *Luis Buñuel*, 122; Buñuel, *My Last Sigh*, 178.

44. See Higginbotham, *Luis Buñuel*, 59–60; see also Mahieu, "El período mexicano de Luis Buñuel," 2–3.

45. Buñuel, *Mon dernier soupir*, 160–61.

46. Buñuel claims credit for the first abridged American version of Leni Riefenstahl's *Triumph of the Will* (see Buñuel, de la Colina, and Perez Turrent, *Conversations avec Luis Buñuel*, 58–59; and Buñuel, *Mon dernier soupir*, 220–22). I subsequently refer to both the original French and to the standard U.S. editions of this work. The English edition tends to simplify, edit, or misinterpret anecdotes; it is, however, useful for some quotations, and I will rely on it when it seems appropriate.

47. Fuentes, *Buñuel*, 58–59.

48. Higginbotham, *Spanish Film under Franco*, 1–6.

49. See Mora, *Mexican Cinema*, 52–74. See also Fox, "The New Border Establishing Shots," 166–207; and Monsiváis, "Mexican Cinema," 141. See also Figueroa and Isaac, *Conversaciones con Gabriel Figueroa*, 24–25.

50. Samples of Buñuel criticism are reprinted in Kyrou, *Luis Bunuel*, 89–93; and Aranda, *Luis Buñuel* 265–75. See also Buñuel, *An Unspeakable Betrayal*.

51. See Buñuel, de la Colina, and Perez Turrent, *Conversations avec Luis Buñuel*, 52.

52. Buñuel, *Mon dernier soupir*, 244 (my translation).

53. Buñuel, *My Last Sigh*, 107.

54. Mora, *Mexican Cinema*, 75.

55. Mexico's most celebrated cultural critic, Carlos Monsiváis, writes:

> Although the star system, the cult of exceptional faces and personalities and the canonization of principal figures was a latecomer [in Mexico], the industry desired, from the beginning and without pretenses, to entertain, creating habits through the reiteration of types of behavior: "Let's give the audience what it wants because, in the end, it always wants the same thing. . . ." During the "Golden Age ". . . the public trusted that its idols would explain how to survive in a bewildering age of modernization." (quoted in Paranaguá, *Mexican Cinema*, 117)

56. García Riera, *Historia documental del cine mexicano* (4:98–101).

57. Mora, *Mexican Cinema*, 83. See also Hershfield, *Mexican Cinema/Mexican Woman*, 77–105.

58. See Ayala Blanco, *Aventura del cine mexicano*.

59. Hershfield, *Mexican Cinema/Mexican Woman*, 77–105.

60. The article is reprinted in its entirety in García Riera, *Historia documental del cine mexicano*, 3:90–91; the translation is my own.

61. García Riera, *Emilio Fernández*, 36–37.

62. Ibid.

63. Buñuel, de la Colina, and Pérez Turrent, *Conversations avec Luis Buñuel*, 63–65.

64. García Riera, *Historia Documental del cine mexicano*, 3:163.

65. Buñuel, de la Colina, and Pérez Turrent, *Conversations avec Luis Buñuel*, 64 (my translation).
66. See Dudley Andrew's analysis in *Mists of Regret*, 43–50.
67. García Riera, *Historia Documental del cine mexicano*, 3:163.
68. Buñuel, *My Last Sigh*, 202.
69. Ibid., 198–99; Buñuel, de la Colina, and Pérez Turrent, *Conversations avec Luis Buñuel*, 63–64.
70. García Riera, *Historia documental del cine mexicano*, 4:68–69.
71. Lillo, *Género y transgresión*, 63, 66 (my translation).
72. D'Amico, *Historia del teatro dramático*.
73. Lillo, *Género y transgresión*, 63.

CHAPTER 3: 'LOS OLVIDADOS' AND THE CRISIS OF MEXICAN CINEMA

1. See Buñuel, de La Colina, and Pérez Turrent, *Conversations avec Luis Buñuel*, 68–78. Buñuel recounts how even the film's producer, Óscar Dancingers, and members of the crew were worried about the amount of "filth" in the film and that it was "blackening" the image of Mexico. See also Buñuel, *My Last Sigh*, 200–202.
2. This scenario would be repeated often during Buñuel's career in Mexico. Films like *Subida al cielo*, *Nazarín*, and even *Viridiana* and Emilio Fernández's *María Candelaria* would have to go through the festival circuits before Mexican recognition.
3. Publicity materials, Centro de Investigación y Enseñanza Cinematográficas, University of Guadalajara.
4. Cosío Villegas, "La crisis de México."
5. Ibid., 29 (my translation).
6. Mary Kay Vaughan, *Cultural Politics in Revolution*.
7. Cosío Villegas, "La crisis de México," 34 (my translation).
8. López-Portillo Tostado, *Estado e ideología empresarial en el gobierno alemanista*, 13 (all subsequent translations from López-Portillo's book are my own).
9. Ibid., 25.
10. Ibid., 64.
11. Ibid., 68–69.
12. Claire F. Fox also brings up the term *neoporfiriato*, coined by Cosío Villegas to refer to the era's "modernization and authoritarianism" and its influence in some cinema of the period (see Fox, *The Fence and the River*, 99–100).
13. López-Portillo Tostado, *Estado e ideología empresarial en el gobierno alemanista*, 128–29. See also Torres Ramírez, *Historia de la revolución mexicana*; Taracena, *La vida en México bajo Miguel Alemán*; Hansen, *La política del desarrollo mexicano*.
14. Hansen, *La política del desarrollo mexicano*, 90.
15. López-Portillo Tostado, *Estado e ideología empresarial en el gobierno*

alemanista, 139–40. See also Enrico Mario Santí's preliminary study in his Introduction to *El laberinto de la soledad*, 65–75.

16. Santí, Introduction to *El laberinto de la soledad*, 13 (this, and all subsequent translations from *El Laberinto de la soledad* are my own). On Octavio Paz and his significance in Mexican intellectual life, see Camp, *Intellectuals and the State in Twentieth Century Mexico*.

17. Santí, Introduction to *El laberinto de la soledad*, 14.

18. Ibid., 19–21.

19. Ibid., 26.

20. Williams, *Figures of Desire*, 3–52. Williams explains the origins of surrealist theories about images, the surrealists interest in dreams, and the importance of dreams in the early works of Freud, particularly his *The Interpretation of Dreams*.

21. Santí, Introduction to *El laberinto de la soledad*, 32.

22. André Bazin's first review of *Los olvidados* was originally published in *Esprit* in 1951; quote is from the translated article, reprinted in Bazin, *The Cinema of Cruelty* (55, 57). The Buñuel quote is from a 1954 interview, also in *The Cinema of Cruelty* (90).

23. Santí, Introduction to *El laberinto de la soledad*, 40.

24. Ibid., 100.

25. Ibid., 102–3 (emphasis in original); see also Clifford, *The Predicament of Culture*, 145.

26. Andrew, *Mists of Regret*, 45–46.

27. Octavio Paz, letter to Alfonso Reyes, 23 July 1949, cited in Santí, Introduction to *El laberinto de la soledad*, 44–45.

28. Santí, Introduction to *El laberinto de la soledad*, 46.

29. Ibid., 96.

30. Remember the ubiquitous skeleton of a high-rise building under construction, that foolproof sign of modernization which dominates the background of the scenes depicting the deaths of Julián and Jaibo; remember, as well, the Jaibo gang's attack on the blind man, don Carmelo.

31. I am borrowing this expression from López, "Celluloid Tears."

32. His "conventional" movies played with the practices of their generic roots while at the same time finding a middle ground, a mediation between parody and discipline, in order to dissect Mexican popular cinema and comment on Mexican political and social issues. However, all of the generic movies, with the exception of the transitional films *Gran Casino* and *El gran calavera*, were made after *Los olvidados*—after Buñuel's reputation had been restored and secured, and after he had been welcomed into the small clique of the Mexican film directors with international prestige in the festival circuits.

33. "*J'ai une profonde horreur des chapeaux mexicains. Je veux dire par là que je déteste le folklore officiel et organisé*" (Buñuel, *Mon dernier soupir*, 283–84 [emphasis in original]).

34. Buñuel, *My Last Sigh*, 133.

35. See Blanco Aguinaga, Rodríguez Puértolas, and Zavala, *Historia social de*

la literatura española, 1:264–73, 384–99. As much as Buñuel admired De Sica, he was admittedly far more interested in the Spanish picaresque novel, and he was an admirer of *Lazarillo de Tormes* (1554) and Francisco de Quevedo's *Historia de la vida del buscón* (1626). Buñuel's admiration for the Spanish picaresque novel was probably a narrative and structural influence in *Los olvidados*. When it came to the influence of Italian neorealism, Buñuel stated that it was, at best, negligible (see Buñuel, "Cinema as an Instrument of Poetry"). In any case, *Las Hurdes* is much more evidently a strong influence in *Los olvidados*, and that film, produced in Spain in 1932, predates neorealism by at least eleven years.

36. Recall producer Dancigers's concerns with "too much filth" (see Buñuel, de La Colina, and Pérez Turrent, *Conversations avec Luis Buñuel*).

37. Buñuel, de La Colina, and Pérez Turrent, *Conversations avec Luis Buñuel*, 68–71.

38. Buñuel, *Mon dernier soupir*, 283–84.

39. The connections of Buñuel with the Spanish picaresque are well documented in many scholarly works; see, for example, Fuentes, *Luis Buñuel*. I think it is relevant to point out that the Indian boy is literally a picaresque character, since the Spanish word for a blindman's guide is *lazarillo* and comes from the character of the same name, Lázaro de Tormes, of the original picaresque novel of 1554.

40. See Medina, *Historia de la revolución mexicana*, 231–81; see also Becker, *Setting the Virgin on Fire*, 61–76.

41. García Canclini, *Hybrid Cultures*, 52–53.

42. Rozado, *Cine y realidad social en México*.

43. Rozado, *Cine y realidad social en México*, 60–61 (my translation).

44. *Río Escondido* deals, in part, with a rural teacher's struggle to put in practice revolutionary politics while having to face a powerful local *caudillo*, a type of local strongman the Revolution unwillingly helped to keep in power. And *Pueblerina* beautifully tells the story of two poor, small-town Indians struggling for acceptance in a "Porfirian-thinking" town and also dealing with the difficulties of the power structure of the town boss.

45. See Galindo's *Campeón sin corona* (1945), *¡Esquina, bajan!* (1948), and *Espaldas mojadas* (1953–55).

46. The films of Galindo present their protagonists in a "modernization" dilemma (see *Campeón sin corona* and *Espaldas mojadas*), opposing "tradition," in the form of "Mexico," to the dangers of "modernization," coming primarily from the United States. Thus, in the films of Galindo, the moral predicament takes a Manichean–nationalistic shape.

47. Mora, *Mexican Cinema*, 57.

48. García Canclini, *Hybrid Cultures*, 52–53.

49. Jean Franco analyzes *Los olvidados* partly in the Mexican context. In her book, *Plotting Women*, Franco compares the film to other Mexican films (Emilio Fernández's *Enamorada*). Franco emphasizes the role of Pedro's mother to show how women characters, even when allowed a cohesive role in a collapsing soci-

ety, are denied narrative agency. Franco recognizes that the film takes a sensitive look at the contradictions of modernity within an Oedipal structure (153–59).

50. It is, however, José Clemente Orozco's murals that are known to have been more influential in Gabriel Figueroa's work. Of "the three muralists," David Alfaro Siqueiros was known to be openly opposed to government policies and was imprisoned during the presidency of Adolfo López Mateos.

51. Buñuel, de la Colina, and Pérez Turrent, *Conversations avec Luis Buñuel*, 76–78.

52. See Buñuel, "El cine, instrumento de poesía." See also Octavio Paz's original review of *Los olvidados,* "El poeta Buñuel," originally written in Cannes in April 1951.

53. Paz, "El Poeta Buñuel" (my translation).

54. Santí, Introduction to *El laberinto de la soledad,* 29.

55. André Bazin, *L'Observateur* (August 1952), quoted in Bazin, *The Cinema of Cruelty,* 59–60.

56. Andrew, *André Bazin,* 213–14. Buñuel's comments on criticism in *Mon dernier soupir* (274) are far from friendly: "*Je déteste le pédantisme et le jargon. Il m'est arrivé de rire aux larmes en lisant certains articles des Cahiers du Cinéma*" *(I hate pedantism and jargon. Sometimes I weep with laughter in reading certain articles in the Cahiers du Cinéma)* (emphasis in original; for my translation, I referred to the original French in order to keep the judgmental spirit of Buñuel's words).

57. In 1958, for example, the film *La cucaracha,* a "revolutionary epic" by Ismael Rodríguez, and starring a literal "Who's Who" of Mexican classical cinema (Dolores del Río, María Félix, and Emilio Fernández), was prepackaged and sent as the shoo-in "official" Mexican entry to the Cannes Film Festival. It was chosen over Buñuel's *Nazarín*. Due, in part, to John Huston's interest in the film, *Nazarín* was presented at Cannes (but not as a Mexican film), where it was given the first "International Critics Prize" in 1959. *La cucaracha,* the official Mexican entry, was ignored by the jurors.

58. Bazin, *The Cinema of Cruelty,* 59–60.

59. Vaughan, *Cultural Politics in Revolution,* 25.

60. Interview with Professor Eduardo de la Vega by the author, July 1996, Centro de Investigación y Enseñanza Cinematográfica, Universidad de Guadalajara.

CHAPTER 4: GENRE, WOMEN, NARRATIVE

1. See "Ley de la Industria Cinematográfica," in García Riera, *Historia documental del cine mexicano,* 4:11–15.
2. Hershfield, *Mexican Cinema/Mexican Woman,* 119–29.
3. López, "Tears and Desire," 156–57.
4. Ibid., 157.
5. Williams, " 'Something Else Besides a Mother.' "
6. Mora, *Mexican Cinema,* 57.

7. Williams, "Melodrama Revised," 42.
8. See their works in Gledhill, *Home Is Where The Heart Is*.
9. Martín-Barbero, *Communication, Culture, and Hegemony*, 116.
10. See Vardac, *From Stage to Screen*, 20–66; see also Altman, "Dickens, Griffith, and Film Theory Today."
11. Monsiváis, "Mythologies," 117.
12. López, "Tears and Desire," 147–63.
13. Ibid., 150–51.
14. See Sommer, "Irresistible Romance"; see also Sommer, *Foundational Fictions*.
15. Martín-Barbero, *Communication, Culture, and Hegemony*, 167.
16. Ibid., 166.
17. See Ávila-Dueñas, *El cine mexicano de Luis Buñuel*; Fuentes, *Buñuel en México*; Lillo, *Género y transgresión*.
18. Buñuel, *Mi último suspiro*, 202.
19. In his autobiography and in his *Conversations avec Luis Buñuel* (with José de la Colina and Tomas Pérez Turrent), Buñuel claimed that *Susana* had been misunderstood, that the ending was supposed to be "a joke," and that he wished he had been openly ironic about it.
20. López, "Tears and Desire," 151.
21. Martín-Barbero, *Communication, Culture, and Hegemony*, 119.
22. See, for example, Elsaesser, "Tales of Sound and Fury."
23. Martín-Barbero, *Communication, Culture, and Hegemony*, 165–71; Monsiváis, "Mythologies"; and Monsiváis, "Mexican Cinema."
24. The campaign advertisement for *Susana*, which I saw at the University of Guadalajara's Centro de Investigación y Enseñanza Cinematográfica, states that "in the life of every man there is a woman like Susana" and invites audiences to see "why naïve women like Susana are dangerous."
25. The Doña Bárbara character is adapted from the 1929 novel of the same name, written by the Venezuelan Rómulo Gallegos and considered to be one of the landmark novels of twentieth-century Latin American letters. The film's treatment of the character, nevertheless, corresponds to that of similar female characters in Mexican cinema, masculinized women who are ultimately chastised by either patriarchal institutions or, in this case, the patrimonial land itself.
26. López, "Tears and Desire," 153.
27. Williams, *Figures of Desire*, 103.
28. Robert Lachenay, *Cahiers du Cinéma*, no. 30 (1954), quoted in Ayala Blanco, *Aventura del cine mexicano*, 144. Lachenay is a pseudonym for François Truffaut and refers to Ninón Sevilla's performance in Alberto Gout's 1949 film, *Aventurera*.
29. By 1951 Buñuel was working mainly for Dáncigers, with the exception of *Susana*, which he directed for producer Sergio Kogan, specifically as a vehicle for the producer's wife, Rosita Quintana (see Ávila Dueñas, *El cine mexicano de Luis Buñuel*, 63).
30. López, "Tears and Desire," 159.

31. Monsiváis, *Mexican Postcards*, 31.

32. García Riera, *Historia documental del cine mexicano*, 7:309 (my translation). Actually, García Riera mistakenly states that Marta is leaning on an electric pole; she is, in fact, against the wall. But the design of the shot (a woman standing alone on a darkly lit street corner at night, apparently waiting for someone) does suggest a prostitute/customer scenario, especially when the husband drives by and the couple (now married) jokingly feign a street pickup scene.

33. Mora dates *Aventurera* to 1952, but Emilio García Riera, Jorge Ayala Blanco, and Francisco Sánchez all place the date as 1949 (see Sánchez, *Crónica antisolemne del cine mexicano*).

34. Franco, *Plotting Women*, 153–55.

35. Buñuel, de la Colina, and Pérez Turrent, *Conversations avec Luis Buñuel*, 76–77.

36. See Doane, "Pathos and the Maternal," 70–95.

37. Franco, *Plotting Women*, 153–55.

38. See Fregoso, *The Bronze Screen*, 16–17; see also Cypess, *La Malinche in Mexican Literature*.

39. See, for example, Todorov, *The Conquest of America*, 98–123; see also Thomas, *Conquest*.

40. Paz, *El laberinto de la soledad*, 217 (my translation).

41. Buñuel, de la Colina, and Pérez Turrent, *Conversations avec Luis Buñuel*, 91.

42. See, for example, Buñuel's comments on the film in *My Last Sigh* (202), and in Buñuel, de la Colina, and Pérez Turrent, *Conversations avec Luis Buñuel* (86). *A Woman Without Love* was called by Buñuel himself "quite simply the worst movie I ever made" (*My Last Sigh*, 202) and is almost unanimously forgotten by the critics.

43. Cypess, *La Malinche in Mexican Literature*, 110.

44. López, "Tears and Desire," 151.

45. Sánchez, *Crónica antisolemne del cine mexicano*, 12.

46. Cypess, *La Malinche in Mexican Literature*, 153 (my emphasis).

47. The exile of Rosario's lover to Brazil emphasizes his literal meaning as a man who is moving ahead with the (brief) postwar boom in Latin America. On the topic of the postwar economies, see Halperín-Donghi, *The Contemporary History of Latin America*, 247–91.

48. Buñuel, *My Last Sigh*, 202.

49. The film was assigned to him at CLASA (Cinematográfica Latino Americana, S.A.), where Buñuel had just made *La ilusión viaja en tranvía*.

50. Buñuel's original French edition of *Mon dernier soupir* (254–56; my translation). Some specific references and opinions about Mexico found in the original French edition are avoided or significantly toned down in the English translation by Abigail Israel.

51. Buñuel, *Mon dernier soupir*, 255.

52. Buñuel, *My Last Sigh*, 209. Buñuel emphasizes the anecdote between

Reyes and Vasconcelos, adding similar stories about other men of arts and letters, among them Diego Rivera and Emilio Fernández. Fernández killed a man in Coahuila in the 1970s and served time in prison for it (Mora, *Mexican Cinema*, 126).

CHAPTER 5: ON THE ROAD

1. See López-Portillo Tostado, *Estado e ideología empresarial en el gobierno alemanista*.
2. Monsiváis, "Cantinflas: That's the Point!"
3. Monsiváis, "Tin Tan: The Pachuco."
4. Mexican film comedy was based on a strict star system in the classic era. Mario Moreno ("Cantinflas"), Adalberto Martínez ("Resortes"), Germán Valdés ("Tin-Tán"), Fernando Soto ("Mantequilla"), and many other comedians *became* specific types of characters (hence the nicknames by which they were known), yet they individually represented a particular sector of the working class in each of their pictures: Tin-Tán is the "pachuco," Cantinflas the "pelado," and Resortes is the "slum dweller," or *arrabalero* (see Ayala Blanco, *La aventura del cine mexicano*, 225–34).
5. Ávila Dueñas, *El cine mexicano de Luis Buñuel*, 95.
6. López-Portillo Tostado, *Estado e ideología empresarial en el gobierno alemanista*, 38.
7. Ayala Blanco, *Aventura del cine mexicano*, 137–38; López, "Celluloid Tears," 44–45.
8. See, for example, Bailey, *¡Viva Cristo Rey!*
9. President Cárdenas's most famous speeches are published in several collections. See, for example, Cárdenas, *Lázaro Cárdenas*, 125, 177, 282–88; see also Cárdenas, *¡Cárdenas Habla!*, 113–16. For an excellent historical and contextual analysis of President Cárdenas's popularity, see Gilly, *El cardenismo*.
10. López-Portillo Tostado, *Estado e ideología empresarial en el gobierno alemanista*, 69–80.
11. Buñuel, de la Colina, and Pérez Turrent, *Conversations avec Luis Buñuel*, 88–89; Ávila Dueñas, *El cine mexicano de Luis Buñuel*, 96; García Riera, *Historia documental del cine mexicano*, 4:366–67.
12. See Lázaro Cárdenas's speeches in Cárdenas, *¡Cárdenas Habla!*, and Cárdenas, *Lázaro Cárdenas*.
13. Monsiváis, *Mexican Postcards*, 96.
14. Buñuel, de la Colina, and Pérez Turrent, *Conversations avec Luis Buñuel*, 91.
15. This scene, I believe, is a lampoonish reference to the solemnity of a similar dancing sequence in Emilio Fernández's *Pueblerina* (1948). The provocation really lies in calling attention to the forced intimacy of the scene in *Pueblerina* (their guests never show up, so they perform the dance alone) by turning the scene in *Subida al cielo* into an impromptu spectacle.

16. López-Portillo Tostado, *Estado e ideología empresarial en el gobierno alemanista*, 80–101.

17. See Halperín-Donghi, *The Contemporary History of Latin America*, 247–51, 274–76. Furthermore, Ana López and Claire Fox have commented to me that it is revealing to see the introduction of "free trade" and the smuggling of U.S. goods into Mexico as a problem in this film, foreseeing by four decades the debates on NAFTA in the early 1990s.

18. Ayala Blanco, *Aventura del cine mexicano*, 137.

19. García Riera, *Historia documental del cine mexicano*, 7:309.

20. Zuzanna Pick suggested to me that in *Mexican Bus Ride* the road-movie structure points to the importance of travel narratives in Latin American culture. From precolonial times, when Columbus's and Cabeza de Vaca's diaries were written, to the premodern times of the explorers Alexander Von Humboldt and Robert and Richard Schomburgk, to the modern tales of Alejo Carpentier (*The Lost Steps*, 1953), travel narratives have structured "recognizance" ventures into "unknown" territories of America's landscapes and cultures. It seems appropriate that Buñuel and Altolaguirre's collaboration should take the form of a discovery trip through Mexico, where the two Spaniards go indeed to "find" the culture, the people, and the landscape.

21. Monsiváis, *Mexican Postcards*, 107.

CHAPTER 6: MASCULINITY AND CLASS CONFLICT

1. These "virtues of the ideal patriarch" are listed in O'Malley, *The Myth of the Revolution*, 139.

2. Ibid., 133–45; see also Paz, *El laberinto de la soledad*, 211–27.

3. O'Malley, *The Myth of the Revolution*, 139–40.

4. On this topic, see Ayala Blanco, *Aventura del cine mexicano*; Sánchez, *Crónica antisolemne del cine mexicano*; Hershfield, *Mexican Cinema, Mexican Woman*; Berg, *Cinema of Solitude*; O'Malley, *The Myth of the Revolution*; and Mora, *Mexican Cinema*.

5. Berg, *Cinema of Solitude*, 107.

6. Franco, *Plotting Women*, 131.

7. See Buñuel, *My Last Sigh*, 213; and Buñuel, de la Colina, and Pérez Turrent, *Conversations avec Luis Buñuel*, 94.

8. García Riera, *Emilio Fernández*, 33.

9. Buñuel, *My Last Sigh*, 206–12.

10. O'Malley, *The Myth of the Revolution*, 137.

11. Ibid., 137.

12. Ávila Dueñas, *El cine mexicano de Luis Buñuel*, 109.

13. Buñuel, de la Colina and Pérez Turrent, *Conversations avec Luis Buñuel*, 99.

14. By comparison, *El Bruto* cost 600,000 pesos (approx. U.S. $70,000) and was shot in eighteen days; and *The Adventures of Robinson Crusoe* cost 1,900,000 pesos (approx. U.S. $220,000) and was shot in three months.

15. See, respectively, González Dueñas, *Luis Buñuel*, 59–65; Roudinesco, *Jacques Lacan and Co.;* Tesson, *Luis Buñuel;* Tesson, *Él;* and Williams, *Figures of Desire*, 43–45, 150, 151, 154.

16. Césarman, *L'oeil de Buñuel*, 121–22 (my translation).

17. See Freud, "Psychoanalytic Notes on an Autobiographical Account of a Case of Paranoia," and "On the Mechanism of Paranoia," both in *Case Histories II*, 129–49 and 196–205, respectively.

18. As I have pointed out, both villains and antiheroes with links to the pre-revolutionary regime come up in *Los olvidados, Susana, Subida al cielo*, and *El bruto*. In Buñuel's films, these characters seem to represent generally retrograde attitudes and not necessarily a specific political position.

19. See Tesson, *Él*, 78–80; Césarman, *L'oeil de Buñuel*, 122–23.

20. I feel the need to clarify that I am not validating Freud's study on paranoia, which I am not qualified to judge. But I need to refer to it because it was Freud that Buñuel read. Perhaps, in the light of four decades of further developments in psychology and psychiatry, Francisco is untenable as a "case study" today, but that is irrelevant in the context in which Mercedes Pinto in the 1930s and Buñuel and Alcoriza in the 1950s wrote about Francisco. As a matter of fact, Pinto's descriptions of "Him" were praised by the psychiatric community in the 1930s; Buñuel's were praised by Jacques Lacan in the 1950s. The third edition of Mercedes Pinto's *Él* was published, along with praising commentary from professors of psychiatry, physicians, and experts in jurisprudence, because the book was written as something of an apology in her divorce procedures.

21. Usigli, *Ensayo de un crimen*.

22. Buñuel, de la Colina, and Pérez Turrent, *Conversations avec Luis Buñuel*, 127.

23. Usigli, *Ensayo de un crimen*, 20 (my translation).

24. Ávila Dueñas, *El cine mexicano de Luis Buñuel*, 175.

25. Buñuel, de la Colina, and Pérez Turrent, *Conversations avec Luis Buñuel*, 130–31. In *Los olvidados*, for example, an apparent pedophile approaches Pedro on the street in an attempt to prostitute him, which is just about the most direct reference to homosexuality in Buñuel's films.

26. See Freud, "The Sexual Aberrations," in *On Sexuality*, 45–87. On Archibaldo's specific "symptoms," see ibid., 80–81. Again, I am not judging the validity of Freud's claims, but I need to state them as contextually relevant to Buñuel's formation in light of Freud's importance for surrealist thought, in general, and for Buñuel's thought, in particular.

27. See Cosío Villegas, "La crisis de México."

28. Berg, *Cinema of Solitude*, 121–25.

CONCLUSION

1. Ávila Dueñas, *El cine mexicano de Luis Buñuel*, 125.

2. See Víctor Fuentes's discussion of the American movies *(Robinson Crusoe* and *The Young One)* in his book, *Buñuel en México*.

3. Barbachano is highly regarded as a maverick producer of quality cinema, even in the worst times of Mexican cinema, such as the *sexenio* of Luis Echeverría in the 1970s. His credits include Benito Alazraki's *Raíces* (1953); *Cuba baila* (1959), a rare, documentary effort produced in association with ICAIC; Paul Leduc's *Frida* (1985); and Jaime Humberto Hermosillo's *Doña Herlinda y su hijo* (also 1985).

4. See García Riera, *El cine de Silvia Pinal*, 101–8; see also Rodríguez Castañeda, "*Viridiana* dividió la vida de Buñuel y la mía."

5. Specifically, Buñuel's *Abismos de pasión* is an adaptation of chapters 8–16 and chapter 22 of Brontë's novel (see Brontë, *Wuthering Heights*). In the late 1980s a popular Mexican television soap opera, also entitled *Abismos de pasión*, was a modern-day adaptation of Brontë's novel with a Mexican setting. Buñuel's film is also known as *Cumbres borrascosas*, which is the Spanish title of Brontë's novel. I have used the more common title, *Abismos de pasión*, following Buñuel, de la Colina, and Pérez Turrent *(Conversations avec Luis Buñuel)*; Mora *(Mexican Cinema)*; Baxter *(Buñuel)*; and others.

6. Buñuel, de la Colina, and Pérez Turrent, *Conversations avec Luis Buñuel*, 116, 120.

7. Martín-Barbero, *Communication, Culture, and Hegemony*, 165–66; see also López, "Cellulloid Tears"; Monsiváis, "Mythologies"; and Monsiváis, "Dolores del Río."

8. *Nuevo Cine*, no. 1, April 1961.

9. *Nuevo Cine*, no. 4–5, November 1961, p. 1 (my translation).

10. Paranaguá, *Arturo Ripstein*. Buñuel's presence is constant in Paranaguá's book, but see, especially, pp. 53–78. See also Isaac, *Conversaciones con Gabriel Figueroa*, 104; Berg, *Cinema of Solitude*, 183–84; Sánchez, *Crónica antisolemne del cine mexicano*, 165. Landmark events from this period include the founding of *Nuevo Cine*; the first generation of film-school-trained directors (1964–66); and the first national screenplay competition, sponsored by the Banco Nacional Cinematográfico and the association of film producers and held in 1965 (Berg, *Cinema of Solitude*, 46–47).

11. Berg, *Cinema of Solitude*, 28.

12. Ibid., 29 (my emphasis).

13. See Paranaguá, *Arturo Ripstein;* and Figueroa and Isaac, *Conversaciones con Gabriel Figueroa*, 103–6.

14. Figueroa and Isaac, *Conversaciones con Gabriel Figueroa*, 104.

Bibliography

Altman, Rick. "Dickens, Griffith, and Film Theory Today." *South Atlantic Quarterly* 88 (spring 1989): 321–58.
———. *Film/Genre*. London: BFI, 1999.
Anderson, Benedict. *Imagined Communities: Reflections on the Origins and Spread of Nationalism*. London: Verso, 1990.
Andrew, Dudley. *André Bazin*. New York: Columbia University Press, 1990.
———. *Mists of Regret: Culture and Sensibility in Classic French Film*. Princeton, N.J.: Princeton University Press, 1995.
Anghelo, Zachary. "Carta de Roma: Mi viejo amigo Buñuel." *Nuevo Cine* (Mexico City), no. 4–5, November 1961, 45.
Aranda, J. Francisco. *Luis Buñuel: Una biografía crítica*. Barcelona: Lumen, 1969.
———. "Luis Buñuel, productor, actor, guionista." *Programa Mensual/Cineteca Nacional* (Mexico City), May 1980, 25–30.
Armes, Roy. *Third World Filmmaking and the West*. Berkeley: University of California Press, 1987.
Aub, Max. *Conversaciones con Buñuel*. Madrid: Aguilar, 1984.
Ávila Dueñas, Iván H. *El cine mexicano de Luis Buñuel*. Mexico City: IMCINE/CNCA, 1994.
Aviña, Rafael. "Cien años de cine en México." *Uno Más Uno* (Mexico City), 28 December 1995, 19.
Avrich, Paul. *Sacco and Vanzetti: The Anarchist Background*. Princeton, N.J.: Princeton University Press, 1991.
Ayala Blanco, Jorge. *Aventura del cine mexicano*. Mexico: Era, 1968.
Bailey, David C. *¡Viva Cristo Rey! The Cristero Rebellion and Church–State Conflict in Mexico*. Austin: University of Texas Press, 1974.
Barbachano Ponce, Manuel. "Cine mexicano indigenista." *La Jornada* (Mexico City), 27 February 1994, 29.
———. "Nacionalismo cinematográfico." *La Jornada* (Mexico City), 29 May 1995, 27.

Baxter, John. *Buñuel*. New York: Carrol and Graf, 1998.
Bazin, André. *What Is Cinema?* Berkeley: University of California Press, 1967.
———. *The Cinema of Cruelty: From Buñuel to Hitchcock.* New York: Seaver, 1982.
Becker, Marjorie. *Setting the Virgin on Fire: Lázaro Cárdenas, Michoacán Peasants, and the Redemption of the Mexican Revolution.* Berkeley: University of California Press, 1995.
Berg, Charles Ramírez. *Cinema of Solitude: A Critical Study of Mexican Film, 1967–1983.* Austin: University of Texas Press, 1993.
Bhabha, Homi K., ed. *Nation and Narration.* London: Routledge, 1990.
Blanco Aguinaga, Carlos, Julio Rodríguez Puértolas, and Iris M. Zavala. *Historia social de la literatura española.* 2 vols. Madrid: Editorial Castalia, 1984.
Breton, André. *Manifestes du surréalisme.* Paris: Editions Gallimard, 1990.
———. *What Is Surrealism?* New York: Haskell House, n.d.
Brontë, Emily. *Wuthering Heights.* New York: Bantam Classics, 1981.
Buache, Freddy. *Luis Buñuel.* Lyon: Serdoc, 1960.
Buñuel, Luis. "El cine, instrumento de poesía." *Nuevo Cine* (Mexico City), no. 4–5 (1961): 46–48.
———. *Los olvidados.* Mexico City: Era, 1980.
———. "Buñuel por Buñuel." *Uno Más Uno* (Mexico City), 2 May 1982, supplement.
———. *Mi último suspiro.* Translated by Ana M. de la Fuente. Barcelona: Plaza y Janés, 1982.
———. *Mon dernier soupir.* Paris: Robert Laffont, 1982.
———. *Buñuel 83.* Mexico City: UNAM, 1983.
———. *My Last Sigh.* Translated by Abigail Israel. New York: Knopf, 1984.
———. "Cinema as an Instrument of Poetry." In *An Unspeakable Betrayal,* 136–41. Berkeley: University of California Press, 2000.
———. *An Unspeakable Betrayal.* Berkeley: University of California Press, 2000.
Buñuel, Luis, Jose de la Colina, and Tomas Perez Turrent. *Conversations avec Luis Buñuel.* Paris: Cahiers du Cinéma, 1993.
Cañizal, Eduardo Peñuela, ed. *Um jato na contramão: Buñuel no México.* São Paulo: Editora Perspectiva, 1993.
Cárdenas, Lázaro. *¡Cárdenas habla!* Mexico: Partido Revolucionario Mexicano, 1940.
———. *Lázaro Cárdenas: Palabras y documentos públicos.* Mexico City: Siglo XXI, 1978.
Carrouges, Michel. *André Breton and the Basic Concepts of Surrealism.* University City: University of Alabama Press, 1974.
Césarman, Fernando. *L'Oeil de Buñuel.* Paris: Dauphin, 1982.
Cineteca Nacional. *Buñuel en México.* Mexico City: Cineteca Nacional, 1974.
———. *Testimonios para la historia del cine mexicano.* Mexico City: Cineteca Nacional, 1975.

———. "Buñuel: 80 años, retrospectiva." *Programa Mensual / Cineteca Nacional* (Mexico City), May 1980, 3.
———. "Buñuel crítico, Buñuel escritor." *Programa Mensual / Cineteca Nacional* (Mexico City), May 1980, 7–9.
———. "El cine, instrumento de poesía." *Programa Mensual / Cineteca Nacional* (Mexico City), May 1980, 10–15.
———. "Buñuel, el ojo de la imagen." *Programa Mensual/Cineteca Nacional* (Mexico City), July 1990, 51–59.
Clifford, James. *The Predicament of Culture: Twentieth Century Ethnography, Literature, and Art.* Cambridge, Mass.: Harvard University Press, 1988.
Cobián, Felipe. "Gustavo Alatriste." *Proceso*, no. 976, 17 July 1995, 68–69.
Cosío Villegas, Daniel. "La crisis de México." *Cuadernos Americanos* (March 1947): 29–51.
Cypess, Sandra M. *La Malinche in Mexican Literature: From History to Myth.* Austin: University of Texas Press, 1991.
Dalí, Salvador. *The Secret Life of Salvador Dalí.* New York: Dover Publications, 1993.
D'Amico, Silvio. *Historia del teatro dramático.* Mexico: Hispanoamericana, 1961.
de la Vega Alfaro, Eduardo. Interview by author. Guadalajara, Mexico, 10 July 1996.
de los Reyes, Aurelio. *Cine y sociedad en México.* Mexico: UNAM and Cineteca Nacional, 1981.
———. *80 años de cine en México.* Mexico City: UNAM, 1977.
de la Colina, José. "Cuando la muerte dejó de ser absoluta." *Época* (Mexico City), no. 237, 18 December 1995, 54–63.
———. "La agonía del amor romántico." *Nuevo Cine* (Mexico City), no. 4–5, November 1961, 13–21.
de la Colina, José, and Tomás Pérez Turrent. "Prohibido asomarse al interior." *Dicine* (Mexico City), no. 2, September 1983, 3–4.
Doane, Mary Ann. "Pathos and the Maternal." In *The Desire to Desire: The Woman's Film of the 1940s,* 70–95. Bloomington: Indiana University Press, 1987.
Drouzy, Maurice. *Luis Buñuel: Architecte du rêve.* Paris: Lherminier, 1978.
Edwards, Gwynne. *The Discreet Art of Luis Buñuel.* London: Marion Boyars, 1982.
Elizondo, Salvador. "Moral sexual y moraleja en el cine mexicano." *Nuevo Cine* (Mexico City), no. 1, April 1961, 4–11.
———. "Luis Buñuel, un visionario." *Nuevo Cine* (Mexico City), no. 4–5, November 1961, 2–7.
Elsaesser, Thomas. "Tales of Sound and Fury." In *Home Is Where the Heart Is: Studies in Melodrama and the Woman's Film,* ed. Christine Gledhill, 43–69. London: BFI, 1987.
Evans, Paul W. *The Films of Luis Buñuel: Subjectivity and Desire.* Oxford: Oxford University Press, 1995.

Figueroa, Gabriel. "Los discursos de Gabriel Figueroa." *Proceso*, no. 958, 13 March 1995, 60–61.
Figueroa, Gabriel, and Alberto Isaac. *Conversaciones con Gabriel Figueroa*. Guadalajara: Universidad de Guadalajara, 1993.
Florescano, Enrique. *Memoria mexicana*. Mexico: Fondo de Cultural Económica, 1994.
Fox, Claire, F. *The Fence and the River: Culture and Politics at the U.S.–Mexico Border*. Minneapolis: University of Minnesota Press, 1999.
Franco, Jean. *Plotting Women: Gender and Representation in Mexico*. New York: Columbia University Press, 1989.
Fregoso, Rosa Linda. *The Bronze Screen: Chicana and Chicano Film Culture*. Minneapolis: University of Minnesota Press, 1993.
Freud, Sigmund. *The Interpretation of Dreams*. New York: Avon, 1972.
———. *On Sexuality*. New York: Penguin, 1977.
———. *Case Histories II*. New York: Penguin, 1981.
Fuentes, Carlos. *Revista de la Universidad de México* (Mexico City), 1954–56 (collection).
Fuentes, Víctor. *Buñuel en México: Iluminaciones sobre una pantalla pobre*. Teruel: Instituto de Estudios Turolenses, 1993.
———. *Buñuel: Cine y literatura*. Barcelona: Salvat, 1989.
Galeota, Vito. *Galdós e Buñuel: Romanzo, film narratività in Nazarín e Tristana*. Napoli: Istituto Universitario Orientale, 1988.
García Canclini, Néstor. *Hybrid Cultures: Strategies for Entering and Leaving Modernity*. Minneapolis: University of Minnesota Press, 1995.
García Riera, Emilio. "Buñuel y la política." *Nuevo Cine* (Mexico City), no. 4–5, November 1961, 8–12.
———. "La eterna rebelión de Luis Buñuel." *Tiempo de Cine* (Mexico City), no. 13, 1962, 8–11.
———. *La guía del cine mexicano*. Mexico City: Patria, 1984.
———. *Historia del cine mexicano*. Mexico City: SEP, 1986.
———. *Emilio Fernández: 1904–1986*. Mexico City: Cineteca Nacional; Guadalajara, Jalisco: Universidad de Guadalajara, 1987.
———. *Historia documental del cine mexicano*. 18 vols. Guadalajara: Universidad de Guadalajara, 1992.
———. *El cine de Silvia Pinal*. Guadalajara: Universidad de Guadalajara, 1996.
———. "Crisis del cine nacional." *México en la cultura* (Mexico, D.F.), 21 September 1959.
———. Interview by author. 12 July 1996, Guadalajara.
Gilly, Adolfo. *El cardenismo: Una utopía mexicana*. Mexico City: Aguilar, León y Cal Editores, 1994.
Gledhill, Christine, ed. *Home Is Where The Heart Is: Studies in Melodrama and the Woman's Film*. London: BFI, 1987.
Gómez Mesa, Luis. "La generación cinematográfica del '27." *Cinema 2002* (Madrid), no. 37 (1978): 52–58.

González Dueñas, Daniel. *Luis Buñuel: La trama soñada*. Mexico City: Cineteca Nacional, 1993.

———. "Una década sin Buñuel." *Programa Mensual/Cineteca Nacional* (Mexico City), August 1993, 24–37.

Gruzinski, Serge. *The Conquest of Mexico*. London: Polity Press, 1993.

Halperín-Dongui, Tulio. *The Contemporary History of Latin America*. Durham, N.C.: Duke University Press, 1993.

Hansen, Roger D. *La política del desarrollo mexicano*. Mexico City: Siglo XXI, 1971.

Hart, Stephen, ed. *"¡No Pasarán!" Art, Literature, and the Spanish Civil War*. London: Tamesis Books, 1988.

Hayes, Joy E. "Touching the Sentiments of Everyone: Nationalism and State Broadcasting in Thirties Mexico." *The Communication Review* 1, no. 4 (1996): 411–40.

Hayward, Susan. *French National Cinema*. London: Routledge, 1993.

Hershfield, Joanne. *Mexican Cinema/Mexican Woman: 1940–1950*. Tucson: University of Arizona Press, 1996.

Higginbotham, Virginia. *Luis Buñuel*. New York: Twayne, 1979.

———. *Spanish Film under Franco*. Austin: University of Texas Press, 1988.

Íñiguez Mendoza, Ulises. "Cine, surrealismo y Luis Buñuel." *El occidental* (Guadalajara), 25 June 1995, 8.

Isaac, Alberto. "Gabriel Figueroa habla sobre Luis Buñuel." *Dicine* (Mexico City), no. 50, March 1993, 16–17.

Joseph, Gilbert, and Daniel Nugent, eds. *Everyday Forms of State Formation: Revolution and the Negotiation of Rule in Modern Mexico*. Durham, N.C.: Duke University Press, 1994.

———. "Popular Culture and State Formation in Revolutionary Mexico." In *Everyday Forms of State Formation: Revolution and the Negotiation of Rule in Modern Mexico*, ed. Gilbert Joseph and Daniel Nugent, 3–23. Durham, N.C.: Duke University Press, 1994.

Julián, Pablo. "El mundo religioso de Luis Buñuel." *Programa Mensual/ Cineteca Nacional* (Mexico City), May 1980, 19–24.

Karetnikova, Inga, and Leon Steinmentz. *Mexico According to Eisenstein*. Albuquerque: University of New Mexico Press, 1991.

Kinder, Marsha. *Blood Cinema*. Berkeley: University of California Press, 1993.

Knight, Alan. *The Mexican Revolution*. Lincoln: University of Nebraska Press, 1990.

———. "Popular Culture and the Revolutionary State in Mexico, 1910–1940." *Hispanic American Historical Review* 74, no. 3 (1994): 393–444.

King, John. *Magical Reels: A History of Cinema in Latin America*. London: Verso, 1990.

King, John, Ana López, and Manuel Alvarado, eds. *Mediating Two Worlds: Cinematic Encounters in the Americas*. London: BFI, 1993.

Kuenzli, Rudolf, ed. *Dada and Surrealist Film*. Cambridge, Mass.: MIT Press, 1996.

Kyrou, Ado. *Luis Buñuel*. Paris: Seghers, 1962.
Larrea, Juan, and Luis Buñuel. "Ilegible hijo de flauta." *Nuevo Cine* (Mexico City), no. 4–5, November 1961, 43–44.
Lillo, Gastón. *Género y transgresión: El cine mexicano de Luis Buñuel*. Paris: Montpelier Université Paul Valéry, 1994.
Lizalde, Eduardo. *Luis Buñuel*. Mexico City: UNAM, 1962.
López, Ana M. "Celluloid Tears: Melodrama in the 'Old' Mexican Cinema." *Iris* 13 (summer 1991): 29–51.

———. "Tears and Desire: Melodrama in the 'Old' Mexican Cinema." In *Mediating Two Worlds: Cinematic Encounters in the Americas*, ed. John King, Ana López, and Manuel Alvarado, 147–63. London: BFI, 1993.

López-Portillo Tostado, Felícitas. *Estado e ideología empresarial en el gobierno alemanista*. Mexico: UNAM, 1995.
Mahieu, José A. "El período mexicano de Luis Buñuel." *Cuadernos Hispanoamericanos* (Madrid), no. 358, 1980, 1–16.
Martín-Barbero, Jesús. *Communication, Culture, and Hegemony: From the Media to Mediations*. London: Sage, 1995.
Maupassant, Guy de. *Pierre and Jean*. New York: Scribner's, 1936.
Mauriac, Claude. *L'amour du cinéma*. Paris: Albin Michel, 1954.
Mayne, Judith. *Directed by Dorothy Arzner*. Bloomington: Indiana University Press, 1994.
Medina, Luis. *Historia de la revolución mexicana: Del Cardenismo al Avilacamachismo*. Mexico City: Colegio de México, 1978.
Méndez Berman, León, and Santos Mar. *El embrollo cinematográfico*. Mexico City: Cooperación, 1953.
Méndez Leite, Fernando. *Historia del cine español*. Madrid: Rialp, 1965.
Mergier, Anne Marie. "La crítica de la historiografía fílmica de México." *Proceso*, no. 835, 2 November 1992, 58–59.
Moctezuma de la Villa, P. "La crítica perdurable." *Cine* (Mexico City) 2, no. 19 (October 1979): 66–67.
Monsiváis, Carlos. *Amor perdido*. Mexico City: Era, 1984.

———. "Mexican Cinema: Of Myths and Demystifications." In *Mediating Two Worlds*, ed. John King, Ana López, and Manuel Alvarado, 139–46. London: BFI, 1993.

———. *Los rituales del caos*. Mexico City: Era, 1994.

———. "Mythologies." In *Mexican Cinema*, ed. Paulo Antonio Paranaguá, 117–27. London: BFI; Mexico: IMCINE, 1995.

———. "Cantinflas: That's the Point!" In *Mexican Postcards*, 105. London: Verso, 1997.

———. "Dolores del Río: The Face as Institution." In *Mexican Postcards*, 71–87. London: Verso, 1997.

———. "Tin Tan: The Pachuco." In *Mexican Postcards*, 107. London: Verso, 1997.

———. *Mexican Postcards*. London: Verso, 1997.

Mora, Carl J. *Mexican Cinema: Reflections of a Society*. Berkeley: University of California Press, 1989.
Muñoz Castillo, Fernando. "Mitos del cine mexicano I." *Sábado* (Mexico City), no. 943, 28 October 1995, 6.
———. "Mitos del cine mexicano II." *Sábado* (Mexico City), no. 944, 4 November 1995, 6.
———. "Mitos del cine nacional [sic] III." *Sábado* (Mexico City), no. 945, 11 November 1995, 6.
Nadeau, Maurice. *The History of Surrealism*. New York: Collier, 1967.
Nascimento, Gerardo Carlos do. "Nos céus da idade média." In *Um jato na contramão: Buñuel no México*, ed. Eduardo Peñuela Cañizal. São Paulo: Com-Arte, 1993.
Niquet, José A. "40 años de *Los olvidados*." *Revista de Revistas* (Mexico City), no. 4181, 16 March 1990, 48–55.
O'Malley, Ilene V. *The Myth of the Revolution: Hero Cults and the Institutionalization of the Mexican State, 1920–1940*. Westport, Ct.: Greenwood Press, 1986.
Paranaguá, Paulo Antonio. *Arturo Ripstein: La espiral de la identidad*. Madrid: Cátedra/Filmoteca Española, 1997.
———, ed. *Le Cinéma mexicain*. Paris: Centre Georges Pompidou, 1992.
———. *Mexican Cinema*. Translated by Ana López. London: BFI, 1995.
Paz, Octavio. "El poeta Buñuel." *Nuevo Cine* (Mexico City), no. 4–5, November 1961, 46–48.
———. "Homenaje a Luis Buñuel." Parts 1–3. *Novedades* (Mexico City), 7, 14, and 21 August 1983.
———. *El laberinto de la soledad*. Madrid: Cátedra, 1993.
Peñuela Cañizal, Eduardo, ed. *Um jato na contramão: Buñuel no México*. São Paulo: Editora Perspectiva, 1993.
Pérez Galdós, Benito. *Tristana*. Barcelona: Carroggio, 1980.
———. *Nazarín*. Mexico City: Origen, 1983.
Pérez Turrent, Tomás. "Luis Buñuel, el instinto y la conversión." *Programa Mensual/Cineteca Nacional* (Mexico City), May 1980, 4–9.
Pick, Zuzanna. *The New Latin American Cinema: A Continental Project*. Austin: University of Texas Press, 1993.
Pina, Francisco. "El viejo y eterno realismo español." *Nuevo Cine* (Mexico City), no. 4–5, November 1961, 26–28.
Pinto, Mercedes. *Él*. 3d ed. Santiago, Chile: Nascimento, 1936.
Rees, Margaret, ed. *Luis Buñuel: A Symposium*. Horsforth: Trinity and All Saints College, 1983.
Ríos Alfaro, Lorena. "La crítica y el melodrama." *Uno Más Uno* (Mexico City), 27 September 1995, 27.
———. "Se hizo cine de milagro." *Uno Más Uno* (Mexico City), 28 December 1995, 17.
Rivera, J. Héctor. "Índice cronológico del cine mexicano." *Proceso*, no. 853, 8 March 1993, 48–49.

———. "Memoria del cine mexicano." *Proceso*, no. 910, 11 April 1994, 74.
———. "Los que hicieron nuestro cine." *Proceso*, no. 910, 11 April 1994, 75.
Rodríguez Castañeda, R. "Viridiana dividió la vida de Buñuel y la mía, dice Gustavo Alatriste." *Proceso*, no. 353, 8 August 1983, 46–51.
Rodríguez Monegal, Emir. "El mito Buñuel." *Tiempo de Cine* (Mexico City), no. 14–15, July 1963, 7–10.
Rotellar, Manuel. "Luis Buñuel en Filmófono." *Cinema 2002*, no. 37 (1978): 36–40.
Rothman, William. *Documentary Film Classics*. Cambridge: Cambridge University Press, 1997.
Roudinesco, Elizabeth. *Jacques Lacan and Co.: A History of Psychoanalysis in France, 1925–1985*. London: Free Association Press, 1985.
Rozado, Alejandro. *Cine y realidad social en México: Una lectura de la obra de Emilio Fernández*. Guadalajara: Universidad de Guadalajara, 1991.
Rucar de Buñuel, Jeanne, and Marisol Martín del Campo. *Memorias de una mujer sin piano*. Mexico City: Alianza Editorial, 1990.
Salcedo Romero, Gerardo. "Una década sin Buñuel." *Programa Mensual/Cineteca Nacional* (Mexico City), July 1993, 27–31.
Sánchez, Francisco. "Imágenes en libertad." *Otro Cine* (Mexico City), no. 3, July–September 1975, 22–24.
———. *Crónica antisolemne del cine mexicano*. Xalapa: Universidad Veracruzana, 1989.
Sánchez Vidal, Agustín. *Luis Buñuel*. Madrid: Cátedra, 1991.
Sandro, Paul. *Diversions of Pleasure: Luis Buñuel and the Crises of Desire*. Columbus: Ohio State University Press, 1987.
Santí, Enrico M. Introduction to *El laberinto de la soledad*, by Octavio Paz. Madrid: Cátedra, 1993.
Sarup, Madan. *Jacques Lacan*. Toronto: University of Toronto Press, 1992.
Schwarze, Michael. *Luis Buñuel*. Barcelona: Plaza y Janés, 1988.
Sommer, Doris. *Foundational Fictions: The National Romances of Latin America*. Berkeley: University of California Press, 1990.
———. "Irresistible Romance: The Foundational Fictions of Latin America." In *Nation and Narration*, ed. Homi K. Bhabha, 86–90. London: Routledge, 1990.
Taibo, Paco Ignacio I. *El Indio Fernández*. Mexico City: Planeta, 1991.
Talens, Jenaro. *The Branded Eye*. Minneapolis: University of Minnesota Press, 1993.
Taracena, Alfonso. *La vida en México bajo Miguel Alemán*. Mexico City: Editorial Jus, 1979.
Tesson, Charles. *Él: Luis Buñuel*. Paris: Éditions Nathan, 1995.
———. *Luis Buñuel*. Paris: Cahiers du Cinéma, 1995.
Thomas, Hugh. *Conquest: Montezuma, Cortés, and the Fall of Old Mexico*. New York: Simon and Schuster, 1993.
Todorov, Tzvetan. *The Conquest of America*. New York: Harper and Row, 1984.

Torres, Salvador. "En la época de oro." *Uno Más Uno* (Mexico City), 21 August 1993, 26.

———. "La censura." *Uno Más Uno* (Mexico City), 22 August 1993, 23.

Torres Ramírez, Blanca. *Historia de la revolución mexicana: México en la segunda guerra mundial*. Mexico City: Colegio de México, 1979.

Troiano, Felice. *Surrealismo e psicanalisi nelle prime opere di Buñuel*. Firenze: Nuova Italia, 1983.

Usigli, Rodolfo. *Ensayo de un crimen*. Mexico: Secretaría de Educación Pública, 1986.

Vardac, A. Nicolas. *From Stage to Screen*. Cambridge, Mass.: Harvard University Press, 1949.

Vasconcelos, José. *La raza cósmica*. Mexico City: Porrúa, 1982.

Vaughan, Mary Kay. *Cultural Politics in Revolution: Teachers, Peasants, and Schools in Mexico, 1930–1940*. Tucson: University of Arizona Press, 1997.

Williams, Alan. *Republic of Images: A History of French Filmmaking*. Cambridge, Mass.: Harvard University Press, 1992.

Williams, Linda. "'Something Else Besides a Mother': *Stella Dallas* and the Maternal Melodrama." In *Home Is Where the Heart Is: Studies in Melodrama and the Woman's Film*, ed. Christine Gledhill, 299–325. London: BFI, 1987.

———*Figures of Desire: A Theory and Analysis of Surrealist Film*. Berkeley: University of California Press, 1990.

———. "Melodrama Revised." In *Refiguring American Film Genres: Theory and History*, ed. Nick Browne. Berkeley: University of California Press, 1998.

Wolfe, Bertram D. *The Fabulous Life of Diego Rivera*. New York: Stein and Day, 1963.

Wood, Michael. "Buñuel in Mexico." In *Mediating Two Worlds*, ed. John King, Ana López, and Manuel Alvarado, 40–52. London: BFI, 1993.

Zea, Leopoldo. *Conciencia y posibilidad del mexicano*. Mexico: Porrúa, 1982.

Index

Page numbers in italics refer to illustrations.

Abismos de pasión, 13, 41, 105, *144*, 145–47, 176n5
Aceves Castañeda, Luis, 147
Aclemar, Lili, 96
The Adventures of Robinson Crusoe: commercial success of, 4, 143–44; cost of, 174n14; international coproduction of, 80, 132; Mexican cinema and, 12–13, 141; popular appeal of, 145; production of, 143, *144*
L'Age d'Or: *Abismos de pasión* and, 147; criticism of, 2; as extraordinary, 33, 54; *Subida al cielo* and, 116; as surrealist film, 32, 37, 38, 63, 165n36
agrarian cooperatives, 69
Alatriste, Gustavo, 144, 147
Alazraki, Benito, 176n3
Alberti, Rafael, 34, 35
Alberto Galán *(María Candelaria)*, 29
Alberto *(Susana)*, 29, 86, 91
Albina *(Subida al cielo)*, 115
Alcoriza, Janet, 51
Alcoriza, Luis, 51, 52, 68, 73, 126, 131, 135, 175n20
Alejandro *(Abismos de pasión)*, 146
Alemán, Miguel: Banco Nacional Cinematográfico and, 54; *cabaretera* films and, 6, 46, 61, 62, 113; cinema laws and, 160n4; modernization and, 6–7, 10, 59–61, 70, 72; working classes and, 113, 120
alemanismo: *Gran Casino* and, 46–47; *La hija del engaño* and, 98; *La ilusión viaja en tranvía* and, 111, 117, 119, 122; *Una mujer sin amor* and, 105; *Los olvidados* and, 59–60, 61, 68, 70, 119; *Río Escondido* and, 24; *Subida al cielo* and, 12, 111, 113, 117; *Susana* and, 119
Alexandrov, Grigori, 38, 162–63n48
Alfredo *(El gran calavera)*, 52
All About My Mother, 89
Allá en el Rancho Grande, 15, 27, 47, 90, 162n41
Almodóvar, Pedro, 89
Alonso, Ernesto, 12, 136, 139, *141*, 147
Altolaguirre, Manuel, 112, 174n20
Álvarez Acosta, Miguel, 106
Amezcua, Javier, 66
anarchism, 36, 164n15
An Andalusian Dog. See *Un chien andalou*
Anderson, Benedict, 18, 160n6
André Bazin (Andrew), 76
Andrés *(El bruto)*, 126–32
Andrew, Dudley, 64, 76, 159n6
El ángel exterminador: criticism of, 3, 4, 7, 8; Mexican cinema and, 111, 116;

187

El ángel exterminador (continued)
  Nuevo Cine and, 13, 150; production of, 145, 146
Angelito *(La hija del engaño)*, 95–98, 97
Anguiano family, 107–8
El apando, 150
Apu trilogy, 4
Aragon, Louis, 37
Araquistain, Luis, 41
Archibaldo de la Cruz *(Ensayo de un crimen)*, 11, 12, 29, 136–39, 144, 175n26
Ariel awards, 143
Armendáriz, Pedro, 12, 16, 28, 126, 127, 129–31
Arniches, Carlos, 40, 54, 94, 145, 165n32
arrabalera films: *El bruto* and, 126, 131; Buñuel and, 148; modernization and, 54, 113; *Los olvidados* and, 67–68, 72; Resortes and, 173n4
Artaud, Antonin, 63
"artisan" mode of production, 16
Aub, Max, 133
auteur criticism, 1, 2–5, 13, 159–60n12
Aventura del cine mexicano (Ayala Blanco), 163n52
Aventurera, 73, 82, 98, 171–72nn28,33
Ávila Camacho, Manuel, 72, 111, 160n4
Ávila Dueñas, Ivan, 131
Ayala Blanco, Jorge, 28, 122, 163n52, 172n33
Aztecs, 18, 19, 24, 25, 100, 160–63nn13,57

Baker, Josephine, 36
Bakhtin, Mikhail, 7
Banco Nacional Cinematográfico, 27, 45–46, 54, 150, 176n10
Barbachano Ponce, Manuel, 144, 147, 176n3
Bataille, Georges, 63–64
Batcheff, Pierre, 36, 43

Bauche, Freddy, 159–60n12
Baudry, Jean-Louis, 7
Bazin, André: on crisis of Mexican cinema, 77; influence on Buñuel, 5, 75–76, 159n6, 170n56; *Nuevo Cine* and, 149; *Los olvidados* and, 32, 63, 75–76, 168n22
Bazin, André (Andrew), 159n6
Belle de jour, 12, 33, 163–64n3
Berg, Charles Ramírez, 11, 126, 132, 142, 150–51
Bhabha, Homi, 25, 160n6
Bicycle Thieves, 67
Bildungsroman, 67
Blockade, 42
Bolívar, Ignacio, 34
Bolshevik revolution, 163n50
Bracho, Julio, 70, 73
The Branded Eye (Talens), 5
Breton, André, 37, 39, 63, 106, 112, 165n37
Broken Blossoms, 89
Brontë, Emily, 13, 146, 176n5
Brooks, Peter, 7
El bruto: Alcoriza, Luis, and, 126; Buñuel scholarship on, 7; censorship and, 132; contextuality of, 11, 12; machismo and, 10, 12, 117, 129–30, 132; as macho-drama, 126–32, 127; Mexican cinema and, 144, 147, 148; Mexican Revolution and, 126–32; national crisis/male trauma and, 136; production of, 174n14; slaughterhouse in, 122, 126
Buñuel, Luis, 9, 145, 151; birth and childhood of, 33–34; Catholicism of, 3, 33, 34; family life of, 39, 41–42, 55, 165n34; Mexican citizenship of, 55; Nuevo Cine and, 149–51
Buñuel en México (Fuentes), 8
"Buñuel Fracasa en México" (Mendoza), 48, 51, 166n60
"Buñuel in Mexico" (Wood), 159–60n12
Buñuel scholarship, 2–5, 7–9, 11, 159–60nn9,12. *See also* film criticism

Bustillo Oro, Juan, 15, 26, 70, 82
Butler, Hugo, 143

cabaretera films: Alemán associated with, 6, 46, 61, 62, 113; Buñuel's appropriation of, 12; of Gout, 9, 30, 54; *Gran Casino* and, 51; *La hija del engaño* as, 10, 94–98; male identity and, 109; Mexican cinema and, 6, 7, 46–48, 82; *Los olvidados* and, 73; *Susana* and, 10, 89–90; urban population growth and, 61, 90
cabareteras: in *La hija del engaño*, 94, 96, 97, 97–98; in *La ilusión viaja en tranvía*, 122; in Mexican cinema, 16, 81; in *Subida al cielo*, 113; in *Susana*, 90, 91, 93
Cahiers d'Art, 35
Cahiers du Cinéma, 4, 5, 75–76, 133
Caillois, Roger, 63–64
Caireles *(La ilusión viaja en tranvía)*, 120, 122
Calles, Plutarco Elías, 59
Caloca, Lauro, 160n3
Campeón sin corona, 67, 126
Cannes Film Festival, 27, 30, 58, 74, 76, 143, 170n57
Cantinflas, 6–7, 15, 22, 65, 112, 117, 160n3, 173n4
Capital (Marx), 35
Cárdenas, Lázaro: nationalization and, 44, 60, 114–15, 173n9; *Los olvidados* and, 10; speeches of, 117, 173nn9,12; utopian goals of, 58, 59; working classes and, 111, 113
El cardenismo (Gilly), 162n42
Cargo of Innocence, 42
Caro, Alicia, 95
Carpentier, Alejo, 62, 174n20
Carranza, Venustiano, 20–21
Carrière, Jean-Claude, 55, 66
Cartel, 48, 51
El castillo de la pureza, 30
Catalina *(Abismos de pasión)*, 146
Catholicism: Buñuel and, 3, 33, 34; Cristero Rebellion and, 114; in *Él*, 133, 134; in family melodrama, 6; Mexican Revolution and, 22; Spanish Civil War and, 42; surrealism and, 36, 37; in *Susana*, 88, 90, 91–93
Cayatte, André, 101
Cazals, Felipe, 150
Cela s'appele l'aurore, 13, 80, 143, 144
censorship, 39, 80, 132, 144, 164n28
Centro Sperimentale de Cinematografia (Rome, Italy), 5
Cervantes, Miss *(Ensayo de un crimen)*, 139
Césarman, Fernando, 5, 133, 135, 159–60n12
Cet obscur objet du désir: criticism of, 2, 4; man-woman relationships in, 12; melodramatic tradition and, 33, 163–64n3; Mexican cinema and, 12
Chaplin, Charles, 34, 41, 42, 123
Charisse, Cyd, 149
Le charme discret de la bourgeoisie, 116
charros, 11, 16, 48, 51, 90, 109
Un chien andalou: Batcheff in, 36, 43; criticism of, 2; as debut film, 32; dream sequences and, 92; as extraordinary, 33, 54, 116; public screening of, 34; surrealists and, 36–37, 63, 165n37
"la chingada," 57, 84, 101, 102–3, 104
churros, 48, 94, 150
Churubusco Studios, 122, 150
cine-club, 34
cine de arrabal, 22, 51, 70
cinema laws, 16, 22, 84, 160–61nn3,4,15
Cinema Nôvo (Brazil), 5, 151
Cine y realidad social en México (Rozado), 71
CLASA films, 106, 144, 172n49
class conflict, 124–42
classical cinema: Bazin on, 75–76; Buñuel and, 30, 33, 51, 58, 66, 68, 77; cultural nation and, 26–29, 30, 163n52; ideological positions of, 46, 166n55; melodramas and, 83–84;

classical cinema *(continued)*
  Mexican Revolution and, 21–26, 147, 162n41; modernization and, 70–73; Nuevo Cine and, 150; *Los olvidados* and, 73–76, 77; transition from, 5, 8, 30, 48, 54, 76–77, 170n57. *See also* Mexican cinema; national cinema
Clifford, James, 64
Coatlicue, 74
Cobo, Roberto, 66, 75
Cocteau, Jean, 34
Collège de sociologie, 63
comedias rancheras, 6, 15, 46–48, 51, 90, 109, 119
comedies. *See* social comedies
compadrazgo, 107–8
El compadre Mendoza, 90, 162n41
contextuality, 7, 9–14, 112, 120
Contla, Nacho, 97, 97
Cooper, Gary, 149
Cordero, Joaquín, 108
Córdova, Arturo de, 133, *135*
Corner, Getting Off, 67, 113
Cortázar, Ernesto, 132
Cortés, Hernán, 19, 65, 100, 103
Cortés, Martin, 100
Cosío Villegas, Daniel: on cultural nation, 25; on failure of Revolution, 10, 58–60, 69, 70, 77, 78, 167n12; on Mexicanness, 29, 65, 162n43
The Cosmic Race (Vasconcelos), 22
Count Schwartzemberg *(Ensayo de un crimen)*, 138
creoles, 18, 19, 25, 128
"La crisis de México" (Cosío Villegas), 58, 162n43
Cristero Rebellion, 114
Crónica antisolemne del cine mexicano (Sánchez), 27, 163n52
crossover films, 4, 80
Cuadernos Americanos, 58, 61
Cuando los hijos se van, 15, 82
Cuarón, Alfonso, 119
Cuauhtémoc, 19
Cuba baila, 176n3
La cucaracha, 170n57

cultural nation, 26–29, 30, 78
Cultural Politics in Revolution (Vaughan), 22, 162n42
cultural production, 18–26, 160–62nn13,15,18,26,34
Cumbres borrascosas. See Abismos de pasión
Cypess, Sandra Messinger, 103, 104

Dada, 34
Dalí, Salvador, 34, 36, 38, 39, 43, 55, 165n37
Dancigers, Oscar: *Abismos de pasión*, 144; *The Adventures of Robinson Crusoe* and, 143, 144; Buñuel and, 147, 171n29; *El gran calavera* and, 144; *Gran Casino* and, 44, 46, 144; *La hija del engaño* and, 94, 144; *La mort en ce jardin*, 144; *Los olvidados* and, 57, 58, 74, 167–69nn1,36
Darwin, Charles, 34
Daughter of Deceit. See La hija del engaño
Davis, Frank, 41
Davison, Tito, 97
Day of the Dead fiesta, 107
Death and the River. See El río y la muerte
de la Cabada, Juan, 112
de la Colina, José, 50, 68, 147
Del Rio, Dolores, 16, 28, 44, 68, 170n57
De Sica, Vittorio, 67, 168–69n35
Desnos, Robert, 62
Destiny, 35
The Devil and the Flesh. See Susana
devoradoras, 16, 81, 88, 90, 113
Díaz, Porfirio, 20, 26, 69. *See also porfirismo*
Díaz Morales, José, 98
Díaz Ordaz, Gustavo, 150
Dieterle, William, 42
Directed by Dorothy Arzner (Mayne), 13
The Discreet Art of Luis Buñuel (Edwards), 3, 33
Disney, 39
Distinto Amanecer, 73

Diversions of Pleasure (Sandro), 2, 7
documentaries: *Las Hurdes* and, 45, 50–51, 58, 63; *Los olvidados* and, 68
Domínguez, Columba, 16, 108
Doña Barbara, 88, 90, 171n25
doña Carmen *(Susana)*, 86, 88, 91–93, 99, 136
doña Ester *(Subida al cielo)*, 115, 117–18
Doña Herlinda y su hijo, 176n3
don Andrés *(El bruto)*, 126–32
doña Sixta *(Subida al cielo)*, 117–18
don Carmelo *(Los olvidados)*, 11, 69, 70, 128, 131, 168n30
Dondé, Manuel, 12, 113, 117, 133
don Eladio *(Subida al cielo)*, 11, 113, 116–17, 128
don Francisco *(Él)*. *See* Francisco *(Él)*
don Guadalupe *(Susana)*, 86, 87, 90–93, 128, 134, 136
don Jaime *(Viridiana)*, 12
don Lope *(Tristana)*, 12
don Nemesio *(Subida al cielo)*, 113, 115, 116
Don Quintín, el amargao, 40, 94, 145, 165n32
don Quintín *(La hija del engaño)*, 94–98, 134
don Santos Luzardo *(Doña Barbara)*, 171n25
"drama of identification," 66, 168n31
dream sequences, 2, 92–93
Dreyer, Carl Theodore, 89
Drouzy, Maurice, 5
Duverger, Albert, 35, 36
dyad, moral, 72–73, 169n46

Echeverría, Luis, 176n3
education. *See* public education
Edwards, Gwynne, 3, 33, 159–60n12
Eisenstein, Sergei: Buñuel and, 35, 38; "folkloric" customs and, 101, 107, 118; indigenist films and, 26–27, 162–63nn48,50; *Nuevo Cine* and, 149
ejidos, 69, 114
Él: Buñuel scholarship on, 10; characters in, 11, 12; contextuality of, 11; criticism of, 1, 4, 5, 8; machismo in, 10, 12; as macho-drama, 132–36, 135; Mexican cinema and, 7, 147, 148, 149; Mexican Revolution and, 134–35; national crisis/male trauma and, 138; *Nuevo Cine* and, 149; production of, 144
Elizondo, Salvador, 149
Él (Pinto), 132, 133, 135–36, 175n20
Elsaesser, Thomas, 82
Eluard, Paul, 37, 39, 165n37
Enamorada, 15, 68, 82, 169–70n49
En este pueblo no hay ladrones, 150
Ensayo de un crimen, 141; Buñuel scholarship on, 7; characters in, 11, 12, 29; contextuality of, 1, 11, 12; criticism of, 4, 5, 8; machismo and, 10, 12, 117, 138–39; as macho-drama, 136–42; Mexican cinema and, 148; Mexican Revolution and, 137–38, 140
Ensayo de un crimen (Usigli), 7, 136–37
Epstein, Jean, 35, 36, 38, 40
Ernst, Max, 37
Espaldas mojadas, 67, 119
¡España, leal en armas!, 41
¡Esquina, bajan!, 67, 113
Estado e ideología empresarial en el gobierno alemanista (López-Portillo), 59, 162n42
ethnographic surrealism, 62, 63–64
Etievant, Henri, 36
Evans, Peter W., 8, 159n10
exile community, Spanish, 8, 43–44, 147
The Exterminating Angel. *See El ángel exterminador*

The Fall of the House of Usher, 35
Una familia de tantas, 82
family melodramas: *El bruto* as, 124, 126–32; Buñuel and, 82, 148; classical cinema and, 33, 163–64n3; *Él* as, 124; genre politics and, 81–98; *El gran calavera* as, 51–54; *Gran*

family melodramas *(continued)*
Casino as, 46–48; *La hija del engaño* as, 94–98; Mexican cinema and, 6, 7, 15, 26, 51, 82–83, 160n2; mother characters in, 99–110; *Una mujer sin amor* as, 65, 101–5; *Los olvidados* and, 70; patriarchy and, 125; *El río y la muerte* as, 65, 105–10; *Susana* as, 85–93, 87
Le fantôme de la liberté, 2, 12, 119
fascism, 41–42
Felisa *(Susana)*, 88, 91–93
Félix, María, 16, 24, 68, 170n57
female characters: in *Doña Barbara*, 88, 90, 171n25; in *La hija del engaño*, 10, 94–98, 97; Kinder on, 41; in Mexican cinema, 30, 81, 83–84; in *Una mujer sin amor*, 10, 101–5; in *Los olvidados*, 74, 75, 99, 104; in *El río y la muerte*, 10, 105–10; in *Susana*, 10, 85–93. *See also* La Malinche
La femme et le pantin (Louqs), 163–64n3
femmes fatales, 16, 81, 88, 90, 113
Fernández, Emilio ("El Indio"): Armendáriz and, 126, 129; Buñuel and, 151; classical cinema and, 27–28, 163nn51,57; Eisenstein's influence on, 26–27; genres of Mexican film and, 15; international criticism of, 75–76, 77, 167n2, 170n57; machismo and, 130; Magdaleno and, 49; Mexican Revolution and, 2, 16, 26; modernization and, 71–73; muralism and, 22, 24–25, 69, 78, 161–62nn34,36; official folklore and, 68; *Los olvidados* and, 72–73, 75–76, 80; revolutionary melodramas and, 15, 82; scholarship on, 5; violence and, 172–73n52; World War II and, 44
fetishes, 139–40
feuilleton, 82
fiestas, 118, *118*, 173n15
La fièvre monte à El Pão, 13, 81, 143
Figueroa, Gabriel, *151*; classical cinema and, 27–28; international criticism of, 75–76; Mexican Revolution and, 16; muralism and, 22, 24, 161n29, 170n50; scholarship on, 5; World War II and, 44
Figures of Desire (Williams), 2
film criticism: auteurist, 3–5, 159–60n12; by Buñuel, 44–45, 166n50; of Buñuel's Mexican melodramas, 85; genre, 7; of *El gran calavera*, 53; of *Gran Casino*, 48–49, 51; of *Una mujer sin amor*, 101, 172n42; of *Los olvidados*, 4, 5, 57–58, 63, 67, 73–76, 167–70nn1,22,49,56; psychoanalytic, 2–3, 8
film legislation, 16, 22, 84, 160–61nn3,4,15
Filmófono (Madrid): Buñuel's years at, 33, 39–41, 42, 165n36; funding at, 45; genre films at, 51, 54, 55; during Spanish Republic, 41, 44
The Films of Luis Buñuel (Evans), 8, 159n10
film studies, 2–5, 7–9, 160n2. *See also* film criticism
Filosofía y Letras, 61
filthiness, 67, 74, 99, 148, 167–69nn1,36
Fitzgerald, Edward, 68, 98
Flaherty, Robert J., 50, 58
Flor silvestre, 27, 28, 29, 54, 72, 77, 126
folklore, official, 58, 63, 66, 68, 101, 118–19, 147–48, 173n15
La fórmula secreta, 150
Foucault, Michel, 7
Fox, Claire F., 167n12, 174n17
Francisco *(Él)*, 11, 12, 133–35, *135*, 175n20; Archibaldo de la Cruz and, 138, 139, 140; don Nemesio and, 115; Mexicanness and, 144
Franco, Francisco, 39, 41, 42, 43, 164n28
Franco, Jean, 84, 99, 100, 125–26, 159n10, 169–70n49
free trade, 121–22, 123, 174n17
French National Cinema (Hayward), 16, 28

French Revolutionary theater, 82
Freud, Sigmund, 35, 63, 133, 139, 140, 168n20, 175nn20,26
Freudian criticism, 2, 8, 63, 65
Frida, 176n3
Fuentes, Carlos, 149
Fuentes, Fernando de, 90; classical cinema and, 27, 162n41; *comedia rancheras* of, 15, 47; family melodramas of, 26, 70, 88, 90; revolutionary hero and, 163n57
Fuentes, Victor, 8, 14, 44, 169n39

Gaceta Literaria, 34, 35
Galindo, Alejandro, 54, 67, 72, 73, 82, 113, 119, 126, 169n46
Gámez, Rubén, 150
Gance, Abel, 35
Gance, Marguerite, 35
Garbo, Greta, 38
Garcés, Delia, 133
García, Sara, 16, 99
García Ascot, Jomí, 149
García Canclini, Néstor: on cultural production, 18–19, 77, 160–62nn13,42; on modernization, 19, 61, 70–71
García-Lorca, Federico, 34, 43
García Márquez, Gabriel, 149
García Riera, Emilio, 49, 97, 122, 149, 172nn32–33
Gaudí, Antonio, 134
'generation of '27,' 34, 112
'generation of '98,' 34
Género y transgresión (Lillo), 7, 53
genre system: Buñuel scholarship on, 2, 3, 7, 11; Buñuel's use of, 1, 45, 80; classification of, 5–7, 15–16, 81–83, 159n7; at Filmófono, 33, 40–41; in Mexican cinema, 10–14, 15, 32, 45–54
Gerardo *(Gran Casino)*, 49
Gerszo, Gunther, 102
Gertrud, 89
Gibbons, Cedric, 102
Gilly, Adolfo, 162n42
Giménez Caballero, Ernesto, 34

Gledhill, Christine, 82
Gloria *(Él)*, 133, 134, 135
The Golden Age. See *L'Age d'Or*
Golden Age. *See* classical cinema
Gómez Mesa, Luis, 40
Gout, Alberto, 9, 30, 54, 73, 82, 98, 171n28
Granados, Rosario, 52, *53*, 102, *103*
El gran calavera: Alcoriza, Luis, and, 126; Buñuel scholarship on, 7; commercial success of, 41, 57; contextuality of, 9; criticism of, 3; as genre movie, 48, 51–55, *53*; patriarchy and, 110; production of, 144; as social comedy, 32
Gran Casino: contextuality of, 1, 9, 11; criticism of, 2, 3; female characters in, 81; Mexican cinema and, 32, 41, 44, 46–51, 47, 52, 54–55, 148; production of, 144
The Great Madcap. See *El gran calavera*
Grierson, John, 50, 58
Griffith, D. W., 83, 89
Guanajuato in *Él*, 12
guiñol, 53–54
Guízar, Tito, 16
gun cult, 108, 130

Hayward, Susan, 16–18, 28, 160n6
Hermosillo, Jaime Humberto, 11, 30, 150, 176n3
Hershfield, Joanne, 88–90
Hidalgo, Miguel, 19
Hidden River, 24–25
Higginbotham, Virginia, 3, 43, 159–60n12
High Heels, 89
High Noon, 127
high-rise building, 69–70, 168n30
La hija de Juan Simón, 40
La hija del engaño: Alcoriza, Luis, and, 126; as *cabaretera* melodrama, 10, 94–98, *97*; contextuality of, 11, 12; as family melodrama, 94–98; Mexican cinema and, 81, 98, 113, 116, 145, 148; mother character in, 99–

La hija del engaño (continued)
  100, 104; patriarchy and, 95, 98, 99, 110, 142; production of, 144; as remake, 40; Soler in, 9, 51, 94, 95
hijos de la chingada, 84, 101, 102–3, 104
Historia de la vida del buscón (Quevedo), 67, 168–69n35
Hollywood: Buñuel and, 32, 33, 37–38, 41–43, 164nn23–24; *¡Que Viva México!* and, 26, 162–63n48; studio politics of, 45, 46; during World War II, 44
Hollywood melodramas, 38, 82–83, 84, 100, 164n24
homicidal behavior, 124, 138–40
homosexual behavior, 124, 129, 133, 136, 138–42, 175n25
The House of Bernarda Alba, 43
Huitzilopocthli, 74
hurdanos, 50
Las Hurdes: censorship of, 39, 164n28; criticism of, 2; *Los olvidados* and, 58, 64–65, 73, 168–69n35; *Subida al cielo* and, 112, 119; as surrealist film, 41, 45, 50–51, 54, 63–64
Huston, John, 170n57
Hybrid Cultures (García Canclini), 61, 77, 162n42
hybridity, 71, 73, 90

I Am Pure Mexican, 126, 131
ICAIC, 176n3
If I Were Senator, 117
La ilusión viaja en tranvía: CLASA films and, 172n49; contextuality of, 11, 12; criticism of, 3, 4; as family melodrama, 7; Mexican cinema and, 111–12, 144, 148; patriarchy and, 110; prostitutes and, 97; as road movie, 10, 116, 119–23, 121, 174n20; slaughterhouse in, 122
Imagined Communities (Anderson), 18, 160n6
Inda, Estela, 75, 75, 99
independence movements, 19, 161n17
Indian heritage, 18, 19, 21–23, 25

Indians, 16, 68–69, 125, 169n39
"indigenismo," 15, 22, 24, 26–29, 73, 163n56
"industrial auteur" criticism, 13
Infante, Pedro, 16
inflation, 120–22, 123
"Institutional Revolution," 17, 21–22, 58–59, 115
Institutional Revolutionary Party. *See* PRI
Instituto de Bellas Artes, 60
Instituto Indigenista, 60
Internacional Cinematográfica, 144
international film criticism: Buñuel and, 1, 143–44, 167n2; cultural nation and, 20; Fernández-Figueroa and, 27, 75–76, 163n51, 170n57; *Los olvidados* and, 30, 57, 74–76
The Interpretation of Dreams (Freud), 35, 168n20
Isaac, Alberto, 30, 149, 150, 161n29
It's Not Enough to Be a Mother, 82

Jaibo (Los olvidados), 66, 67, 69, 75, 129, 136, 168n30
Janitzio, 22, 27, 28
Um jato na contramão: Buñuel no México, 8
Jesús (Susana), 86–88, 90–93
Jodorowski, Alejandro, 150
Jonrón (La hija del engaño), 95–96, 97
Le Journal d'une femme de chambre, 33, 163–64n3
Jovita (La hija del engaño), 95–98
Juan Charrasqueado, 131
Julián (Los olvidados), 66, 69, 168n30
Junco, Tito, 105
Jurado, Katy, 127, 130

Kaplan, E. Ann, 82
Keaton, Buster, 34
Kessel, Joseph, 163–64n3
Kinder, Marsha, 40–41
kiss, 49–50
Knight, Alan, 25, 162n42
Kogan, Sergio, 131, 171n29
Kristeva, Julia, 7

Kurosawa, Akira, 4
Kyrou, Ado, 5

El laberinto de la soledad (Paz), 57, 61–66, 74, 78–79, 84, 106, 163n55
Lacan, Jacques, 2, 133, 175n20
Lachenay, Robert, 171n28
Lamarque, Libertad, 47, 47, 48, 49, 81
Land Without Bread. See *Las Hurdes*
Lang, Fritz, 35
Lavinia *(Ensayo de un crimen)*, 139–40
Lavista, Raúl, 102
lazarillo, 69, 169n39
Lazarillo de Tormes, 67, 168–69nn35,39
Leduc, Paul, 150, 176n3
Lencho *(La hija del engaño)*, 95–96, 98
Lester, Sol, 27
Let's Go with Pancho Villa, 27, 162n41
Lillo, Gastón, 7, 53–54
"Little Tramp," 123
Lloyd, Harold, 34
lo mexicano. See Mexicanness
López, Ana, 83–84, 95, 104, 147, 174n17
López-Portillo Tostado, Felícitas, 59–60, 69, 120, 162n42
López Somoza, Luis, 86
The Lost Steps (Carpentier), 174n20
Louqs, Pierre, 163–64n3
love scenes, 49–50, 52
El lugar sin límites, 30, 150
Luis Buñuel (Fuentes), 169n39
Luis Buñuel (Higginbotham), 3
Luis Buñuel (Kyrou), 5
Luis Buñuel: Architecte du rêve (Drouzy), 5

machismo: *El bruto* and, 10, 12, 117, 129–30, 132; *Él* and, 10, 12, 117, 132–33, 136; *Ensayo de un crimen* and, 10, 12, 117, 138–39; *La hija del engaño* and, 95–96, 130; Mexican cinema and, 110, 141, 148; national identity and, 10, 29, 124–25, 142, 163n57; revolutionary myth and, 20–21, 30, 161–62n34; *El río y la muerte* and, 109, 130; *Subida al cielo* and, 117; *Susana* and, 85, 90, 130
macho-dramas, 10, 124–42; *El bruto* as, 124, 126–32; *Él* as, 124, 132–36, 142; *Ensayo de un crimen* as, 124, 136–42
Maclovia, 68
Madero, Francisco, 20, 24, 59
El maestro rural, 23
Magdaleno, Mauricio, 49
Mahieu, José Agustin, 43
male identity, 10, 99, 100–101, 132
La Malinche: *Una mujer sin amor* and, 103–4; national identity and, 10, 12, 84, 100, 124, 125; Paz on, 65, 74, 106–7; violence and, 106–7
malinchismo, 100, 103
mannequin, 139–40, 141
Mantequilla, 9, 95, 97, 112, 120, 173n4
María *(La hija del engaño)*, 95–96, 99, 104
María Candelaria: Armendáriz and, 126, 131; classical cinema and, 54, 68, 77, 101; cultural nation and, 25; international acclaim for, 27–29, 72, 163n56, 167n2; prostitutes and, 97
María de mi corazón, 30, 150
Marinetti, Filippo Tommaso, 34
Marta *(La hija del engaño)*, 95–98, 172n32
Martín-Barbero, Jesús, 21, 23–24, 82, 84, 89, 147
Martínez, Adalberto. See Resortes
Martínez, Paco, 128
Martínez Solares, Raúl, 102
Marx, Karl, 34, 35–36
masculinity in crisis, 130, 131, 132, 135–36, 140, 142
maternal melodramas, 10, 16, 99–110; *Una mujer sin amor* as, 100, 101–5; *El río y la muerte* as, 100, 101, 105–10
Maupassant, Guy de, 33, 101, 145
Mauprat, 35
Mayas, 18, 25

Mayne, Judith, 13
Meche *(El bruto)*, 128–31
Meche *(Los olvidados)*, 99
Mejía, Alfonso, 66, *66*, 78, *78*
melodramas. See family melodramas
Menchaca family, 107–8
Mendoza, Miguel Ángel, 48, 51, 166n60
Mendoza, Victor Manuel, 86
Mercedes *(Gran Casino)*, 49
mestizo race, 22, 59, 100
Metz, Christian, 7
Mexican cinema: Barbachano and, 144, 176n3; Buñuel and, 9–14, 29–31, 32, 43–56, 75–76, 80–81, 140–42, 147–51; Buñuel scholarship on, 3–4; crisis of, 5–9, 10, 11, 29–30, 57–79; cultural nation and, 26–29, 163n52; cultural production and, 18–26, 160n3; *La hija del engaño* and, 81, 98; mother characters in, 99–100; *Los olvidados* and, 5, 10, 11, 29–30, 57–79, 168nn22,30; *Susana* and, 80, 85, 93. See also classical cinema; national cinema
Mexican Cinema/Mexican Woman (Hershfield), 88
Mexican Cinema: Reflections of a Society (Mora), 82, 163n52
Mexican Congress, 16, 160n3
mexicanidad, 28–29, 150
Mexicanness: Armendáriz and, 129; Buñuel and, 81, 144; cultural nation and, 25, 29, 65; La Malinche and, 103; Paz on, 61–62, 74, 84; philosophy of, 78
Mexican Revolution, 6, 16; Bolshevik revolution and, 163n50; *El bruto* and, 126–32; class conflict and, 130–31; cultural production and, 18–26, 161–62nn17,18,26,34; *Él* and, 134–35; *Ensayo de un crimen* and, 137–38, 140; failure of, 47; national cinema and, 2, 5, 8, 15, 44; Nuevo Cine and, 150; *Los olvidados* and, 12, 58–59
Mexicas, 18, 74, 160–61n13

"Mexico and Mexicanness," 61
Mexico Yesterday, Today, and Tomorrow, 24, 161–62n34
MGM, 37–38, 41, 42
Miguel Inclán *(María Candelaria)*, 29
Mildred Pierce, 100
Miller, Henry, 149
Minotaure, 165n37
Mirbeau, Octave, 163–64n3
misogyny, 103, 124, 125, 139
Mists of Regret (Andrew), 64
modernization: Alemán administration and, 6–7, 10, 59, 61, 167n12; Buñuel's early films and, 55; *Él* and, 134–35; *Ensayo de un crimen* and, 134; Fernández and, 70–73; Galindo and, 72, 73; 169n46; García Canclini on, 19, 70–71; *La hija del engaño* and, 98, 134; *La ilusión viaja en tranvía* and, 122–23; *Una mujer sin amor* and, 104, 105, 135, 172n47; *Los olvidados* and, 66, 69–70, 72–73, 168–70nn30,49; *El río y la muerte* and, 134; *Subida al cielo* and, 117, 123; *Susana* and, 91, 134
Monsiváis, Carlos, 123, 147; on melodramas, 83, 84; on Mexican cinema, 23–24, 159n7; on Mexico City, 95; Nuevo Cine and, 149; on parody, 89; on social comedies, 111–12
Mora, Carl J., 82, 162–63nn48,52, 172n33
Morelos, José María, 19
Moreno, Antonio, 96
Moreno, Mario. See Cantinflas
La mort en ce jardin, 13, 80, 143, 144
Moscow Film School, 5
mother characters, 99–110
motifs, Buñuelian, 8
Der müde Tod, 35
Una mujer sin amor: Alemán administration and, 60; Buñuel scholarship on, 8; contextuality of, 11, 12; criticism of, 3; as family melodrama, 7, 10, 33, 65, 85, 89, *103*; Granados in, 52; as maternal melodrama, 100, 101–5, *103*; Mexican cinema and,

80, 144, 145; national crisis/male trauma and, 136; national identity and, 103–5, 148; patriarchy and, 102, 104, 105, 110
muralism: cultural nation and, 18, 20, 22, 77, 161n26; Fernández-Figueroa and, 22, 24, 69, 78, 161–62nn34,36, 170n50; revolutionary epic and, 6
Murnau, F. W., 35
Museum of Modern Art (New York), 43, 162–63n48
musical dramas, 6, 16, 22
musical melodramas, 32–33, 40, 46–48, 49, 81
My Last Sigh (Buñuel), 41, 55–56, 66, 129, 130
The Myth of the Revolution (O'Malley), 20
"Mythologies" (Monsiváis), 159n7

NAFTA, 174n17
Náhuatl, 100
National Autonomous University, 133
national cinema: blueprint for, 16–18, 160n6; genres of, 5–7; melodramas and, 84. *See also* classical cinema; Mexican cinema
National Cinematographic Bank, 27
National Film Institute, 22
national identity: Buñuel scholarship on, 3; in Buñuel's films, 1, 11–12; García Canclini on, 73; machismo and, 10, 29, 124–25, 163n57; La Malinche and, 10, 12, 84, 100, 124, 125; melodramas and, 84; Mexican Revolution and, 18–26, 29, 59, 161–63nn26,34,57; mother characters and, 100–101, 102, 104; Paz on, 61–66. *See also* Mexicanness
nationalization, 44, 47, 60, 114–15
National Museum of Anthropology, 19, 160–61n13
National Palace, 24, 69
Nation and Narration (Bhabha), 25, 160n6
Navarro, Carlos, 22, 27, 120
Nazarín: Barbachano and, 144, 147; Buñuel scholarship on, 7; criticism of, 2; international acclaim for, 167–70nn2,57; Mexican cinema and, 13, 105, 144, 145; *Nuevo Cine* and, 149; production of, 145, 151
Negrete, Jorge, 16, 47, 47–51, 54, 57
neoporfiriato, 60, 69, 167n12
neorealism, Italian, 67, 151, 168–69n35
Neruda, Pablo, 34
neurosis, 63, 66, 133, 139, 140
New Cinema. *See* Nuevo Cine
new cinema movements, 4–5, 151
1917 Constitution, 60
Noailles, Charles de, 37
Noailles, Marie-Laure de, 37
No basta ser madre, 82
"¡No pasarán!" (Paz), 62
Nosotros los pobres, 81, 113, 126
nouvelle vague, 151
Nuevo Cine: Buñuel and, 7, 77; emergence of, 13, 149–51, 176n10; transition to, 5, 8, 30, 76–77
Nuevo Cine journal, 13, 149–50, 151, 176n10

L'Observateur, 5, 76
Oedipal narrative, 8, 74, 75, 99, 159n10, 169–70n49
L'Oeil de Buñuel (Césarman), 5, 133
Office of Inter-American Affairs, 43
El Ojitos *(Los olvidados)*, 68–69, 169n39
In Old Tampico. See Gran Casino
Oliverio *(Subida al cielo)*, 113, 114–16, 118
Los olvidados: Alcoriza, Luis, and, 126; Buñuel scholarship on, 7, 8, 159n10; crisis of Mexican cinema and, 5, 10, 11, 29–30, 57–79, 66, 75, 168nn22,30; criticism of, 4, 5, 57–58, 63, 67, 73–76, 167–70nn1,22,49; dream sequences and, 92; Fernández and, 72–73, 75–76, 80; homosexual behavior and, 175n25; international acclaim for, 1, 30, 32, 57–58, 73, 74–76, 130, 140–41, 167n2; Mexican

Los olvidados (continued)
cinema and, 7, 55, 113, 116, 147, 148, 149; Mexican Revolution and, 12, 58–59; mother character in, 74, 75, 99; national crisis/male trauma and, 136; *Nuevo Cine* and, 149; patriarchy and, 11, 110; pedophilia and, 175n25; production of, 144; social Darwinism in, 29

O'Malley, Ilene V., 20–21, 124–25, 130–31

180-degree rule, 50

one-hundred families, 59

An Ordinary Family, 82

The Origin of Species (Darwin), 34

Orozco, José Clemente, 20, 22, 27, 71, 170n50

Ortega y Gasset, José, 34

Out at the Big Ranch, 15, 27, 162n41

Ozu, Yazujiro, 4

Pablo *(El gran calavera)*, 52

Pabst, G. W., 35

pachuco, 7, 51, 65, 74, 173n4

Palma, Andrea, 16

Palme d'Or, 143

Paloma *(El bruto)*, 127–31

Paramount Pictures, 39

paranoid behavior, 124, 132–36, 138–39, 175nn20,26

Pardavé, Joaquín, 16

parody: *Ensayo de un crimen* and, 138–39; of genre, 57; *Gran Casino* as, 50–51, 55; *La hija del engaño* and, 96, 97; *Una mujer sin amor* and, 105; *Susana* as, 51, 81, 85, 88–89, 93, 105

patriarchy: *El bruto* and, 128, 129, 130, 131; character types of, 11, 16; class conflict and, 130; *Doña Barbara* and, 90, 171n25; *Él* and, 132, 133, 136; family melodramas and, 125; *El gran calavera* and, 110; *La hija del engaño* and, 95, 98, 99, 110, 142; *La ilusión viaja en tranvía* and, 110; *malinchismo* and, 100; of Mexican Revolution, 20–22, 24, 25, 26, 162n41; *Una mujer sin amor* and, 102, 104, 105, 110; *Los olvidados* and, 11, 110; relationship of state to people, 160n2; revolutionary myth and, 30; *El río y la muerte* and, 107, 109–10; *Subida al cielo* and, 11, 110; subversion of, 41; *Susana* and, 85, 88–91, 93, 99, 142; virtues of, 124, 125, 174n1

Paz, Octavio: cultural nation and, 25; *malinchismo* and, 100; Mexicanness and, 29, 78–79, 83–84, 85, 163n55; national identity and, 61–66, 163n57, 168n16; *Nuevo Cine* and, 149; *Los olvidados* and, 10, 57, 74, 77, 79; on violence, 106–7, 108

pedophilia, 138, 175n25

Pedro *(El bruto)*, 126, 128–32, 136, 140

Pedro *(Los olvidados)*, 66, 67, 69, 78, 99, 131, 136, 175n25

Pedro's mother *(Los olvidados)*, 74, 75, 99, 104

pelado, 7, 65, 113, 173n4

Películas Anáhuac, 46

Peón, Ramón, 82

Pérez-Galdós, Benito, 34, 163–64n3

Pérez Turrent, Tomás, 50, 68, 147

Un perro andaluz (Buñuel), 34

picaresque, Spanish, 67, 168–69nn35,39

Picasso, Pablo, 35

Pick, Zuzanna, 174n20

Pierre et Jean (Maupassant), 33, 101, 145

pilgrimage structure, 112–13, 115

Pinal, Silvia, 144, 146, 147

Pinto, Mercedes, 132, 133, 135–36, 175n20

Plotting Women (Franco), 125, 159n10, 169–70n49

Pons, María Antonieta, 16

Popocatépetl, 69

"Popular Culture and the Revolutionary State in Mexico" (Knight), 162n42

porfirismo: *El bruto* and, 130; *Él* and,

134, 175n18; *Ensayo de un crimen* and, 138; *La hija del engaño* and, 95; *Los olvidados* and, 58, 69, 70; revolutionary melodramas and, 48; *Susana* and, 93
Porter, Edwin S., 83
Posada, José Guadalupe, 18
Prado, Lilia, 113, 118, *118*, 121, 147
PRI (Partido Revolucionario Institucional), 16, 25, 26, 60, 115, 116
Producciones Tepeyac, 143
prostitutes: in *La hija del engaño*, 94, 96–98, 122, 172n32; Mexican cinema and, 81, 122; in *Una mujer sin amor*, 102
psychoanalysis, 133
psychoanalytic criticism, 1, 2, 4, 8, 63, 65
"Psychoanalytic Notes . . . of a Case of Paranoia" (Freud), 133
psychohistory, 62
public education, 21–24, 25, 161–62nn26,34
Public Education Secretariat. *See* SEP
public radio, 20, 21, 161n18
public transportation settings, 112
Pueblerina, 72, 101, 169n44, 173n15

Quevedo, Francisco de, 67, 168–69n35
¡Que Viva México!, 26, 38, 101, 107, 162–63n48
Quintana, Rosita, 85, *87*, 88, 171n29
Quintín *(La hija del engaño)*, 94–97

Rabal, Francisco, 147
radio broadcasting, 20, 21, 39, 161n18
Raíces, 176n3
Ramírez Berg, Charles, 125
Ramiro *(El gran calavera)*, 51–52
Ramos, Samuel, 29
rancheras. See *comedias rancheras*
Raquel *(Subida al cielo)*, 113, *118*
Rashomon, 4
El Rastro, 122, 126
Raúl *(Él)*, 134
Ray, Man, 37

Ray, Satyajit, 4
La raza cósmica, 77
Reachi, Manuel, 112
Redes, 22, 27
Red Scare (U.S.), 36
Reed: México insurgente, 150
Residencia de Estudiantes (Madrid, Spain), 34, 39
Resortes, 173n4
Revista Mexicana de Cultura, 61
revolutionary epics, 124–25; cultural nation and, 22; Mexican cinema and, 6, 26, 170n57; national cinema and, 15–16
revolutionary melodramas, 48, 82–83, 90, 93
revolutionary myth, 20–21, 23, 30, 78, 161–62n34
La Révolution Surréaliste, 36
La Revue du Cinéma, 165n37
Rey, Fernando, 147
Reyes, Alfonso, 29, 77, 78, 108, 172–73n52
Riefenstahl, Leni, 166n46
Río Escondido, 24, *24*–25, 29, 72, 169n44
El río y la muerte: contextuality of, 11, 12; as family melodrama, 7, 10, 65, 85, 105–10, *109*; machismo and, 130; as maternal melodrama, 100, 101, 105–10, *109*; Mexican cinema and, 80, 116, 144, 147, 148; national crisis/male trauma and, 136; violence in, 12, 106–10
Ripstein, Arturo, 11, 30, 150
Rivera, Diego: cultural nation and, 25; influence on Mexican cinema, 27; international acclaim for, 20; *María Candelaria* and, 28; modernization and, 71; *Río Escondido* and, 24, 69, 161–62n34; violence and, 172–73n52
road movies, 10, 111–23, 174n20; *La ilusión viaja en tranvía* as, 119–23; *Subida al cielo* as, 114–19
Roberto de la Cruz *(Ensayo de un crimen)*, 136–37

Rockefeller, Nelson, 43
Rodríguez, Ismael, 81, 113, 126, 131, 170n57
Roll, Phillip Ansel, 143
Romeo and Juliet (Cantinflas), 160n3
Rooner, Charles, 49
Rosario *(Una mujer sin amor)*, 102
Rosario's husband *(Una mujer sin amor)*, 103, 103–4, 135
Rosario's lover *(Una mujer sin amor)*, 102, 105, 172n47
Rosario's sons *(Una mujer sin amor)*, 102–5, 103, 136, 144
Rossellini, Roberto, 149
Rotellar, Manuel, 39–40, 165n36
Rousseau, Jean-Jacques, 34
Rozado, Alejandro, 71–72
Rucar de Buñuel, Jeanne, 39, 41–42, 55, 165n34
rural schools, 23–24

Sacco, Nicola, 36, 164n15
Sáenz de Heredia, José Luis, 39
sainete, 51, 53
Salvador, Jaime, 105
Sánchez, Francisco, 27–28, 104, 163n52, 172n33
Sandro, Paul, 2–3, 7, 159–60n12
San Jeronimito, 114–15
Santa, 96
Santí, Enrico Mario, 62–64, 163n55
Savage, Carlos, 97
Schomburgk, Richard, 174n20
Schomburgk, Robert, 174n20
schools. *See* public education
Schreber, Dr., 133
Sciuscia, 67
Secretaría de Educación Pública. *See* SEP
The Secret Life of Salvador Dalí (Dalí), 43
secularization, 114
Señora tentación, 98
Sensualidad, 73, 82, 98
SEP (Secretaría de Educación Pública), 21, 22, 23, 25, 161n26
Sevilla, Ninón, 16, 98, 171n28

sexenio, 46, 62, 111, 120
Shanghai Express, 38
"Silly Symphonies," 39
Silva Herzog, Jesús, 29, 61
Silvestre (Subida al cielo), 116, 117–18
Simón del desierto: Buñuel scholarship on, 7, 8; Mexican cinema and, 13, 30, 111, 144; Nuevo Cine and, 150; production of, 145
Sinclair, Upton, 162–63n48
Siqueiros, David Alfaro, 20, 27, 71, 74, 170n50
The Siren of the Tropics, 36–37
Sirk, Douglas, 89
Si yo fuera diputado, 117
smuggling, 122, 174n17
social comedies: Buñuel and, 32–33, 40; *Ensayo de un crimen* as, 124; Mexican cinema and, 6–7, 15–16, 22, 111–12, 120, 173n4; road movies and, 111–23
social Darwinism, 25, 29
socialist realism, 6
Solano Galeana, Lilia, 112
Soler, Andrés, 126, 127, 128
Soler, Domingo, 16
Soler, Fernando: in *El gran calavera*, 51, 53, 57; in *Gran Casino*, 48; in *La hija del engaño*, 9, 94, 95, 142; star system and, 16, 125; in *Susana*, 86, 87, 90, 142
Sommer, Doris, 26, 72, 84
Soto, Fernando. *See* Mantequilla
Spanish Civil War, 41–44, 62
Spanish conquerors, 100, 163n57
Spanish Republic, 41–42, 43, 44, 62, 67
Spencer, Herbert, 34
star system: Alonso and, 12, 139; Armendáriz and, 12, 126, 129, 131–32; Buñuel and, 36; Lamarque and, 48; Mexican cinema and, 16, 147, 166n55; Negrete and, 48; social comedies and, 173n4; Soler and, 48, 94
Stella Dallas, 100
Stern, Miroslava, 139, *141*

Storm Over Mexico, 27
Studio 28 (Paris, France), 37
Subida al cielo: contextuality of, 11, 12; criticism of, 3, 4, 5; international acclaim for, 75, 130, 140–41, 167n2; Mexican cinema and, 5, 7, 101, 111–14, 116, 119, 147, 148; patriarchy and, 11, 110; as road movie, 10, 111, 114–19, 118
surrealism: Buñuel's interpretation of, 37, 45; chance and, 31; Freud and, 168n20, 175n26; Mexico and, 65
surrealist, Buñuel as, 32, 33; *La ilusión viaja en tranvía* and, 55, 120; Mexican cinema and, 8, 13, 50, 66, 145–46, 148, 168n32; *Los olvidados* and, 58, 63; scholarship on, 1–2, 3, 4; *Subida al cielo* and, 55, 120; *Susana* and, 55, 92–93
surrealist aesthetics, 55
surrealist ethnography, 62, 63–65
surrealists: Buñuel's alienation from, 39, 40–41, 55, 165nn36–37; communist, 43; in Mexico, 44; in Paris, 35–37; Paz and, 62–65; violence and, 106
Susana: as *cabaretera* melodrama, 10, 89–90, 93; campaign advertisement for, 171n24; characters in, 29; contextuality of, 11, 12; criticism of, 3, 8; dream sequences and, 92–93; as family melodrama, 85–93, 87; Mexican cinema and, 80, 85, 93, 113, 116, 148; mother character in, 99–100; national crisis/male trauma and, 136, 138; opening of, 94; as parody, 51, 81, 85, 88–89, 93, 105; patriarchy and, 85, 88–91, 93, 99, 142; production of, 171n29; Soler in, 51, 86, 87, 90, 142
Susana (*Susana*), 85–93, 87, 95, 129

Talens, Jenaro, 5
Tarrajas *(La ilusión viaja en tranvía)*, 120, 122
"Tears and Desire" (López), 83
Tesson, Charles, 37, 133, 135

This Strange Passion. See *Él*
In This Town There Are No Thieves, 30
The Three Musketeers (Cantinflas), 160n3
Tin-Tán, 6–7, 15, 22, 51, 65, 112, 173n4
Tissé, Edward, 38, 162–63n48
Tívoli, 30
Tokyo Story, 4
Toland, Greg, 44
El topo, 150
Torrado, Adolfo, 51
travel narratives, 174n20
Las tres alegres comadres, 97
Trío Calaveras, 49–50, 54
Tristana, 12, 33, 163–64n3
Triumph of the Will (Riefenstahl), 166n46
Truffaut, François, 93, 171n28
Tual, Denise, 43

Ugarte, Eduardo, 137, 140
Última Tule, 77
Ultraists, 34, 37
Unamuno, Miguel de, 34
unconscious, 2, 35–36, 63, 92
Unik, Pierre, 41, 50, 146
United Artists, 42, 143
urban melodramas. See *cine de arrabal*
Urgoiti, Ricardo María, 39
Usigli, Rodolfo, 7, 25, 136–37

Valdés, Germán. See Tin-Tán
Vámonos con Pancho Villa, 27, 162n41
Van Eckerman *(Gran Casino)*, 49
Vanzetti, Bartolomeo, 36, 164n15
Vasconcelos, José, 22, 23, 77, 78, 108, 161n26, 172–73n52
Vaughan, Mary Kay, 22–24, 161–62nn26,42
Venice Film Festival, 106
La vida criminal de Archibaldo de la Cruz, 137
Vidor, King, 81
Villa, Francisco ("Pancho"), 20, 24, 125
violence, 12, 74, 85, 99, 106–10, 141, 163n57, 172–73n52

Virginia *(El gran calavera)*, 52
Virgin of Guadalupe, 100
Viridiana: characters in, 12; commercial success of, 143; as crossover film, 2, 81; international acclaim for, 167n2; Mexican cinema and, 4, 12, 13, 147; *Nuevo Cine* and, 149; production of, 144, 145
La voie lactée, 112, 119
Von Humboldt, Alexander, 174n20
Von Sternberg, Joseph, 38, 164n23
Von Stroheim, 149

Warner Bros., 39, 41, 42–43
Weber, Michel, 49
Wetbacks, 67, 119
We, the Poor, 81, 113
When the Children Leave, 15, 82
Williams, Linda, 2, 82, 92, 133, 159–60n12, 168n20
Wolfe, Bertram D., 161–62n34
A Woman Without Love. See *Una mujer sin amor*

Wood, Michael, 14, 159–60n12
working classes, 6, 111–23, 131, 173n4
World War II, 42, 44
The Wretched of the Earth (Fanon), 78
Written on the Wind, 89
Wuthering Heights. See *Abismos de pasión*
Wuthering Heights (Brontë), 13, 146, 176n5
Wyler, William, 146

xenophobia, 36

Yaqui communities, 25
The Young and the Damned. See *Los olvidados*
The Young One, 81, 143
Y tu Mamá también, 119

Zapata, Emiliano, 20, 24, 125
Zea, Leopoldo, 29, 78
Zinnemann, Fred, 22, 27, 127

Indexer:	Sharon Sweeney
Compositor:	BookMatters
Text:	10/13 Aldus
Display:	Aldus

www.ingramcontent.com/pod-product-compliance
Lightning Source LLC
Chambersburg PA
CBHW030652230426
43665CB00011B/1064